IBM
Technical Libr
5600 Cottle Rc
San Jose, CA 95193

This Book Features Lay-Flat Binding

For convenience while working at a computer, this book is bound with a high-quality *lay-flat* binding. Simply open to the page you need, press your fingers along the left-hand seam, and the book will stay open to that page until you're ready to move on.

"Information through Innovation"

ASSEMBLER LANGUAGE FOR THE IBM SYSTEM 370
A MODULAR APPROACH

DAVID M. COLLOPY
OHIO UNIVERSITY, LANCASTER

boyd & fraser publishing company

Dedicated to my family, especially Cindy and Ryan

Senior Acquisitions Editor: James H. Edwards
Project Manager: Christopher T. Doran
Production Editor: Barbara Worth
Compositor: Jacqueline Davies
Interior Design: Linda M. Robertson
Cover Design: Mike Fender Design
Manufacturing Coordinator: Tracy Megison
Marketing Manager: Eileen Pfeffer

 © 1994 by boyd & fraser publishing company
A Division of South-Western Publishing Co.
One Corporate Place • Ferncroft Village
Danvers, Massachusetts 01923

 International Thomson Publishing
boyd & fraser publishing company is an ITP company.
The ITP trademark is used under license.

All rights reserved. No part of this work may be reproduced or used in any form or by any means—graphic, electronic, or mechanical, including photocopying, recording, taping, or information and retrieval systems—without written permission from the publisher.

Software, programs, and information described in, and associated with this work are provided *as is*. Any statements made about the utility of the software, programs, or information are not to be considered as expressed or implied warranties. The publisher and author will not be liable for incidental or consequential damages of any kind incurred by you, the consumer, or any other user.

Names of all products mentioned herein are used for identification purposes only and may be trademarks and/or registered trademarks of their respective owners. South-Western Publishing Co. and boyd & fraser publishing company disclaim any affiliation, association, or connection with, or sponsorship or endorsement by such owners.

Manufactured in the United States of America

Library of Congress Cataloging-In-Publication Data

Collopy, David M.
    Assembler language for the IBM system 370 : a modular approach / David M. Collopy.
       p.   cm.
    Includes index.
    ISBN 0-87709-089-0
    1. IBM 370 (Computer)—Programming. 2. Assembler language (Computer program language) I. Title.
QA76.8.I122C65 1994
005.2'25—dc20
                                              93-14281
                                                CIP

1 2 3 4 5 6 7 8 9 10 MT 7 6 5 4 3

BRIEF CONTENTS

1	GETTING STARTED	1
2	NUMBER SYSTEMS AND DATA REPRESENTATION	19
3	INTRODUCTION TO ASSEMBLER LANGUAGE	53
4	FILES, MODULAR STRUCTURE, AND PRINTING OUTPUT	89
5	READING DATA AND PERFORMING LOOPS	128
6	COMPARISON AND CONDITIONAL BRANCHING	168
7	PAGE AND CONTROL BREAK PROCESSING	208
8	PACKED-DECIMAL OPERATIONS	241
9	SEQUENTIAL FILE UPDATING	266

APPENDIXES

A	Entering and Running Your First Program	319
B	Introduction to DOS Job Control Language	323
C	Summary Reference: Assembler Instructions	332
D	Summary Reference: EBCDIC Codes	335
E	Powers of Two and Sixteen Tables	337
F	Hexadecimal and Decimal Conversion Table	339
G	Answers to Asterisked Exercises	341
	Index	349

CONTENTS

PREFACE xiii

1 GETTING STARTED 1

Learning Objectives 2
What Is a Computer? 2
The Computer System 3
    Software Concepts 3
    Hardware Concepts 4
Data Organization 5
Planning the Program 7
    The Programming Development Process 7
Planning Printer Output 9
    Report Planning Guidelines 12
Errors and Debugging 13
The Assembly Process 14
Key Review Terms 16
Review Exercises 17

2 NUMBER SYSTEMS AND DATA REPRESENTATION 19

Learning Objectives 20
The Decimal Number System 20
The Binary Number System 22
    Converting Decimal to Binary 23
    Adding and Subtracting Binary Integers 24
Computer Memory—Bits, Bytes, and Words 26
Two's Complement Notation 27

The Hexadecimal Number System and EBCDIC 29
   Converting Hexadecimal to Decimal 30
   Converting Decimal to Hexadecimal 31
   Adding and Subtracting Hexadecimal Integers 32
   The EBCDIC Coding Scheme 34
Zone-Decimal Data 34
General Instruction Format 36
Machine Language 38
   Machine Code 41
Symbolic Code and Assembler Language 43
General Purpose Registers 44
Assembler Language Coding Format 44
Pseudo-Assembler Programming Examples 45
Key Review Terms 49
Review Exercises 49
Programming Exercises 52

3 INTRODUCTION TO ASSEMBLER LANGUAGE   53

Learning Objectives 54
Fixed-Point Binary Operations 54
Define Constant (DC) Statement 55
   Fullword Numeric Constants 55
   Halfword Numeric Constants 56
   Character String Constants 57
   Hexadecimal Constants 58
Define Storage (DS) Statement 60
Load (L) Instruction 61
Load Register (LR) Instruction 62
Add (A) Instruction 63
Add Register (AR) Instruction 64
Subtract (S) Instruction 65
Subtract Register (SR) Instruction 65
Store Register (ST) Instruction 66
Partial Dump (PDUMP) Macro 67
End-of-Job (EOJ) Statement 69
END Statement 70
Sample Program CHAP3A 70
Multiply (M) Instruction 73
Multiply Register (MR) Instruction 74
Divide (D) Instruction 76

Divide Register (DR) Instruction 78
Sample Program CHAP3B 79
Key Review Terms 82
Review Exercises 82
Programming Exercises 84

4 FILES, MODULAR STRUCTURE, AND PRINTING OUTPUT 89

Learning Objectives 90
Files and Records 90
Defining Files in Assembler 91
OPEN Macro 94
CLOSE Macro 94
Preparing Data for Output 95
Convert to Decimal (CVD) Instruction 95
Unpack (UNPK) Instruction 96
Move Zone (MVZ) Instruction 97
Move Immediate (MVI) Instruction 98
Get (GET) Macro 99
Put (PUT) Macro 99
Equate (EQU) Statement 100
Sample Program CHAP4A 101
Move Character (MVC) Instruction 106
Edit (ED) Instruction 107
  Editing Patterns 107
Modular Structured Programming 110
Branch and Link (BAL) Instruction 111
Branch Register (BR) Instruction 112
Sample Program CHAP4B 113
Additional Sample Programs: CHAP4C and CHAP4D 117
Key Review Terms 122
Review Exercises 122
Programming Exercises 125

5 READING DATA AND PERFORMING LOOPS 128

Learning Objectives 129
Iteration and Loop Processing 129
Branch on Count (BCT) Instruction 130

Sample Program CHAP5A 131
Assigning Data to the Input File 137
Reading Data 138
Pack (PACK) Instruction 140
Convert to Binary (CVB) Instruction 141
Reading a File and Processing Totals 141
  Sample Program CHAP5B 141
  Sample Program CHAP5C 150
Tracking the General Purpose Registers 157
Structured Programming 158
  Programming Guidelines 158
Key Review Terms 159
Review Exercises 160
Programming Exercises 160

6 COMPARISON AND CONDITIONAL BRANCHING 168

Learning Objectives 169
Selecting Alternate Processing Paths 169
Program Flags 170
Unconditional and Conditional Branching 170
Condition Codes and Comparison Statements 171
Branch Statements 172
Compare Logical Character (CLC) Instruction 174
Branch on Equal (BE) and Branch on Not Equal (BNE) Instructions 175
Branch (B) Instruction 176
Compare (C) Instruction 176
Branch on High (BH) and Branch on Not High (BNH) Instructions 177
Sample Program CHAP6A 178
Compare Logical Immediate (CLI) Instruction 185
Compare Register (CR) Instruction 186
Branch on Low (BL) and Branch on Not Low (BNL) Instructions 186
Branch on Zero (BZ) and Branch on Not Zero (BNZ) Instructions 187

Branch on Positive (BP) and Branch on Not Positive (BNP)
  Instructions 188
Branch on Minus (BM) and Branch on Not Minus (BNM)
  Instructions 189
Load and Test Register (LTR) Instruction 189
Sample Program CHAP6B 190
Key Review Terms 198
Review Exercises 199
Programming Exercises 201

7 PAGE AND CONTROL BREAK PROCESSING 208

Learning Objectives 209
Performing Page Breaks 209
Sample Program CHAP7A 211
Performing Control Breaks 220
Sample Program CHAP7B 221
Key Review Terms 233
Review Exercises 233
Programming Exercises 234

8 PACKED-DECIMAL OPERATIONS 241

Learning Objectives 242
Packed-Decimal Data 242
Packed-Decimal Operations 243
Packed-Decimal Define Constant (DC) Statement 244
Packed-Decimal Define Storage (DS) Statement 245
Add Packed (AP) Instruction 246
Zero and Add Packed (ZAP) Instruction 247
Subtract Packed (SP) Instruction 249
Multiply Packed (MP) Instruction 249
Divide Packed (DP) Instruction 250
Compare Packed (CP) Instruction 252
Sample Program CHAP8 253
Key Review Terms 264
Review Exercises 264
Programming Exercises 265

9 SEQUENTIAL FILE UPDATING 266

Learning Objectives 267
Sequential File Maintenance 267
   Creating a File 267
   Updating a File 268
   Processing a File 269
Creating the Master File: Sample Program CHAP9A 269
Reading and Printing the Master File: Sample Program CHAP9B 273
Updating the Master File—Part I 279
   Sample Program CHAP9C 280
Updating the Master File—Part II 289
   Sample Program CHAP9D 290
Updating the Master File—Part III 300
   Sample Program CHAP9E 301
Key Review Terms 312
Review Exercises 312
Programming Exercises 313

APPENDIXES

A. Entering and Running Your First Program 319
B. Introduction to DOS Job Control Language 323
C. Summary Reference: Assembler Instructions 332
D. Summary Reference: EBCDIC Codes 335
E. Powers of Two and Sixteen Tables 337
F. Hexadecimal and Decimal Conversion Table 339
G. Answers to Asterisked Exercises 341

INDEX 349

PREFACE

This book is for any person who wants to program in Assembler, but who has little or no programming background and no mathematics beyond basic algebra. It provides an introduction to programming for the individual who wants to learn to write Assembler programs for business data processing applications.

Overall, the approach is to introduce the reader to the technique of coding modular structured programs. This book can be used as a one-semester introduction to programming in Assembler, either for the first- or second-year computer science or computer information systems major.

SPECIAL FEATURES

Emphasis is placed on the program development process and modular programming. The reader is introduced early to the necessity of planning the logic (pseudocode) and using top-down, modular structured programming to construct high-quality, easy-to-read programs.

Each instruction is introduced using the four step "show-and-tell" process:

1. The general format of the instruction is shown—*what it looks like*.
2. The purpose of the instruction is stated—*what it does*.
3. The mechanics of the instruction are discussed—*how it works*.
4. The instruction is illustrated with one or more examples—*how to use it*.

This text takes a "learn-by-doing" approach to presenting Assembler to the reader. As such, each chapter introduces one or more sample programs that are used to relate concepts by illustrating how the material may be applied to an actual data processing application.

Furthermore, each sample program illustrates the application of the program development process, from start to finish. This includes developing the logic using pseudocode, defining the input/output formats, identifying the processing functions, coding the program, and producing the output results.

Program dissection represents yet another special feature of this text. The author dissects the sample programs and takes the reader through the code, step-by-step, and explains how the program statements work together to produce the output results.

Numerous exercises, review terms, and programming problems appear at the end of each chapter. Answers to the asterisked exercises appear in Appendix G. People learn best by practicing. Hence, the programming exercises have been carefully designed to give the reader the opportunity to apply the textbook material by writing programs.

An Assembler Emulator Disk is made available with the Instructor's Manual for this text. This disk allows the user to write, test, and execute mainframe Assembler programs on the microcomputer. In other words, the user need not have access to a mainframe to use this textbook or to learn how to write mainframe Assembler programs. The sample programs presented in the text are run using the Assembler Emulator Disk.

WHAT IS COVERED

A major part of this text is dedicated to presenting the following material: introduction to computers and programming, data organization, the program development process, number systems and data representation, fixed-point binary operations, modular structured programming, file processing, basic DOS JCL, branching and looping, control break processing, packed-decimal operations, and sequential file updating.

WHAT IS NOT COVERED

This text does not include unnecessary details that might detract from the simplicity of writing high-quality programs. This book focuses primarily on providing an introduction to *basic* Assembler language from the structured programming point of view. Intricate details involving internal housekeeping functions are deferred to a more advanced study of Assembler.

Topics excluded are: table handling, macros and macro language, subprograms, bit manipulation, addressing and address modification, floating-point operations, and relocation. Only a brief discussion of relative addressing is included.

ACKNOWLEDGMENTS

First and foremost, I would like to express my sincere gratitude and thanks to all the people who contributed helpful comments and suggestions for improving this text, including its reviewers Len Bezar, Drexel University; Netiva Caftori, Northeastern Illinois University; Don Myers, Vincennes University; and Norman Rothberg, Drexel University.

A special round of thanks goes to my wise assistant, Cathy Young, who spent many long hours working with me to make this book a success. I honestly don't know what I would have done without her help and support.

I would also like to thank the editorial staff at boyd & fraser—Jim Edwards, Daphne Snow, Barbara Worth, and Chris Doran—for their help and generous support throughout the development of this text, and Rob Jared for making it all happen.

David M. Collopy

1 GETTING STARTED

OVERVIEW

Learning Objectives
What Is a Computer?
The Computer System
   Software Concepts
   Hardware Concepts
Data Organization
Planning the Program
   The Program Development Process
 Planning Printer Output
   Report Planning Guidelines
Errors and Debugging
The Assembly Process
Key Review Terms
Review Exercises

Chapter 1: Getting Started

LEARNING OBJECTIVES

After reading this chapter and completing the exercises, the reader should be able to:

- define the term "computer" and discuss the hardware and software components associated with computers.
- explain the hierarchical organization of data.
- explain the purpose of the program development process and the importance of report planning guidelines.
- understand the difference between syntax and logical errors.
- describe the process that the assembler goes through to convert source statements into an executable program.

WHAT IS A COMPUTER?

A computer is an electronic device that accepts input, processes it according to a given set of instructions, and provides the results of the processing. This process is shown schematically in Fig. 1.1. *Input* is a term used to define the data or unprocessed facts manipulated by the computer. *Output* refers to the processed information or results produced by the computer. Output takes many forms. Some examples of output are a list of names or values, a payroll check, a ticket to a baseball game, a printed report, and an updated file.

Essentially, a computer converts data into meaningful information. It is an electronic data processing device with internal storage for holding data and program instructions. Although a computer can perform complex computations with extraordinary speed and accuracy, it cannot do anything on its own. It must be told what to do every step of the way. The instructions that the computer follows are called a *program*, and the individual responsible for writing computer programs is called a *programmer*.

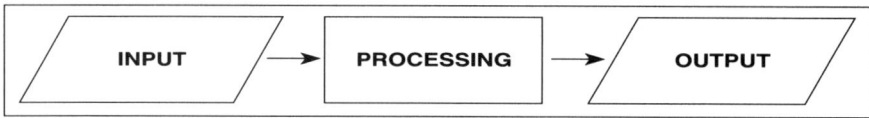

FIGURE 1.1 Basic Functions Performed by the Computer

A computer system consists of *software* (the instructions for processing the data) and *hardware* (the physical equipment used to process the data). Software includes application programs and the operating system. Hardware consists of input/output devices and the central processing or system unit. We will discuss these components in the sections that follow.

THE COMPUTER SYSTEM

SOFTWARE CONCEPTS

Software tells the computer what to do. It issues commands and directs the hardware in performing its work. There are two major types of software: applications and systems software.

Applications Software

Written for end-users, applications software is designed to perform a specific task, such as billing customers, administering payroll, taking inventory, or collecting accounts receivable. An *end-user* is anyone who uses a computer system to perform a task related to data processing. Applications software may be acquired by purchasing off-the-shelf packages or by designing and creating them for one's own purposes.

Packaged programs are prewritten and ready to use. They are available from many retail outlets and software firms. There are thousands of packaged programs on the market today, designed for many different applications.

Custom-made programs are usually written by in-house, trained professionals employed as programmers or by outside consulting firms specializing in custom programming.

In business, applications software has one main objective—to provide management with accurate, up-to-date, and timely information about the operations of the company.

Systems Software

Systems software is normally supplied by the manufacturer of the computer system and consists of utility programs and operating aids that facilitate the use of the computer. It includes the computer's operating system and related software that manages the system's resources and controls the operations of the hardware.

The operating system acts as an interface between the applications software and the computer itself. It allows the user to enter and run application programs. Other functions performed by the operating system include managing internal resources, controlling input/output operations, translating program statements into machine code, scheduling and running jobs, and organizing and manipulating files.

HARDWARE CONCEPTS

Hardware is the physical components of the computer system. It includes input/output devices, the central processing unit, and secondary storage devices. The term *hardware* refers to the actual equipment used to process the input data.

Input/Output Devices

Input devices, such as keyboards, monitors, and tape and disk units, accept and transmit data and program statements to the computer. They translate the input that is written in a form people understand into a code that the computer understands.

On the other hand, output devices, such as printers, monitors, and tape and disk units, translate the electronic signals that the computer understands into a form that people understand.

Central Processing Unit

The *central processing unit* (CPU) is considered to be the heart of the computer. It is responsible for processing the data and producing the output. The CPU is composed of the control unit, the arithmetic/logic unit, and the storage unit as shown in Fig. 1.2.

The *control unit* supervises and monitors the activities performed by the computer system. It does not process the data itself, but directs the processing

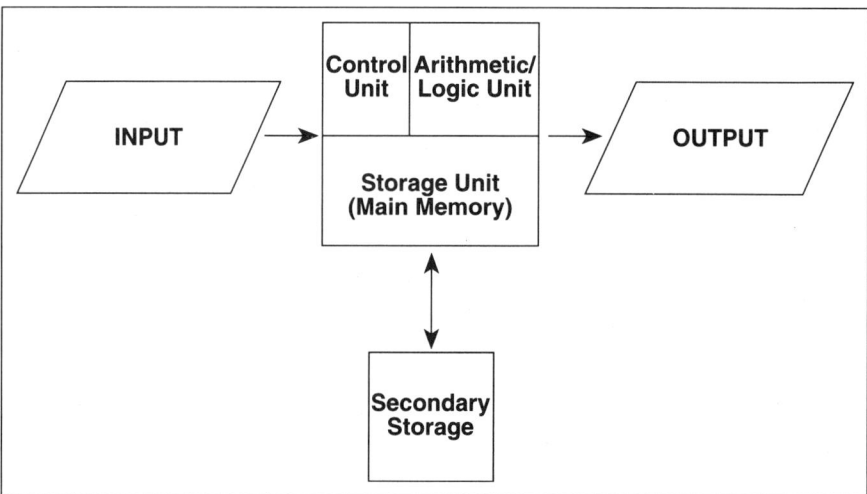

FIGURE 1.2 The Central Processing Unit

operations and coordinates the flow of data to the arithmetic/logic and storage units.

After the control unit instructs the input device to load the program and data, it interprets the program statements one at a time and tells the arithmetic/logic unit to carry out the instructions. It also tells the input device when to read more data and the output device when to write the results.

As the name implies, the *arithmetic/logic unit* (ALU) performs the arithmetic and logical operations required by the program. Arithmetic computations include addition, subtraction, multiplication, and division. Logical operations involve comparing the values of two data items to determine if one value is equal to, less than, or greater than the other. Hence, the major function of the ALU is to do the work, that is, to carry out the processing activities specified by the program.

The *storage unit*, or main memory, accepts input data, program instructions, intermediate results and values, and processed information and temporarily stores them for subsequent processing. Before the computer can execute a program, the instructions and data must reside within the computer's memory.

There are two important facts to know about the storage unit. First, the amount of storage space is limited; only a finite number of characters can be held at any one time. Second, the contents of storage are nonpermanent and are only temporarily maintained while the computer's power is on. Once the computer is turned off, the contents of main memory are lost and cannot be recovered unless they were previously saved to a secondary storage device.

Secondary storage mediums, such as magnetic tape or disks, permanently store data, programs, and processed information so that they are available to the computer on a per-need basis. That is, programs and data may be accessed by and transferred to the computer when they are called by the CPU. The contents of secondary storage remain intact until they are physically removed or deleted by the programmer.

DATA ORGANIZATION

Data is organized in a special way to facilitate processing by the computer. Individual characters entered at the keyboard can be organized into a hierarchical structure ranging from simple data fields to complex networks of integrated databases.

Chapter 1: Getting Started

As shown in Fig. 1.3, fields can be grouped to form a record, and records can be grouped to form a file. Note also that a field is simply a collection of characters.

The following list contains data organization terms and their definitions.

character Any single alphabetic (A–Z), numeric (0–9), or special (#@/*%$#...) symbol entered at the keyboard. For example, the file shown in Fig. 1.3 contains nothing more than a collection of individual alphabetic and numeric characters.

data field A string of character positions grouped together to form a single unit of meaningful information. For example, in Fig. 1.3 five characters have been grouped together to form the customer's account number and eleven characters have been assigned to represent the customer's name.

record A given set of logically related fields grouped together to form a complete unit of information about a particular entity. In Fig. 1.3, five fields comprise a single record that provides information about a customer. Each record consists of the following fields: account number, customer name, credit limit, balance due, and payment made.

file A finite set of related records. When the records for a specific application are grouped together, they are called a file. For example, if the Raintrax Manufacturing Company services 2453 customers, then their customer file would consist of 2453 records.

```
                         ──────── Fields ────────

            Account      Customer       Credit     Balance     Payment
            Number       Name           Limit      Due         Made

   R        12345        Brad Anders    5000.00    2500.00     2500.00
   e        16789        Tara Atkins    7000.00    5748.00     0300.00
   c        20161        Karen Baker    5000.00    0000.00     0000.00
   o          :             :             :          :            :
   r          :             :             :          :            :
   d          :             :             :          :            :
   s        97865        Dave Zephur    3000.00    0125.00     0050.00
```

FIGURE 1.3 Customer Accounts File

database   A large set of integrated records or files. A database consists of a pool of centrally located files that may be accessed and processed by multiple applications. For example, a customer database could be set up to store the customer accounts file for the home office as well as the customer accounts files for all the branch offices.

PLANNING THE PROGRAM

Program logic should be planned. Trial-and-error guesswork has no place in the programming profession. Designing program logic can be compared to building an expressway. The engineer would lay out detailed plans before going to the time, trouble, or expense of building a complex network of highways. Construction would not begin until the completed plan was carefully laid out in writing. Similarly, the programmer should plan carefully and write out the design for a program before sitting down at the computer. A good plan can save hours of frustration at the terminal and produce successful results within a shorter period of time.

Structured program development saves time and increases programmer productivity. Programming can be a complex process involving a multitude of interrelated operations and computations. However, when logic is planned, even the most difficult application can be effectively and efficiently managed. When used properly, the seven-step program development process presented below will help to produce a more reliable program in less time and one that can be maintained more easily throughout its use.

THE PROGRAM DEVELOPMENT PROCESS

Step 1: Defining the Problem
- Determine the objectives of the program. Write a brief statement or paragraph describing the purpose of the program.

Step 2: Analyzing the Problem
- Determine what the output should look like. Sketch a rough draft of the output. Use paper and pencil to lay out the data fields, records, and files. Design and erase as you go.
- Determine the input. Use the output to determine the input data. Focus on identifying the input required by the computer to produce the output.

- Define the processing functions performed by the program. Identify the steps, activities, or calculations required to manipulate the input data and produce the output.
- List the functions on paper. Don't pay attention to their order; simply write them down as they are identified. Once all of the functions have been listed, arrange them in processing order. If possible, group related functions together, but only when it is obvious they belong together.

Step 3: Designing the Program Logic
- Use the ordered list of functions identified in Step 2 to write the *pseudocode* for the program logic. Pseudocode represents English-like statements that are used to outline and describe the logic of a program.
- Desk check the pseudocode and make corrections as needed. When the pseudocode is complete, the programmer checks it over manually by tracing the flow of data through the logic. This process of verifying the logic is called *desk checking*. Of course, corrections are made until the pseudocode produces the desired output.

Step 4: Coding the Program
- Write out the program code on paper. The pseudocode is used to translate the program logic into Assembler statements. That is, the actual program instructions are coded from the logic design. This is accomplished by writing out the program code on paper.
- Desk check the Assembler statements and make corrections as needed.

Step 5: Keying-in the Program
- Enter the program into the computer by keying-in the statements.

Step 6: Testing and Debugging the Program
- Test the statements by running the program. If errors are found during the run, it is the programmer's responsibility to fix those parts of the program that did not work. In programming, an error is called a *bug*, and *debugging* refers to the process of eliminating errors. In short, a bug is any code that prevents a program from producing the correct output.

Step 7: Gathering the Program Documentation
- Gather the documentation that you have created throughout the programming process. Documentation provides information about the program and is used as a reference when updating or maintaining the program. Documentation includes a statement of the problem, input/output definitions, a list of the processing functions, the pseudocode, a program listing, and samples of the output.

PLANNING PRINTER OUTPUT

For the most part, business application programs are written to provide management with meaningful information. Management uses this information to monitor the operations of the company and to assist its employees in making profitable decisions about the business.

But before any information can be produced by the computer, it must first be carefully planned. The data processing results should be organized so that they provide the information that management needs. The output should provide meaningful, relevant, and timely information about the business enterprise.

Take a look at the computer generated report shown in Fig. 1.4. As simple as it may seem, it provides management with relevant information about the company's customers. It consists of column headings that form a four-column report with information about each customer's name, balance due, monthly payment, and new balance.

The body of the report is made up of detail lines. The first detail line of the report gives information about the account belonging to a customer named Ayers. At the time this report was generated, Ayers had a previous balance of $500, made a $200 payment, and currently owes $300. The customer named Walker, on the other hand, has paid in full.

This particular report shows the current status of the accounts receivable system. When customers call to ask their current balance due, management can retrieve this information readily. Similarly, management can use the information in the report to monitor overdue accounts.

The last line in Fig. 1.4 shows report totals for balances due, monthly payments, and new balances.

CUSTOMER NAME	BALANCE DUE	MONTHLY PAYMENT	NEW BALANCE
Ayers	500.00	200.00	300.00
Fontaine	750.00	600.00	150.00
Howard	400.00	300.00	100.00
Ryan	300.00	175.00	125.00
Walker	563.00	563.00	000.00
TOTALS	2513.00	1838.00	675.00

FIGURE 1.4 Accounts Receivable

Reports may vary significantly in design, size, and layout. Usually, clients have a rough idea of what they want the report to look like, as well as the information it should contain. However, it may be necessary for the programmer to sit down and work with a client to design the layout of the report.

The report, shown in Fig. 1.5 for Tamarack Automotive Services was designed with the help of a printer spacing chart (see Fig. 1.6). Forms and reports are designed to fit the horizontal and vertical spacing given for the printer being used.

Common printer specifications for micro- and mainframe computers are shown in Table 1.1. Spacing across the page is measured in characters per inch (CPI); spacing down the page is given as lines per inch (LPI). From the table, we see that the 80-character–line printer for the microcomputer has a horizontal spacing of 10 CPI and a vertical spacing of 6 LPI.

The printer spacing chart in Fig. 1.6 is made up of rows and columns corresponding to the horizontal and vertical print positions of the printer. A programmer uses the chart to design and lay out reports. Once the design is complete, the programmer codes Assembler statements to set up page titles, column headings, detail lines, and so on. Later we'll see how to use special carriage-control characters to control the vertical spacing of the output.

The abbreviations PT, HL, DL, TL, and SL shown on the left side of the printer spacing chart stand for Page Title, Heading Line, Detail Line, Total Line, and Summary Line, respectively. They are notations that remind the

```
                TAMARACK AUTOMOTIVE SERVICES
                     Accounts Receivable
                          mm/dd/yy
        CUSTOMER      BALANCE       MONTHLY        NEW
          NAME          DUE         PAYMENT      BALANCE

        Ayers          500.00       200.00       300.00
        Fontaine       750.00       600.00       150.00
        Howard         400.00       300.00       100.00
        Ryan           300.00       175.00       125.00
        Walker         563.00       563.00       000.00

        TOTALS:       2513.00      1838.00       675.00

        LARGEST NEW BALANCE    $ 300.00
        LARGEST PAYMENT MADE   $ 600.00
```

FIGURE 1.5 Output Report

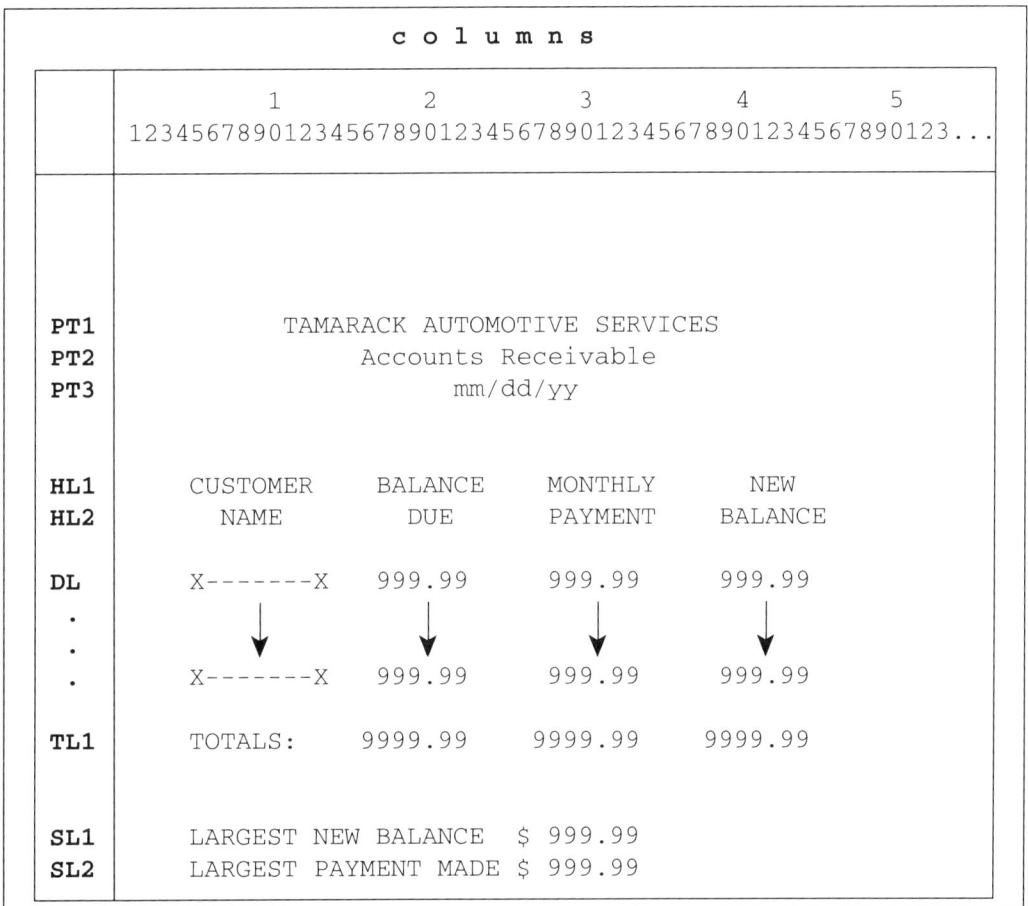

FIGURE 1.6 Printer Spacing Chart

	HORIZONTAL	**VERTICAL**
MICRO:	80-character line with 10 CPI	6 LPI
MAINFRAME:	132-character line with 10–12 CPI	6–8 LPI

TABLE 1.1 Printer Specifications

programmer to define and assign names to the appropriate print lines at coding time. We will discuss this topic further in the section that follows, entitled Report Planning Guidelines.

Also note the use of the Xs and the 9s. They specify the maximum size (print positions) reserved for printing character data (X) and numeric data (9).

REPORT PLANNING GUIDELINES

There are guidelines the programmer should follow when designing printer output for the user. The purpose of the guidelines is to provide a set of standards or procedures that help produce reports that are easier to read and understand. It can be extremely frustrating for the user to thumb through a stack of computer reports that are difficult to read or understand.

The following guidelines were used to design the report shown in Fig. 1.5.

Step 1: Start on a New Page
Start the report at the top of the page. Skip five or six lines before printing the page titles.

Step 2: Page Titles
Center the page title (PT) by subtracting the number of characters in the line from 80. Then compute the starting position of the left margin by dividing the difference by two. Code the line on the printer spacing chart, beginning at the left margin. Single-space multiple page titles and use PT1, PT2, PT3, and so on, to identify them.

Step 3: Heading Lines
Skip two lines and center the heading line (HL). Unless instructed otherwise by the user, leave two blank lines between the last page title and the first heading line. Column headings are normally centered above the data to which they refer. Single-space multiple headings and use HL1, HL2, HL3, and so on., to identify them.

NOTE: Print the page title, column headings, and the page number at the top of each page.

Step 4: Detail Lines
Skip a line and print the first detail line (DL). Detail lines represent the body of the report and are normally single spaced. They should be centered on the printer spacing chart before coding the column headings. Use the following method to center detail lines: First, print the detail line on a piece of scrap paper. Second, decide how many spaces you want between the data items; usually 3–5 blank spaces will do. Third, use the method described in Step 2 to center the line. Center each column heading above the data to which it refers.

Step 5: Total Lines
Use one or two blank lines to separate the last detail line from the first total line (TL). Single-space multiple total lines and use TL1, TL2, TL3, and so on, to identify them.

Step 6: Summary Lines
Skip two lines and print the summary line (SL). Single-space multiple summary lines and use SL1, SL2, SL3, and so on, to identify them.

ERRORS AND DEBUGGING

During program execution, one of three things may occur:

1. Errors are detected by the assembler.
2. Errors are not found, but the output is incorrect.
3. Errors are not found, and the output is correct.

Case 1: Syntax Errors
If an error was detected by the assembler error checker, then the program contains one or more syntax errors. A *syntax error* is an error that violates the rules of the programming language. In other words, a statement was incorrectly coded and has been rejected as erroneous. Often, syntax errors are the result of misspelling or miskeying. Whatever the cause, syntax errors must be corrected and the program reassembled before the program will run successfully.

Case 2: Logic Errors
A *logic error* is an error in the design of a program. At times, logic errors can be extremely difficult to locate. Unlike syntax errors, the error checker has no way of detecting logic errors. Logic errors are usually the result of poor program planning and design. Even though the statements coded are syntactically correct, the program produces incorrect output.

For example, if the programmer assigns the numeric value 4 to HOURS WORKED when 40 should have been assigned, then the program would run but produce output different from what was expected. Also, if PAYRATE and HOURS WORKED were added when they should have been multiplied, the program would run but produce incorrect results.

Case 3: Clean Run
A clean run occurs when the program produces the correct output. It is often a surprise to the novice programmer to discover that programs normally do not run clean on the first try. Programming involves managing a multitude of

detail and complex logic. Once this is understood, it is no longer a surprise to the novice to see errors during a run. The major purpose of the program development process is to reduce the number and complexity of errors by applying a structured approach to managing the programming application.

THE ASSEMBLY PROCESS

The assembly process that follows has been simplified to provide a basic understanding of how programs are executed by the CPU. The exact details of this process are involved and complex and therefore beyond the scope of this text. Such topics would normally be presented in a course on operating systems.

Programmers write instructions in a programming language for the computer to follow. These English-like instructions, called the *source program*, are read by the computer and stored in main memory for subsequent processing. Since the computer cannot execute the source program in this form, each statement must undergo a series of transformations before it can be processed by the assembler. In Fig. 1.7, we see that the source statements are translated into object form by the assembler. The object module represents the machine

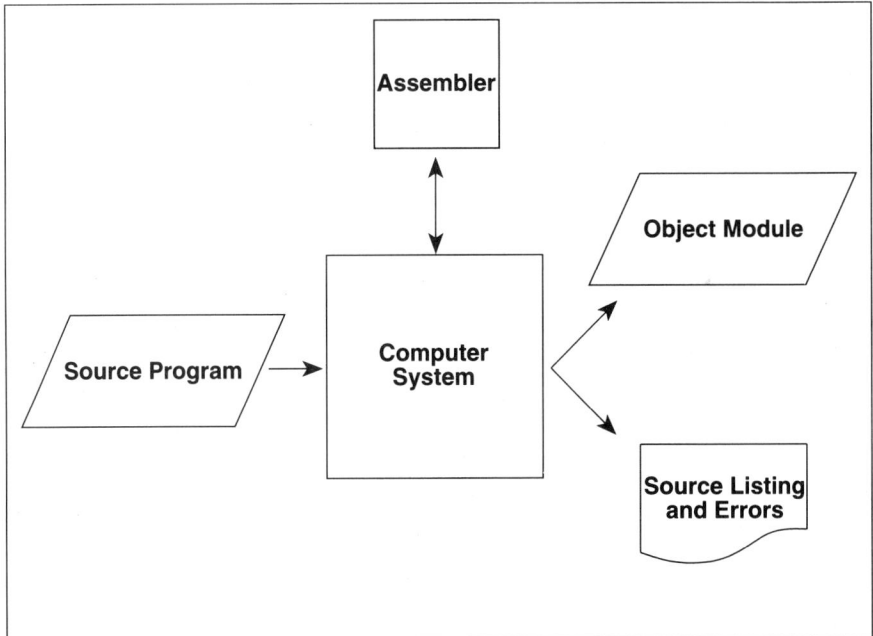

FIGURE 1.7 Assembling the Program

code equivalent of the source program. Actually, each statement in the source program is read and scanned twice by the assembler. During the scanning process, assembler translates the source program into machine code, prints a listing of the source statements, allocates storage space in memory for the object module, and checks for syntax errors.

If errors are detected, assembler flags each statement found in error and, at the end of the source listing, prints a list of diagnostic error messages that briefly describe any syntax errors. At this point, it is up to the programmer to fix the errors and reassemble the program. This process of locating and fixing errors is called *debugging* and continues until the source listing indicates that no errors were found during the assembly.

Even though the object module exists in machine code form, it cannot be executed directly by the computer. It must first undergo further transformation by the linkage editor before the program is ready for execution. The primary objective of the linkage editor is to create a load module from the object module produced by the assembler. As shown in Fig. 1.8, the linkage editor reads the object module, performs several preliminary housekeeping operations, creates an executable load module, and stores it on a disk for later use. When needed, the load module may be retrieved and executed by the computer.

The final step in the assembly process is the execution of the program. In Figure 1.9, the load module is placed in memory by the loader and executed. The loader retrieves the load module, performs the final housekeeping operations, creates an executable program, stores it in main memory, and then

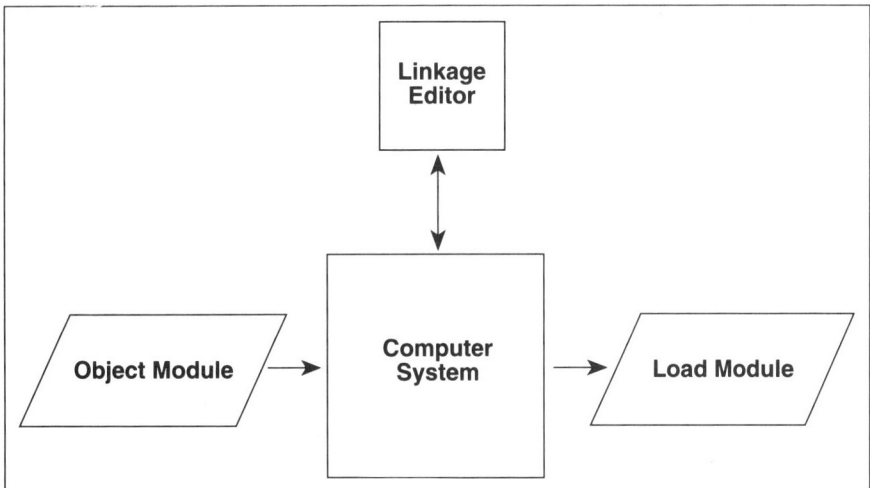

FIGURE 1.8 Linking the Program

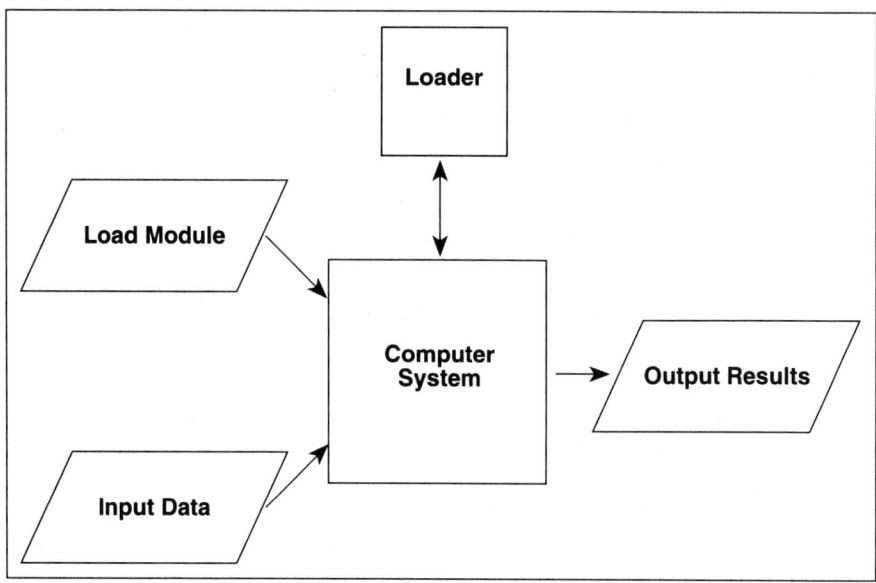

FIGURE 1.9 Executing the Program

executes each program statement in succession. Note that it is during the final step in the assembly process that the input data is read and processed by the program to produce the output results.

KEY REVIEW TERMS

Define the following terms:

load module	information	systems software
data	assembler	CPU
program	pseudocode	printer spacing chart
database	control unit	program development
syntax error	end-user	process
source program	record	input
application software	debugging	logic error
CPI/LPI	output	object module
storage unit	software	computer
input device	file	field
character	linkage editor	desk checking
packaged program	output device	hardware
loader	arithmetic/logic unit	
documentation	custom-made program	

REVIEW EXERCISES

Answers to asterisked exercises are given in Appendix G.

TRUE/FALSE QUESTIONS

*1. A computer is an electronic device that converts input data into meaningful information.

*2. Software consists of input/output devices and the central processing unit.

*3. Input devices accept and transmit program statements and data to the storage unit.

4. The central processing unit is the heart of the computer system; it is responsible for manipulating input data and producing output results.

*5. The control unit reads the source statements and performs the processing specified by the program.

6. Arithmetic operations and logical comparisons are performed by the ALU.

*7. One major function performed by the storage unit is to convert the source program into machine code.

8. Before the computer can execute a program, the program instructions and data must reside within main memory.

9. Main memory, for most computer systems, is unlimited in storage capacity and is often used to temporarily hold programs and data for subsequent processing.

*10. When the power is turned off, the contents of internal storage remain intact and can be recovered once the power is restored.

*11. Packaged software is available through retail outlets and consists of a variety of application programs that are pre-written and ready to use.

12. Custom-made software is often developed and produced by end-users.

*13. Systems software, supplied by the computer manufacturer, includes an operating system and related software that manage the system resources and control the overall operation of the hardware.

14. The operating system supervises input/output operations, translates source programs, schedules and runs programs, and organizes and manipulates files.

*15. Data is normally organized into files to facilitate processing by the computer.

16. A database is a collection of logically related data items or fields.

*17. The purpose of the program development process is to provide a structured approach and organized methodology for planning and creating custom-made programming applications.

18. Pseudocode is a design tool used by the programmer to describe each detailed instruction required by the program.

*19. Testing and debugging refers to the process of running a program to see if it produces the correct output and fixing errors when the program produces incorrect output.

20. Documentation provides detailed information about the input/output devices and operating system used to test and debug a program.

*21. Basically, the assembler checks for logic and syntax errors in the source program.

22. The assembler accepts the source code as input and produces two output items—the object module and a listing of the source program.

*23. When errors are found during the linking step, the linkage editor prints a list of diagnostic error messages along with the source program.

24. The load module represents, in executable format, a machine code equivalent of the source program.

*25. During the final step of the assembly process, the input data is read and processed by the computer to produce the output results.

26. A printer spacing chart is used not only to format reports, but to set up print lines for a program.

2 NUMBER SYSTEMS AND DATA REPRESENTATION

OVERVIEW

Learning Objectives
The Decimal Number System
The Binary Number System
   Converting Decimal to Binary
   Adding and Subtracting Binary Integers
Computer Memory—Bits, Bytes, and Words
Two's Complement Notation
The Hexadecimal Number System and EBCDIC
   Converting Hexadecimal to Decimal
   Converting Decimal to Hexadecimal
   Adding and Subtracting Hexadecimal Integers
   The EBCDIC Coding Scheme
Zone-Decimal Data
General Instruction Format
Machine Language
   Machine Code
Symbolic Code and Assembler Language
General Purpose Registers
Assembler Language Coding Format
Pseudo-Assembler Programming Examples
Key Review Terms
Review Exercises
Programming Exercises

Chapter 2: Number Systems and Data Representation

LEARNING OBJECTIVES

After reading this chapter and completing the exercises, the reader should be able to:

- understand the operational mechanics behind the decimal number system.
- convert binary constants to decimal and convert decimal constants to binary.
- convert hexadecimal constants to binary and decimal and convert binary and decimal constants to hexadecimal.
- add and subtract binary and hexadecimal numbers.
- describe how internal storage, or computer memory, is organized and how the computer represents data in EBCDIC.
- discuss the evolution of programming languages from machine code to high-level languages.
- explain how Assembler uses general purpose registers to process binary data.
- describe the Assembler language coding format.

THE DECIMAL NUMBER SYSTEM

The decimal number system represents integer values with the digits 0 through 9. Even though we use the decimal system on a regular basis, most of us would find it difficult to explain its operational mechanics. We are so accustomed to the decimal system that we do our mathematical computations without considering how the system works.

Let's take time now to see how the operational mechanics of the decimal system actually work. In so doing, we hope to find a common algorithm that can be applied to all number systems.

As an example, let's consider the decimal integer 1458. Each digit position represents a power of ten, which is the base of the system. The actual value represented by the integer is derived by multiplying each digit by its appropriate power of ten and then adding the results. This concept

The Decimal Number System

is illustrated below:

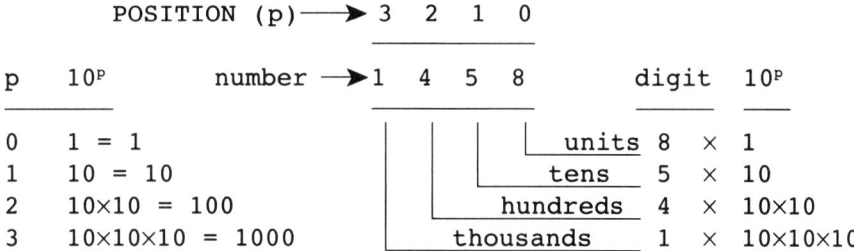

According to the example, the 8 is in the units position, the 5 is in the tens position, the 4 is in the hundreds position, and the 1 is in the thousands position.

In base ten, we may show the *positional notation* for the integer 1458 as:

```
                              powers of 10
                    8 × 1    =    8
                    5 × 10   =   50     (multiply each digit
                    4 × 100  =  400      by its respective
                    1 × 1000 = 1000      power of ten)
       digits of
    the number system            1458   add the results
```

We may also express an integer in *expanded form*, a shortened version of positional notation. The expanded form for 1458 is shown below:

$$1 \times 10^3 + 4 \times 10^2 + 5 \times 10^1 + 8 \times 10^0 = 1458$$

$$1 \times 1000 + 4 \times 100 + 5 \times 10 + 8 \times 1 = 1458$$

There are two basic rules of algebra we must keep in mind when expressing integers in either positional notation or expanded form. First, any number N raised to the 0th power is equal to 1. Second, any number N raised to the 1st power is equal to N.

1. $N^0 = 1$
2. $N^1 = N$

Let's look at a second example. The positional notation and expanded form for the decimal integer 659 is:

```
POSITIONAL NOTATION              EXPANDED FORM

6 5 9
│ │ └── 9×1   =   9              6×10² + 5×10¹ + 9×10⁰ = 659
│ └──── 5×10  =  50
└────── 6×100 = 600
                ───
                659
```

THE BINARY NUMBER SYSTEM

Base two, the binary number system, represents numeric values with the digits 0 and 1. The computer performs all work in binary. It interprets and translates all commands, constants, and variables into binary code before processing them.

As an exercise, let's convert the binary integer 110100 to decimal. From the previous section, we know each digit represents a power of the base (in this case, base two). Furthermore, we know the decimal value of an integer can be found by multiplying each digit by its respective power of the base and then adding the results.

The illustration below shows how this process works for base two.

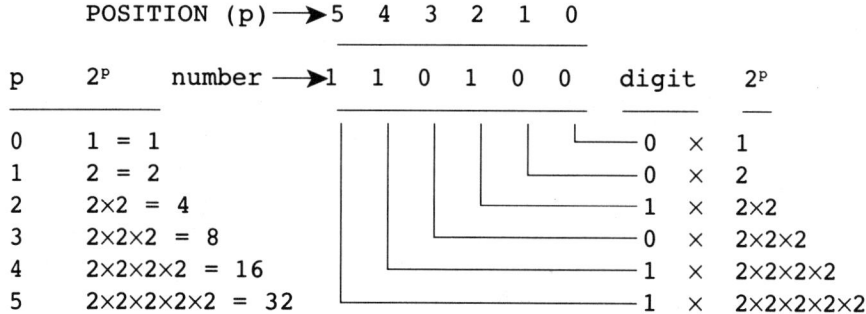

```
           POSITION (p) ──▶ 5  4  3  2  1  0
                           ───────────────────
 p    2ᵖ           number ──▶1  1  0  1  0  0    digit    2ᵖ
───────────────            ───────────────────
 0    1 = 1                                 └──── 0  ×  1
 1    2 = 2                              └─────── 0  ×  2
 2    2×2 = 4                         └────────── 1  ×  2×2
 3    2×2×2 = 8                    └───────────── 0  ×  2×2×2
 4    2×2×2×2 = 16              └──────────────── 1  ×  2×2×2×2
 5    2×2×2×2×2 = 32         └─────────────────── 1  ×  2×2×2×2×2
```

            DECIMAL RESULT OF BINARY 110100 IS 52

When we add the powers of two for the digits with a coefficient of one, we get the decimal sum 52. In other words, the positional notation of a binary number shows the conversion of the number to base ten. That is, the binary integer

110100 is equal to the decimal integer 52.

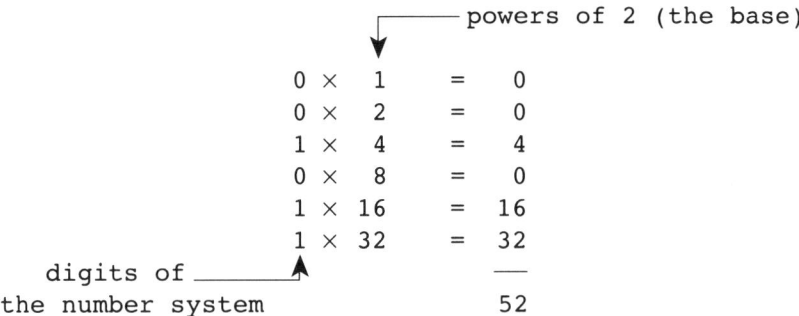

We may express the binary integer 110100 in expanded form as:

$$1\times 2^5 + 1\times 2^4 + 0\times 2^3 + 1\times 2^2 + 0\times 2^1 + 0\times 2^0 = 52$$

$$1\times 32 + 1\times 16 + 0\times 8 + 1\times 4 + 0\times 2 + 0\times 1 = 52$$

CONVERTING DECIMAL TO BINARY

In the previous section, we learned how to convert a binary integer to a decimal value. Now let's reverse the process and convert a decimal integer to binary. The simplest way to do this is to perform a series of repeated divides until the quotient equals zero. The following examples illustrate this process.

Example 1. Converting Decimal 52 to Binary

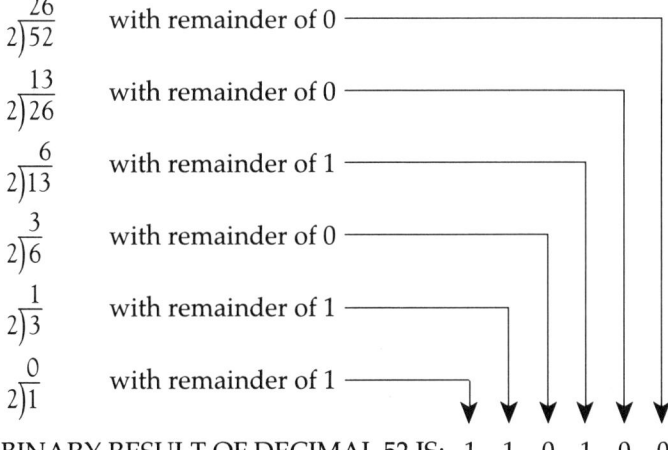

For Example 1, the decimal integer 52 is repeatedly divided by two, the target base of the conversion. Note that each quotient is subsequently divided by the base and its corresponding remainder is recorded. This process continues until the quotient equals zero. The binary digits for the result are made up of the remainders. Hence, decimal 52 is equivalent to 110100 in binary.

Example 2. Converting Decimal 37 to Binary

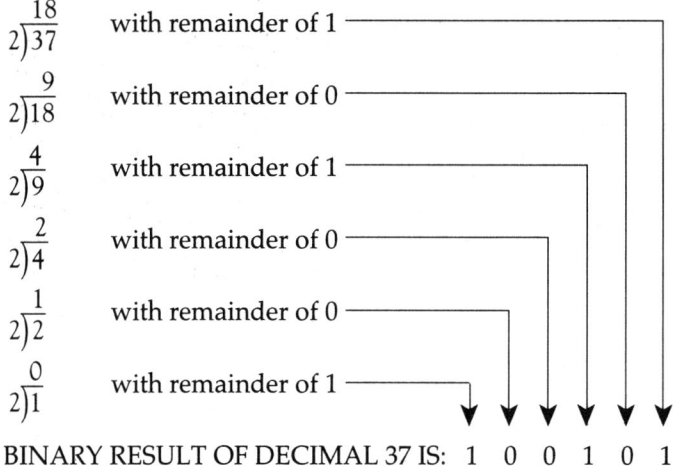

BINARY RESULT OF DECIMAL 37 IS: 1 0 0 1 0 1

ADDING AND SUBTRACTING BINARY INTEGERS

Binary addition and subtraction resemble decimal addition and subtraction in a fundamental way: In both, we carry and borrow digits from the position on the left as required. The best way to explain this concept is to cite a few examples. But first, let's take a look at the fundamental rules of binary addition.

```
Binary Addition Rules:    A.    B.    C.    D.    E.

                                                   1
                          0     0     1     1     1
                         +0    +1    +0    +1    +1
                         ──    ──    ──    ──    ──
                          0     1     1    10    11
```

The first three rules are relatively straightforward. However, the last two rules are not.

Adding and Subtracting Binary Integers

Rule D: 1 + 1 = 10. In binary, 1 + 1 = 0 with a carry of 1. We can verify this in decimal by adding the digits and converting the result to binary. For example, in decimal form, 1 + 1 = 2. When you convert 2 from decimal to binary, the result is 10.

Rule E: 1 + 1 + 1 = 11. We may use parentheses and express 1 + 1 + 1 as (1 + 1) + (1). Then, by substitution and application of Rule D we have (10) + (1) = 11. In other words, in decimal, 1 + 1 + 1 = 3, and 3 is equivalent to binary 11.

This would be a good time to pause and work the problems below. Compare your answers with the decimal equivalents shown.

```
                                                              110
   011       1100100      1111      111111     10110         111
  +100      +1001011     +1011     +101010    +11111        +011
  ----      --------     -----     -------    ------        ----
   111      10101111     11010     1101001    110101       10000


                                                             6
     3          100        15          63         22         7
    +4        + 75        +11         +42        +31        +3
    --        ----        ---         ---        ---        --
     7         175         26         105         53         16


Binary Subtraction Rules:     A.     B.     C.     D.

                               0      1      1     10
                              -0     -0     -1     -1
                              --     --     --     --
                               0      1      0      1
```

The first three rules involve ordinary subtraction operations, whereas the last one may seem a little odd. Let's take a closer look at Rule D: 10 − 1. Before we can subtract 1 from 0, we must borrow two (the base value) from the digit on the left (reducing 1 to 0) and then add the base value to the 0 on the right. Hence, 10 − 1 = 02 − 1 or 2 − 1, which equals 1. Therefore, in binary 10 − 1 = 1, or in decimal 2 − 1 = 1.

Let's work the subtraction problems below. Be sure to verify your answers.

```
  101      1101      1111     11011    10011110     1001
 -001     -1011     -1011    -10100   -01111111    -0111
 ----     -----     -----    ------   ---------    -----
  100      0010      0100     00111    00011111     0010


    5       13        15        27        158         9
   -1      -11       -11       -20       -127        -7
   --      ---       ---       ---       ----        --
    4        2         4         7         31         2
```

COMPUTER MEMORY—BITS, BYTES, AND WORDS

Think of computer memory as a huge storage area (even though it is small in physical size) reserved for holding data and program instructions. It acts as a gigantic repository of binary digits. A binary digit, 0 or 1, is called a *bit* and represents the most basic element of memory. Bit is an acronym for binary digit.

Most computers group eight bits together to form a unit called a *byte*. A byte represents a single character and is the smallest addressable unit that may be accessed by the CPU. The terms byte and character are often used interchangeably and refer to the same thing—a string of eight contiguous bits.

Furthermore, computer architectures group four bytes together and call this group a *word*, or *fullword*. A *halfword* is two bytes, and a *doubleword* is eight bytes (Table 2.1).

Binary integers normally occupy fullwords or halfwords. Figure 2.1 shows that fullwords consist of a sign bit and 31 bits for data. Halfwords consist of a

Bits	Bytes	
8	1	Character
16	2	Halfword
32	4	Fullword
64	8	Doubleword

TABLE 2.1 Grouping Bits into Bytes and Words

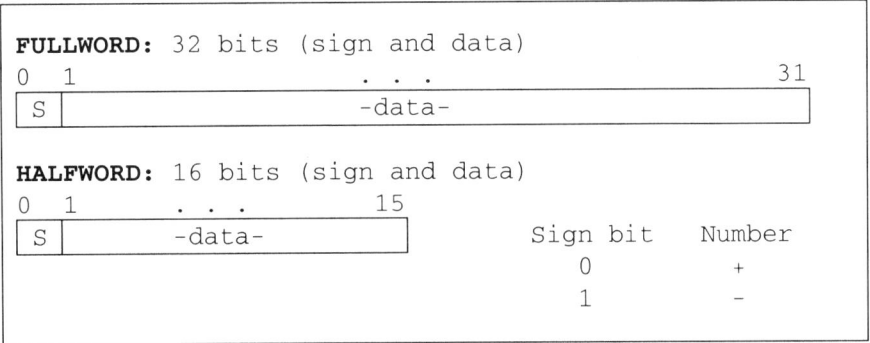

FIGURE 2.1 Fullword and Halfword Formats

sign bit and 15 bits for holding data. The bits are numbered from left to right, starting with 0. Zero is always assigned to the leftmost bit. This is an important convention to remember: The first bit is labeled 0, not 1. For example, the 16 bits for a halfword are numbered 0 through 15, while the bits for a fullword are numbered 0 through 31.

TWO'S COMPLEMENT NOTATION

Positive binary numbers have a sign bit of zero and are always stored internally in their true binary form. On the other hand, negative binary numbers have a sign bit of one and are always stored in memory in two's complement notation. Finding the two's complement of a negative integer involves the following:

1. Take the absolute value of the negative decimal integer and convert it to binary.
2. Pad the number on the left with zeros to complete either a halfword or fullword, whichever is appropriate.
3. Flip the bits—change all 1 bits to 0 and all 0 bits to 1.
4. Add 1 to the binary number.

As an exercise, let's compute the two's complement of –75. Using the conversion technique given in the previous section, we discover that the binary equivalent for the absolute value of –75 is 1001011. The two's complement process is shown below:

```
                                              binary digits for
1. Binary code:                1001011 ◄──── absolute value
2. Pad to halfword: 0000000001001011             of -75
3. Flip the bits:   1111111110110100
4. Add 1:                           +1
                    ──────────────────
                    1111111110110101
```

The binary integer 1111111110110101 represents the two's complement of –75. Note the sign bit is set to 1, as it should be for any negative number. For additional practice, let's find the two's complement of –135.

```
                                              binary digits for
1. Binary code:                10000111 ◄──── absolute value
2. Pad to halfword: 0000000010000111             of -135
3. Flip the bits:   1111111101111000
4. Add 1:                           +1
                    ──────────────────
                    1111111101111001
```

TWO'S COMPLEMENT OF -135 IS: 1111111101111001

Suppose we have the two's complement of a number and we wish to find its corresponding decimal value. We can do this easily by reversing the process: flip the bits, add one, convert the resulting binary value to decimal, and place a minus sign in front of the result.

```
            1111111101111001  =  ? in decimal

1. Given:           1111111101111001
2. Flip the bits:   0000000010000110
3. Add 1:                         +1
                    ──────────────────
4. Evaluate:               10000111  =  135
```

Hence, the decimal equivalent of 1111111101111001 is –135.

THE HEXADECIMAL NUMBER SYSTEM AND EBCDIC

Hexadecimal, base sixteen, is made up of the digits 0 through 9 and the letters A through F, representing the hexadecimal values 10 through 15. Base sixteen can be used as shorthand notation for base two. As shown in Table 2.2, four binary digits can be condensed into one hexadecimal digit.

For example, the 32-bit binary integer shown below may be reduced to 8 digits in base sixteen: CF4BA983.

```
binary:       1100 1111 0100 1011 1010 1001 1000 0011
hexadecimal:    C    F    4    B    A    9    8    3
```

This reduction explains an important benefit of the hexadecimal system: It saves both processing time and storage space.

Let's work a second example to clarify the conversion process. Given the binary value 1010001101, we will convert it to hexadecimal.

Begin on the right and mark off groups of four bits. As necessary, pad the leftmost group with enough zeros to expand it to four positions. Now convert each group of bits to one hexadecimal digit. The steps are shown below.

```
1. group into four digits:    10 1000 1101
2. expand with zeros:       0010 1000 1101
3. convert to hexadecimal:    2    8    D

HEXADECIMAL RESULT OF 1010001101 IS: 28D
```

Decimal	Hexadecimal	Binary	Decimal	Hexadecimal	Binary
0	0	0000	10	A	1010
1	1	0001	11	B	1011
2	2	0010	12	C	1100
3	3	0011	13	D	1101
4	4	0100	14	E	1110
5	5	0101	15	F	1111
6	6	0110			
7	7	0111			
8	8	1000			
9	9	1001			

TABLE 2.2 Hexadecimal digits

We may convert a hexadecimal value to binary by reversing the process. Given the hexadecimal number FA7CE, convert each digit into its four-bit binary equivalent.

```
hexadecimal:      F    A    7    C    E
     binary:    1111 1010 0111 1100 1110
```

CONVERTING HEXADECIMAL TO DECIMAL

The following example, using the hexadecimal integer A9C5, shows how to convert a hexadecimal integer to a decimal integer. The decimal equivalent of A9C5 can be found by adding the products of its digits and their corresponding powers of sixteen.

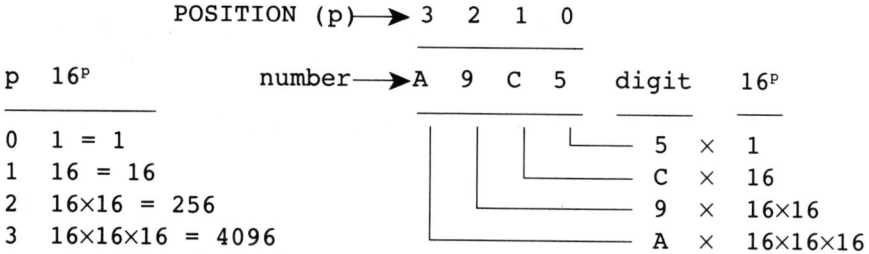

From this exercise, we see that the positional notation of a hexadecimal number shows the conversion of the number to base 10. The simplified version of the positional notation shown below converts A9C5 to 43,461 in decimal.

```
                          ┌──── powers of 16 (the base)
                          ▼
              5 × 1    =   5 × 1    =       5
              C × 16   =  12 × 16   =     192
              9 × 256  =   9 × 256  =    2304
              A × 4096 =  10 × 4096 =   40960
  digits of   ▲                           ─────
the number system                         43461
```

The expanded form for A9C5 is given below:

| A×16³ + 9×16² + C×16¹ + 5×16⁰ = 43461 |

```
    10×4096  +  9×256  +  12×16  +  5×1  =  43461
```

The Hexadecimal Number System and EBCDIC

CONVERTING DECIMAL TO HEXADECIMAL

We may convert a decimal integer to hexadecimal by performing the same series of repeated divides shown earlier. When we apply this technique to a base-sixteen conversion, note that we divide by 16:

Example 1. Converting Decimal 1196 to Hexadecimal:

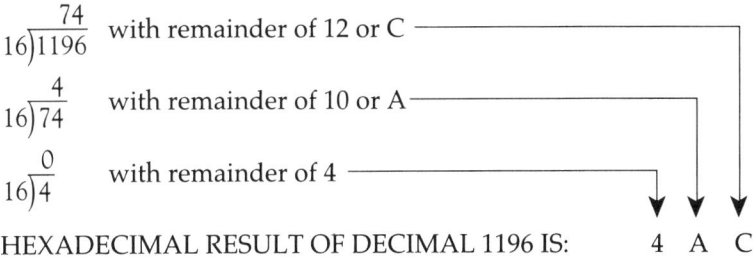

HEXADECIMAL RESULT OF DECIMAL 1196 IS: 4 A C

For the first example, the dividend 1196 is divided by 16, the target base. Each quotient thereafter is subsequently divided by 16 and its corresponding remainder is noted. This process continues until the quotient equals zero. Hence, 1196 in base ten equals 4AC in base sixteen.

Example 2. Converting Decimal 4627 to Base Sixteen:

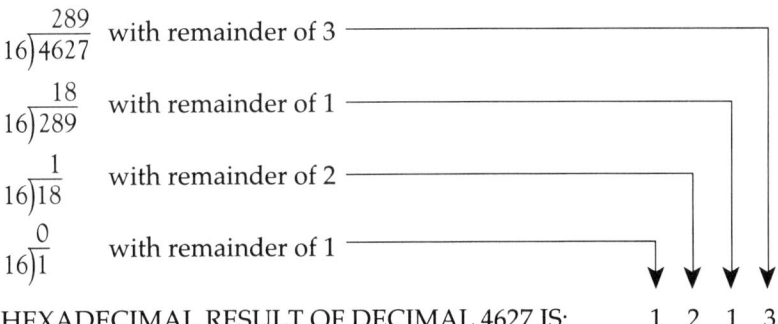

HEXADECIMAL RESULT OF DECIMAL 4627 IS: 1 2 1 3

Conversions such as these can be accomplished easily by using either a hexadecimal and decimal conversion table (see Appendix F) or a calculator with hexadecimal functions.

ADDING AND SUBTRACTING HEXADECIMAL INTEGERS

Regardless of the number system used, the mathematical operations for addition and subtraction remain the same.

Hexadecimal Addition

The following four examples demonstrate the mechanics of hexadecimal addition.

```
Example 1       Example 2       Example 3       Example 4
DEC----HEX      DEC----HEX      DEC----HEX      DEC----HEX
 10      A      10       A       6       6      15       F
 +1     +1     +14      +E     +14      +E     +15      +F
 ---    ---    ---      ---    ---      ---    ---      ---
 11      B     24       18     20       14     30       1E
```

To help clarify the hexadecimal addition process, study the illustrations shown here for Examples 2 and 3.

```
Example 2:      DEC----HEX
                 10      A  ----> 10
                +14     +E  ----> +14
                ---     ---       ---
                 24     18         24
                                  -16 (base)
                                  ---
                                    8 with a carry of 1
```

We want to add A to E (hexadecimal) or 10 to 14 (decimal). The decimal sum of 10 and 14 is 24. Since 24 is a decimal value, we need to subtract 16 from it to convert it to hexadecimal. This leaves 8 with a carry of 1. Thus, in hexadecimal A + E = 18, and decimal 24 is equivalent to hexadecimal 18.

NOTE: We can obtain the same results by converting the hexadecimal values to decimal, adding them (using decimal addition), and then converting the result back to hexadecimal. However, it is faster and more convenient to use the technique just described.

The Hexadecimal Number System and EBCDIC

Example 3 shows how 6 + E = 14 using hexadecimal arithmetic.

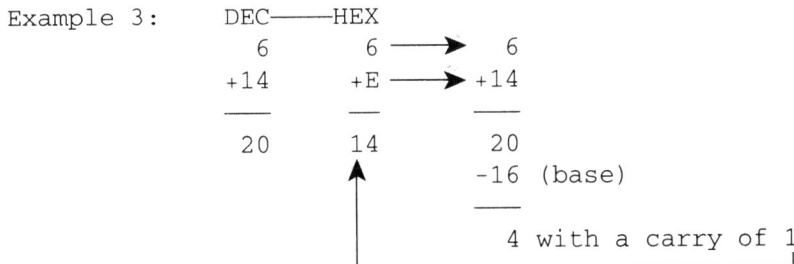

When you are ready, cover the answers in the following problem set and work the second row of problems. Convert the problems to decimal and verify the results.

```
  5A      B7      CA      73     188     391    1AF6    D493C
 +21     +28     +DE     +A9    +13B     +5D    +CFE    +9AEB
 ---     ---     ---     ---    ----    ----    ----    -----
  7B      DF     1A8     11C     2C3     3EE    27F4    DE427
```

Hexadecimal Subtraction

For hexadecimal subtraction, we often borrow 16 from the digit on the immediate left of the current digit and add 16 to the current digit.

In the following example, 24 – 5, we must borrow 1 from 2 (the digit on the left) and carry 16 to the units position, before we can subtract 5 from 4. Because of the borrowing, 2 is reduced to 1 and 16 is added to 4, so that the new minuend is 20. Now we can perform the subtraction: 20 – 5, which gives us the result: 15, or F in hexadecimal. Therefore, in base 16, 24 – 5 = 1F.

```
Example:        DEC———HEX
                 36     24  ——>   1 20   (16 + 4)
                 -5     -5  ——>    -5
                 --     --        ----
                 31     1F        1 15   or   1F
```

For practice, try the following subtraction problems. Verify your answers.

```
    73      97     27C    E52FA    DCC9    C4AEE3
   -11     -58    -13F    -614C   -A51F   -B57D05
   ---     ---    ----    -----   -----   ------
    62      3F     13D    DF1AE    37AA    0F31DE
```

THE EBCDIC CODING SCHEME

For IBM Systems/370 series computers and clones, each character is represented by a unique eight-bit code called the Extended Binary-Coded Decimal Interchange Code, or EBCDIC.

In EBCDIC, each character occupies one byte (eight bits). A byte may represent up to 256 unique combinations of 0s and 1s, or 256 different characters. By definition, a character is anything that can be entered at the keyboard: the twenty-six letters of the alphabet, the numeric digits 0 through 9, and the remaining special characters and symbols.

Refer to Table 2.3 for a partial list of the EBCDIC coding scheme.

The EBCDIC coding scheme classifies or ranks characters from smallest to largest. To determine whether a character is greater than, less than, or equal to another, the computer compares both characters' internal EBCDIC codes. Since each character has a unique 8-bit code, and the computer has an established ranking order, comparisons can be made between letters, numeric digits, and special characters. The ranking order used by the computer is called the *collating sequence*.

According to the collating sequence, A is less than B, R is greater than D, 9 is greater than V, and the SPACE character is less than any letter or numeric digit. See Appendix D for a detailed list of EBCDIC codes and the EBCDIC collating sequence.

ZONE-DECIMAL DATA

Input data is transformed from a form that can be interpreted by humans into character representation, which is then converted into zone-decimal format.

Alphabetics			Decimal Digits			Special Characters		
Hex	Char	EBCDIC	Hex	Char	EBCDIC	Hex	Char	EBCDIC
C1	A	1100 0001	F0	0	1111 0000	5A	!	0101 1010
C2	B	1100 0010	F1	1	1111 0001	5B	$	0101 1011
C3	C	1100 0011	F2	2	1111 0010	5C	*	0101 1100
	:			:		5D	)	0101 1101
	:			:		5E	;	0101 1110
E9	Z	1110 1001	F9	9	1111 1001		:	
							:	

TABLE 2.3 EBCDIC Coding Scheme

Zone-Decimal Data

As an example, suppose we enter the decimal integer +197 at the keyboard.

Input or Readable Form		Character Representation		Zone Decimal Format
+197	→	4EF1F9F7	→	F1F9C7

The following conversion takes place: The integer is transformed into character representation, 4EF1F9F7, which is then converted into a zone-decimal character string, F1F9C7. The transformation process is automatic and transparent to the programmer.

Zone-decimal data is stored internally, one character per byte. Note that the input data +197 is stored in memory as a 3-byte, zone-decimal character string, F1F9C7. Also note that the zone character F occupies the left part of the first two bytes, while the numeric digits occupy the right.

```
  1st byte      2nd byte      3rd byte
  F    1        F    9        C    7
  ZONE-DIGIT    ZONE-DIGIT    SIGN-DIGIT
  1111 0001     1111 1001     1100 0111
```

The zone character C in the third byte represents the sign of the integer. In zone-decimal format, the sign always occupies the zone portion of the rightmost byte. The zone characters F and C specify a plus sign, while B and D specify a minus sign.

Hence the general format for storing numeric values in zone-decimal notation is,

```
ZD ZD ZD ZD....SD
```

where Z and D represent the zone and digit portions of each byte, respectively, and S represents the sign.

Let's look at a few more examples.

	INPUT	CHARACTER	ZONE-DECIMAL
1.	10	F1F0	F1F0
2.	+10	4EF1F0	F1C0
3.	-10	60F1F0	F1D0
4.	NUM = +3	D5E4D4407E404EF3	D5E4D4407E40C3
		N U M = + 3	N U M = 3

Note that in the fourth example, the input contains both alphabetic and numeric characters. Letters and special characters are stored internally in zone-decimal format according to their EBCDIC codes.

Zone-decimal data must either be converted to binary or packed-decimal, before they can be processed by the computer. Assembler can process data in either format. Chapters 2–7 cover the details of binary data processing operations, while Chapter 8 presents the packed-decimal operations.

GENERAL INSTRUCTION FORMAT

Each program instruction, regardless of the language used to write the program, must specify the operation (what to do) and the operands, or data, used to perform the operation.

Programming languages can be categorized by levels, or generations, ranging from low to high. Low-level programming languages are closely related to the design of the computer and are similar in structure to the binary codes used by the computer itself. On the other end, high-level languages are more closely related to the languages that people use. In other words, high-level programming languages resemble human languages, such as English.

For now, let us briefly consider the development of the following programming languages: (1) machine languages, (2) symbolic languages, and (3) procedural languages.

Machine Languages

Machine languages are low-level programming languages that are tedious and time consuming to code. Using a machine language requires a great deal of patience and expertise. All instructions, data, and addresses are coded in binary. The program code consists of seemingly endless strings of 0s and 1s. Obviously, it is easy to make errors and extremely difficult to find them. The following example illustrates what one line of machine code could look like.

```
11110100000000001011000000101100101110100010111
```

NOTE: An *address* is a location in the computer's memory. Just as the postal service uses an address to locate a specific individual residing within a zip code, the computer uses an address to locate specific data residing within computer memory.

Symbolic Languages

Programming languages at the next highest level are called symbolic languages. Programs written in symbolic languages are easier to code and debug than those written in machine code. The programmer writes instructions in symbolic notation, as opposed to strings of 0s and 1s. Mnemonic abbreviations are used for operations and operands. Abbreviations are much easier to understand than long strings of binary code.

Assembler is a symbolic language. Operations and program data are expressed in English-like abbreviations that remind the programmer of their meanings. As an example, the Assembler statement AP (add packed) shown below instructs the computer to add (A) the scores for the midterm and final grades, which are stored as packed-decimal (P) operands. (See Chapter 8 for a discussion about packed-decimal operations.)

```
            AP    FINAL,MIDTERM
```

Procedural Languages

Instructions coded in high-level languages such as BASIC and COBOL often look like statements in English rather than mnemonic expressions. It is relatively easy to learn and use procedural languages. Because of this advantage, procedural languages help boost programmer productivity. In addition, each command coded in a high-level language may cause the computer to perform more than one operation, while a command written in a machine language results in the execution of only one operation.

The following statements are coded in BASIC and COBOL, respectively. Both commands compute overtime hours and are easy to understand.

```
BASIC:   OVERTIME.HOURS = HOURS.WORKED - 40
COBOL:   SUBTRACT 40 FROM HOURS-WORKED
             GIVING OVERTIME-HOURS.
```

Whether high level or low level, all programming statements require an operation, or instruction code, and operands. The operation code, or opcode, tells the computer what to do (for example, add, subtract, move, compare, branch), while the operand represents either the data itself or the address where the data can be found. Once the data has been retrieved, it can be processed by the computer.

	operation	operands
Instruction:	ADD	TOTAL,COUNT

While executing the ADD statement in the example above, the computer retrieves the value stored at COUNT and adds it to the contents located at TOTAL. The resulting sum is placed in TOTAL and destroys the previous value stored there. This particular statement assigns the sum to the operand located at TOTAL. We will discuss this process in the sections that follow.

MACHINE LANGUAGE

To explain the basic concepts and difficulties associated with coding even the simplest of programs in machine language, we present the following example.

Suppose we are faced with the task of coding the following arithmetic expression in machine language:

$$15 \div 3 - 1 + 8$$

At first, this task seems simple enough. But before we proceed, let's briefly outline the required programming steps. The programmer must:

1. memorize (know where to find) the binary equivalents for the machine language opcodes.
2. allocate storage space for all data items and remember the addresses (coded in binary) of each.
3. be careful not to assign a storage location to more than one data item.
4. code (in binary notation) one command for each data processing operation required.

You can see from this example how complicated even the simplest of programs can become when coded in machine language.

Computers have what is commonly referred to as a "scratch pad" memory—a special area reserved in primary storage for holding intermediate results and totals. We shall refer to this special area as the *accumulator*. For our program, the accumulator will be used to hold intermediate results as they develop.

	OPCODE	OPERAND	Accumulator (ACCUM)
1.	START		0
2.	LOAD	15 into ACCUM	15
3.	DIVIDE	3 into ACCUM	5
4.	SUBTRACT	1 from ACCUM	4
5.	ADD	8 to ACCUM	12
6.	END		12

TABLE 2.4 Processing Table: $15 \div 3 - 1 + 8$

Opcodes	Binary
ADD	01011010
SUBTRACT	01011011
MULTIPLY	01011100
DIVIDE	01011101
START	11110100
END	11110101
LOAD	01011000

TABLE 2.5 Opcode Conversion Table

Table 2.4 shows the steps necessary to transform the arithmetic expression into machine code. Note how the values in the accumulator change as each step is processed.

Our first task is to convert the opcodes shown in Table 2.4 into binary. As you may recall, we must code the binary equivalents of the opcodes. To keep things simple, assume we have access to the opcode conversion table shown in Table 2.5.

Let's also assume that the first available location in memory starts at 00001010, the tenth byte. Therefore, we may begin coding the first instruction at this location.

Each instruction consists of two parts, an opcode and an operand, and we must assign each part to one byte of memory. Therefore, all instructions will have a fixed length of two bytes, one for the opcode and one for the operand address. Data values, however, will occupy only one byte of storage each.

With the starting address known, we can then assign opcodes and data values to memory locations as shown in Table 2.6. Note that START is assigned to the first available location in memory and occupies two bytes (10 and 11). The other opcodes and data items are assigned to adjacent memory locations.

		Location		Location
Opcodes:	START →	10-11	Data value 15 →	22
	LOAD →	12-13	Data value 3 →	23
	DIVIDE →	14-15	Data value 1 →	24
	SUBTRACT →	16-17	Data value 8 →	25
	ADD →	18-19		
	END →	20-21		

TABLE 2.6 Memory Allocation Table

10-11 **START** opcode opr-addr 11110100 00000000 Accum = 0 (0)	12-13 **LOAD** opcode opr-addr 01011000 00010110 Accum = 15 (22)	14-15 **DIVIDE** opcode opr-addr 01011101 00010111 Accum = 5 (23)
16-17 **SUBTRACT** opcode opr-addr 01011011 00011000 Accum = 4 (24)	18-19 **ADD** opcode opr-addr 01011010 00011001 Accum = 12 (25)	20-21 **END** opcode opr-addr 11110101 00000000 Accum = 12 (26)
22 DATA =15(00001111)	23 DATA = 3(00000011)	24 DATA = 1(00000001)
25 DATA = 8(00001000)	unused memory	

FIGURE 2.2 Equation: 15 ÷ 3 − 1 + 8

The machine code shown in Fig. 2.2 represents the completed program. For convenience, the first twelve bytes (10–21) have labels that correspond to the opcodes shown in Table 2.4. The decimal values in the upper, left corner specify memory addresses in bytes.

Also note that the operand addresses (opr-addr) are shown in binary as well as in decimal. (Decimal values are enclosed in parentheses.) Each operand is actually an address pointer to a location in memory where the data is stored.

DISSECTION OF SAMPLE PROGRAM IN FIGURE 2.2

```
START:   opcode   opr-addr
         11110100 00000000              Accumulator = 0
```

START marks the beginning of the executable statements and sets the accumulator to zero. Notice the binary opcode for START (11110100) and the value coded for the operand. Since START doesn't process data, the operand address has been set to zero.

```
        LOAD:    opcode    opr-addr
                 01011000  00010110              Accumulator = 15
```

The above statement means: Load the value (15) stored at the operand address 00010110 (22nd byte) into the accumulator.

```
        DIVIDE:  opcode    opr-addr
                 01011101  00010111              Accumulator = 5
```

The above statement means: Divide the contents of the accumulator (15) by the value (3) stored at the operand address 00010111 (23rd byte), and replace the accumulator with the quotient.

```
        SUBTRACT:   opcode    opr-addr
                    01011011  00011000           Accumulator = 4
```

The above statement means: Subtract the value (1) stored at the operand address 00011000 (24th byte) from the accumulator (5), and replace the contents of the accumulator with the result.

```
        ADD:     opcode    opr-addr
                 01011010  00011001              Accumulator = 12
```

The above statement means: Add the value (8) stored at the operand address 00011001 (25th byte) to the accumulator (4), and replace the contents of the accumulator with the sum.

```
        END:     opcode    opr-addr
                 11110101  00000000              Accumulator = 12
```

The opcode 11110101 marks the end of the executable instructions and the start of the program data. Since END doesn't process any data, the operand address is zero.

The program data follows the END statement and is stored in bytes 22, 23, 24, and 25; these bytes contain the integer values 15, 3, 1, and 8, respectively.

MACHINE CODE

The program statements shown in Fig. 2.2 do not represent true machine language code. Labels, accumulator values, and decimal equivalents of binary addresses were included to document the code and help the reader understand the program. The actual program would look more like the code shown in Fig. 2.3.

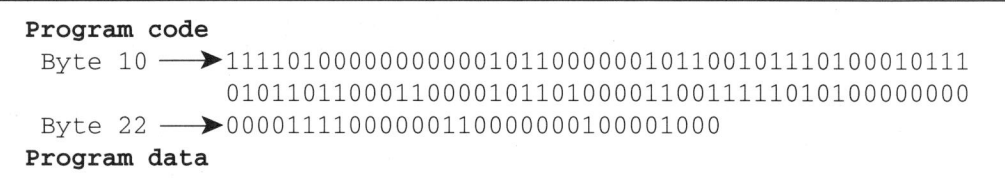

FIGURE 2.3 Machine Code

If you compare the binary code shown in Fig. 2.3 to the program statements shown in Fig. 2.2, you will discover that they are exactly the same.

It is easy to make mistakes when entering data for machine code, even with a program as short as our example. Digits can be transposed and addresses miskeyed.

In addition, debugging machine code is a grueling task. Imagine the frustration of tracing your way through hundreds of lines of binary code searching for the cause of an error. At times, it is difficult to determine where one instruction ends and another begins.

For the sample program shown in Figure 2.3, imagine that we suddenly realize that the formula should have been 15 ÷ 3 − 1 + 20 + 8. Can we simply add 20 to the program code and be done with it? Unfortunately, we cannot.

If we attempt to insert "+ 20" into the equation, then all the addresses in the program after the point of insertion will change. In fact, the addresses coded for the instructions prior to the insertion may also change, since data may have been moved to different locations. To make this change, we will have to go into the program code and change the address locations for most of the instructions and the data.

Obviously, even a simple change to a short machine-language program can turn into a major project. Can you imagine the amount of time needed to insert one instruction into a large program?

Machine language is tedious and time consuming to write, as well as highly prone to error. Nevertheless, it does have the advantage of storage efficiency and fast processing speeds. Timewise, programs written in machine code out-perform programs written in high-level languages, such as BASIC and COBOL. However, high-level languages offer greater flexibility and are much easier to learn. One must consider the trade off, then, between ease of use and changeability versus code efficiency and speed.

SYMBOLIC CODE AND ASSEMBLER LANGUAGE

Table 2.7 shows the machine instructions for the arithmetic expression: 15 ÷ 3 − 1 + 8 in tabular form. (Of course, the actual machine code would not look like this.) Obviously, the 0s and 1s do not remind us of what they represent. It would be far more helpful if we could replace the binary opcodes and operands with abbreviations that are self-descriptive.

That's exactly what symbolic languages allow us to do. The programmer can code descriptive symbols for opcodes and self-documenting abbreviations for operands. Table 2.7 shows the symbolic codes for the machine instructions on the left. Opcodes such as START, LOAD, DIVIDE, SUBTRACT, ADD, and END are self-descriptive and easy to remember. Operand names, too, can be made easier to read. For example, the statement "LOAD NUM15" instructs the computer to load the integer value 15 into the accumulator.

Before the computer can execute a program, the program must be translated into machine code. Computers understand and execute binary commands only. Fortunately for us, symbolic languages have their own internal translator which will, at run time, automatically convert the symbolic code into machine code instructions.

Assembler is a unique symbolic programming language that allows us to write programs that resemble machine code, without the burden of memorizing binary codes and data addresses. Assembler statements are automatically translated into machine code on a one-to-one basis; that is, each Assembler statement translates into one machine code instruction.

	Machine Code				Symbolic Code	
Steps	**Bytes**	**Opcode**	**Operands**		**Opcode**	**Operands**
1	10-11	11110100	00000000		START	
2	12-13	01011000	00010110		LOAD	NUM15
3	14-15	01011101	00010111		DIVIDE	NUM3
4	16-17	01011011	00011000		SUBTRACT	NUM1
5	18-19	01011010	00011001		ADD	NUM8
6	20-21	11110101	00000000		END	
	22	00001111		NUM15	EQUALS	15
	23	00000011		NUM3	EQUALS	3
	24	00000001		NUM1	EQUALS	1
	25	00001000		NUM8	EQUALS	8

TABLE 2.7 Machine Code versus Symbolic Code

GENERAL PURPOSE REGISTERS

The central processing unit for the IBM Systems/370 series computers and compatible machines contains sixteen general purpose registers. Each register occupies four bytes of memory and may hold a fullword of data. These registers are labeled 0–15. We may reference a register by specifying either the register number alone or the register number with the prefix "R." For example, we may reference register six, by coding either 6 or R6.

Registers 0, 1, and 13–15 are used by the operating system and Assembler to provide and establish address linkage and general systems control. We should avoid using them for binary arithmetic, since we may unwittingly alter their contents and cause errors that may prove difficult to locate and correct. We may, however, use registers 2–12 to perform arithmetic operations on binary integers.

In the sections that follow, we shall see how Assembler uses the general purpose registers to process binary data.

ASSEMBLER LANGUAGE CODING FORMAT

The general format for coding Assembler statements is:

    column-1:   L A B E L
    column-9:   \<blank\>
    column-10: O P C O D E
    column-15: \<blank\>
    column-16: O P E R A N D S
    column-72: C O N T I N U A T I O N
    column-73: S E Q U E N C E   N U M B E R S

The optional LABEL field (1–8) contains data and operand names. When used, it must begin in column 1. The rules for forming labels are:

1. Each data name must be unique.
2. A name may contain 1–8 characters.
3. A name must begin with a letter.
4. A name may consist of letters, numeric digits, and the characters $, #, or @.

5. Embedded blanks are not permitted.
6. Each name should be self-descriptive.

Examples of valid names are LOOP, PROG01, DOLLAR$, PAYRATE, ACCOUNT#, and NUMBER2. Examples of invalid names are 1TIME, ID-NBR, AMOUNT?, $VALUE, NET PAY, *TOTAL, and CREDITHOURS.

The OPCODE field (10–14) is required and must begin in column 10. The opcode tells the computer whether the statement is a program instruction or a data definition. Program instructions tell the computer what to do. Data definitions allocate storage space or assign values to constants.

The OPERANDS field (16–39) is optional, but when present, it must begin in column 16. Operands may be coded beyond column 39, but such a situation is unlikely. Multiple operands are separated by commas, and embedded blanks are not permitted. The operand field specifies the data processed by the instruction.

Statements included in the COMMENTS field are optional and may begin anywhere, as long as they are separated from the operand(s) by at least one blank space. Line comments may be specified by coding an asterisk in column 1. They may be placed anywhere to document the program source code.

Any nonblank character may be coded in the CONTINUATION field (72) to indicate the operand is continued on the next line. We normally code an "X" in column 72 to indicate line continuation.

During the days of card processing, the SEQUENCE NUMBER field (73–80) was used to punch sequence numbers into the cards. This made it possible to rearrange the cards in proper order, if they were ever dropped. The SEQUENCE NUMBER field is rarely used today.

PSEUDO-ASSEMBLER PROGRAMMING EXAMPLES

This chapter concludes with two pseudo-Assembler programs to illustrate the programming concepts presented so far. These programs are called "pseudo-Assembler," because they are not truly Assembler programs. At this time, we do not have the tools necessary to begin writing actual Assembler programs. After completing Chapter 3, we will code our first Assembler program.

Sample Program 1, Fig. 2.4, evaluates the arithmetic expression: 20 + 7 − 4. Once the program is executed, the decimal result 23 is stored in register 5.

Chapter 2: Number Systems and Data Representation

```
Label    Opcode  Operands  Comments
1--------10------16-------------------------
         START             start of program
         L       5,NUM20   load 20
         A       5,NUM7    add 7
         S       5,NUM4    subtract 4
         END               end of program
NUM20    DC      F'20'     fullword constant 20
NUM7     DC      F'7'      fullword constant 7
NUM4     DC      F'4'      fullword constant 4
```

FIGURE 2.4 Assembler Program to Evaluate: 20 + 7 − 4

DISSECTION OF SAMPLE PROGRAM 1

```
         START
```

START marks the beginning of the executable instructions.

```
         L       5,NUM20
```

The above statement means: Load the binary constant stored at NUM20 into register number 5 (R5 = 20).

```
         A       5,NUM7
```

The above statement means: Add the binary constant stored at NUM7 to the contents of register 5 and replace the original value of the register with the sum 27 (R5 = 20 + 7).

```
         S       5,NUM4
```

The above statement means: Subtract the binary constant stored at NUM4 from the contents of register 5 and replace the value of the register with the difference 23 (R5 = 27 − 4).

```
         END
```

END marks the end of the executable instructions. The statements that follow define the data processed by the program.

```
NUM20     DC        F'20'
```

The above statement means: Define the fullword binary variable NUM20 and initialize it to 20 (NUM20 = 20).

```
NUM7      DC        F'7'
```

The above statement means: Define the fullword binary variable NUM7 and initialize it to 7 (NUM7 = 7).

```
NUM4      DC        F'4'
```

The above statement means: Define the fullword binary variable NUM4 and initialize it to 4 (NUM4 = 4).

Sample Program 2, Fig. 2.5, evaluates the expression $3 \times (42 \div 6) + 9$. For now, assume opcodes M and D specify multiplication and division, respectively. Furthermore, assume multiplication and division require only one register each (as shown) to perform their operations.

DISSECTION OF SAMPLE PROGRAM 2

```
          START
```

START marks the beginning of the executable instructions.

```
Label     Opcode    Operands   Comments
1-------10------16--------------------------
          START                start of program
          L         7,FORTY2   load 42
          D         7,SIX      divide by 6
          M         7,THREE    multiply by 3
          A         7,NINE     add 9
          END                  end of program
THREE     DC        F'3'       fullword constant 3
FORTY2    DC        F'42'      fullword constant 42
SIX       DC        F'6'       fullword constant 6
NINE      DC        F'9'       fullword constant 9
```

FIGURE 2.5 Assembler Program to Evaluate the Arithmetic Expression: $3 \times (42 \div 6) + 9$.

Chapter 2: Number Systems and Data Representation

```
         L        7,FORTY2
```

The above statement means: Load the binary constant stored at FORTY2 into register number 7 (R7 = 42).

```
         D        7,SIX
```

The above statement means: Divide the contents of register 7 by the binary constant stored at SIX and replace the original value of the register with the quotient 7 (R7 = 42 ÷ 6).

```
         M        7,THREE
```

The above statement means: Multiply the contents of register 7 by the constant stored at THREE and replace the contents of the register with the product 21 (R7 = 7 × 3).

```
         A        7,NINE
```

The above statement means: Add the binary constant stored at NINE to the contents of register 7 and replace the value of the register with the sum 30 (R7 = 21 + 9).

```
         END
```

END marks the end of the executable instructions.

```
THREE    DC       F'3'
```

The above statement means: Define the fullword binary constant THREE and initialize it to 3 (THREE = 3).

```
FORTY2   DC       F'42'
```

The above statement means: Define the fullword binary constant FORTY2 and initialize it to 42 (FORTY2 = 42).

```
SIX      DC       F'6'
```

The above statement means: Define the fullword binary constant SIX and initialize it to 6 (SIX = 6).

```
          NINE    DC      F'9'
```

The above statement means: Define the fullword binary constant NINE and initialize it to 9 (NINE = 9).

KEY REVIEW TERMS

Define the following:

sign bit
hexadecimal number system
statement and line comment
decimal number system
bits
EBCDIC
accumulator
high-level language
byte
zone-decimal format
label
Assembler language
END statement
general purpose register
binary digit
machine language
doubleword
low-level language
address location
data definition
opcode
binary number system
continuation indicator
executable statement
expanded form
operand
sequence numbers
symbolic language
zone character
scratch-pad memory
computer memory
digit bits
halfword
positional notation
fullword
storage location
two's complement notation
zone bits

REVIEW EXERCISES

Show the positional notation and expanded form for each of the following:

*1. decimal 409
 2. decimal 1776
*3. binary 1101101
 4. binary 1110000
*5. hexadecimal 123
 6. hexadecimal 4BFC

Fill in the blanks by converting the numeric values shown below to the number system specified:

	Decimal	Binary	Hexadecimal
*7.	123	_____	_____
8.	_____	11011101	_____
*9.	_____	_____	5A7
10.	6308	_____	_____
*11.	_____	1111101	
12.	_____	_____	2A4C
*13.	1000	_____	_____
14.	_____	10010110	_____
*15.	_____	_____	ABCD

Perform the binary and hexadecimal addition and subtraction problems below:

	Binary	Hexadecimal	Binary	Hexadecimal
*16.	10001	A42	110010	53FC1
	+1011	−931	−11000	+B123
17.	10110111	591278	11111	4A9C
	−1111001	+243A42	+10110	−1F2F
*18.	1101	FFAC	100001	1A5B
	+1111	−A69E	−11110	+F78B
19.	10000010	3ABCEF5	111111	E123456
	−1111111	+A1CBFFF	+101111	−FCBAEE
*20.	101110	45924	110000	FFFF
	+111111	−3EC39	−00111	+FFFF

Find the halfword binary equivalents for the decimal values given:

*21. −125 _____

 22. −63 _____

*23. −10 _____

 24. −100 _____

*25. −2741 _____

Find the decimal equivalents for the halfword and fullword storage areas below. (Don't forget to add the correct sign.)

*26. 0000000011010110 _____

 27. 1111111101011101 _____

*28. 1111111101100011 _____

 29. 0000000000000000 0000000001111011 _____

*30. 1111111111111111 1111111100110001 _____

Convert the following hexadecimal values to binary:

*31. F1A49ECB _____

 32. A0123AFCD9 _____

Convert the following binary values to hexadecimal:

*33. 11110110110100010111101110001100 _____

 34. 0100110111110101110010101100110101110100 _____

Translate the input data into zone-decimal form:

*35. ASSEMBLER _____

 36. VALUE = −92 _____

*37. CTCH 238 _____

 38. +5498.341 _____

*39. 198 CR _____

 40. your name _____

PROGRAMMING EXERCISES

Instructions: For each exercise, write the program code for the specifications given. Model your program after the examples shown in the section entitled "Pseudo-Assembler Programming Examples." Desk check your code to be sure that it produces the correct results.

1. Write an assembler program to solve the equation: $5 \times 6 + 10 - 27$.

2. Change the program in Exercise 1 to include the following change: $5 \times 6 + 10 \div 2 - 27$.

3. Write the program code to solve the following algebraic expression, given $A = 7$, $B = 10$, and $C = 6$: $A^2 - B + C^2 - 4$.

4. Code Assembler statements to evaluate the expression: $2W + X + Y - Z$, given $W = 10$, $X = 4$, $Y = 5$, and $Z = 11$.

5. Write a program to compute the volume of a cube, given a height of 11 centimeters.

6. Compute the perimeter of a small wood lot bounded by five contiguous property lines of 60, 100, 110, 80, and 70 feet.

7. Calculate the gross weekly pay for an employee who is paid at the rate of twelve dollars per hour, has payroll deductions totalling $219 per week, and has worked a total of forty hours during the week.

8. Write a program to compute the six-week test-score average for a student who has earned the following test scores over a six-week period: 70, 50, 100, 80, 65, and 85.

9. Compute the area of a triangle with a base of 16 inches and a height of 10 inches. (*Hint:* The area of a triangle = base × height ÷ 2)

10. Code an Assembler program to compute the surface area of the cube described in Exercise 5.

3 | INTRODUCTION TO ASSEMBLER LANGUAGE

OVERVIEW

Learning Objectives
Fixed-Point Binary Operations
Define Constant (DC) Statement
   Fullword Numeric Constants
   Halfword Numeric Constants
   Character String Constants
   Hexadecimal Constants
Define Storage (DS) Statement
Load (L) Instruction
Load Register (LR) Instruction
Add (A) Instruction
Add Register (AR) Instruction
Subtract (S) Instruction
Subtract Register (SR) Instruction
Store Register (ST) Instruction
Partial Dump (PDUMP) Macro
End-of-Job (EOJ) Statement
END Statement
Sample Program CHAP3A
Multiply (M) Instruction
Multiply Register (MR) Instruction
Divide (D) Instruction
Divide Register (DR) Instruction
Sample Program CHAP3B
Key Review Terms
Review Exercises
Programming Exercises

LEARNING OBJECTIVES

After reading this chapter and completing the exercises, the reader should be able to:

- define binary constants and storage variables using Define Constant (DC) and Define Storage (DS) statements.
- define non-numeric constants and storage items using DC and DS statements.
- code statements to load binary data into registers and store register values in program variables.
- dump program registers and storage variables.
- use pseudocode to plan and develop program logic.
- design, write, and test simple Assembler language programs using fixed-point binary operations.

FIXED-POINT BINARY OPERATIONS

Assembler provides a set of instructions that performs integer arithmetic and processes data in binary form. A major portion of this book, Chapters 3–7, focuses on presenting Assembler's fixed-point (integer) binary operations.

In this chapter, we will examine in detail the following data definitions and programming statements:

```
DC   DEFINE CONSTANT
DS   DEFINE STORAGE
L    LOAD
LR   LOAD REGISTER
A    ADD
AR   ADD REGISTER
S    SUBTRACT
SR   SUBTRACT REGISTER
ST   STORE REGISTER
M    MULTIPLY
MR   MULTIPLY REGISTER
D    DIVIDE
DR   DIVIDE REGISTER
```

DEFINE CONSTANT (DC) STATEMENT

There are two types of constants, numeric and alphanumeric (or character string). A constant is a variable that has been assigned a value. The values of constants do not change during the execution of a program.

In the following examples, five variables (data items) have been defined and assigned constant values.

1. COUNT = 0
2. MAXLINES = 45
3. HEADING = COLMAX TOOL COMPANY
4. MONTH = FEBRUARY
5. PHONE = 614-453-1959

The first two variables, COUNT and MAXLINES, have been assigned the numeric constants 0 and 45, respectively. However, the last three variables have been assigned character string constants that define a report heading, a month of the year, and a telephone number, respectively.

FULLWORD NUMERIC CONSTANTS

Format:

```
1--------10----16-----------columns
Label    DC    F'constant'              Label = constant
```

Purpose: To define fullword binary constants. Binary constants are defined and initialized with the Define Constant (DC) statement. The general format is shown above.

The notation on the right (`Label = constant`) indicates that the label field, which assigns a symbolic name to a storage area, is initialized to the value specified by the constant. The label allows the constant to be referenced by other statements in the program.

The `F` in column 16 specifies four bytes (fullword) of storage are allocated to the variable. The constant enclosed within single quotes is assigned to the variable.

Examples:

```
   Label      DC      F'constant'          -HEX-
   1--------10----16----------          ----------
1. FIRST      DC      F'100'               00000064
2. NUM        DC      F'53'                00000035
3. ACCOUNT    DC      F'23'                00000017
4. MINUS7     DC      F'-7'                FFFFFFF9
```

Examples 1–4 define the variables FIRST, NUM, ACCOUNT, and MINUS7 as fullword numeric constants and assign to each the values 100, 53, 23, and –7 respectively. Upon assembling the DC statements, the computer internally stores the binary equivalents of the decimal constants. For convenience, the binary values are shown in hexadecimal.

From Chapter 2, we recall that positive binary integers are stored internally in their true binary format, whereas negative integers, such as MINUS7, are represented in two's complement notation.

HALFWORD NUMERIC CONSTANTS

Format:

```
1--------10----16-----------columns
Label     DC    H'constant'               Label = constant
```

Purpose: To define halfword binary constants. Assembler also allows us to define and initialize halfword numeric constants with the DC statement. The general format is shown above.

Once again, the notation on the right indicates that the label, which assigns a symbolic name to a storage area, is initialized to the value specified by the constant.

For the examples below, the H in column 16 specifies that a 2-byte storage area will be allocated for the halfword variables. Note that the constant enclosed within single quotes is assigned to the variable identified by the label.

Define Constant (DC) Statement

Examples:

```
    Label      DC      H'constant'        -HEX-
    1--------10----16----------         ------
 1. HALF       DC      H'100'             0064
 2. NEXT       DC      H'5'               0005
 3. ANOTHER    DC      H'19'              0013
 4. MINUS7     DC      H'-7'              FFF9
```

Upon assembly, DC statements allocate space, convert the constants to binary, and store them in memory. The contents of the variables are shown on the right in hexadecimal notation.

NOTE: H, F, and D constants establish automatic boundary alignment. A constant is aligned on a boundary when the address assigned to it is evenly divisible by 2, 4, or 8, respectively. For example, fullword constants (F) are automatically stored at addresses that are evenly divisible by 4. Hence, DC and DS statements may be used to define fixed-length data and to establish boundary alignment for those instructions that require it.

CHARACTER STRING CONSTANTS

Format:

```
1--------10----16-----------columns
Label     DC    C'string'                 Label = string
```

Purpose: To define variable-length, non-numeric constants. Alphanumeric or character string constants are defined in Assembler with the Define Constant (DC) statement. The general format is shown above.

The C in column 16 indicates that the character string will be stored internally in zone-decimal (EBCDIC) format. Enough space will be allocated to hold the entire string. The actual number of characters in the string determines the length in bytes reserved for the constant. For example, a 10-character alphanumeric constant would be assigned to a 10-byte storage area.

The Label field refers to the name given to the storage area and may be referenced by other statements in the program.

Examples:

```
                                                        -LENGTH-
1. NAME     DC    C'RYAN'
      NAME = D9E8C1D5                                   4 bytes
2. TITLE    DC    C'COLMAX TOOLS'
      TITLE = C3D6D3D4C1E740E3D6D6D3E2                  12 bytes
3. ADDR     DC    CL14'477-A LINX ST.'
      ADDR = F4F7F760C140D3C9D5E740E2E34B               14 bytes
4. SHORT    DC    CL10'HELLO'
      SHORT = C8C5D3D3D64040404040                      10 bytes
5. LONG     DC    CL4'BARBARA'
      LONG = C2C1D9C2                                   4 bytes
```

For Examples 1 and 2, the lengths (in bytes) of the string constants are implicitly determined by the number of characters in the string itself. Each character enclosed within single quotes is converted into its 1-byte, zone-decimal equivalent. Then the entire zone-decimal string is stored in memory at the address reserved for the variable.

Examples 3–5 are slightly different. Each has its length defined explicitly by the instruction. The L in column 17 indicates that the decimal value that follows specifies the length (in bytes) for the string constant.

Consider, for example, the variable ADDR; it has the explicit length of 14 bytes. Now look at SHORT; its length has been defined as 10 bytes, even though the string itself is only five characters long. Assembler will pad the field with five blanks on the right before storing it as a 10-character string. When necessary, string constants will be padded with blanks on the right in order to expand their lengths as defined by their DC statements.

Let's look at the last example. The DC statement for LONG specifies a length of four bytes for a string constant that has a total of seven characters. In this case, the last three characters of the string constant will be truncated, without error or warning. Hence, it pays to be careful. When writing a DC statement, make sure you assign enough bytes to hold the entire string.

HEXADECIMAL CONSTANTS

Format:

```
1--------10----16-----------columns
Label    DC    X'string'                Label = string
```

Define Constant (DC) Statement

Purpose: To define variable-length, hexadecimal constants. The general format is shown above.

The X in column 16 indicates that the value enclosed within single quotes is coded in hexadecimal (EBCDIC). Enough space will be allocated to hold the entire string. However, EBCDIC requires two digits per character. Hence, a 12-digit hexadecimal constant will be assigned to a 6-byte storage area.

Examples:

```
                                                        -LENGTH-
1. VALUE      DC      X'F5F7F6'
      VALUE = F5 F7 F6                                  3 bytes
2. MESSAGE   DC      X'C9C2D440F3F7F0'
      MESSAGE = C9 C2 D4 40 F3 F7 F0                    7 bytes
3. SMALL     DC      XL5'F4F7'
      SMALL = 00 00 00 F4 F7                            5 bytes
4. LARGE     DC      XL2'C4C3F1F0'
      LARGE = F1 F0                                     2 bytes
```

In both Examples 1 and 2, the lengths of the hexadecimal constants are implicitly determined by the number of digits in the string divided by two. The hexadecimal string is stored in memory at the address (label) reserved for the variable.

It is interesting to note that hexadecimal constants could be coded as character string constants; that is, Example 1 could be written as: VALUE DC C'576'.

Examples 3 and 4 have their lengths explicitly defined by their instructions. The Ln in columns 17 and 18 indicate the length n in bytes of the hexadecimal constant.

Take another look at Example 3. SMALL has an explicit length of 5, even though the constant itself is only two bytes. Assembler will pad the first three bytes on the left with zeros before storing the constant as a 5-byte field. As a rule, a constant that has fewer bytes than explicitly specified by the instruction will be padded on the left with zeros.

Look at Example 4. Note the actual length of LARGE—four bytes cannot be stored in a two-byte field. Without giving a warning, Assembler will truncate the first two bytes on the left. You must count those bytes carefully to avoid making an error.

DEFINE STORAGE (DS) STATEMENT

Format:

```
1--------10----16--------columns
Label    DS   F                    Label = storage area
```

Purpose: To define fullword binary variables. We can reserve storage space for program variables and temporary data items with the Define Storage (DS) statement.

Normally, DS statements are coded to define variables, other than input or output, that are used by the program to process data. Temporary storage items are often used to hold intermediate results and values for subsequent processing.

Let's briefly review the meanings of the terms "input" and "output." For the payroll application shown in Fig. 3.1, the input includes two items: hours and payrate. The input is processed by the computer to produce the output: the employee's take-home pay. (For this application, we will assume there are no deductions and no overtime.) The appropriate output for each employee is printed on a check and given to the employee.

Hence, input consists of those data items that are processed by the program to produce the output. Output can be defined as the objective of the program or the results of the processing.

Let us continue with our discussion of DS statements. From the previous section, we know that label specifies the name of the storage item. According to the formats shown in Fig. 3.2, column 16 specifies the various format types and their associated lengths. For binary variables, format types H, F, and D specify lengths of 2, 4, and 8 bytes, respectively.

On the other hand, character and hexadecimal variables can be defined by placing either a C or an X in column 16. The Ln in columns 17 and 18 specifies the length of the variable in bytes.

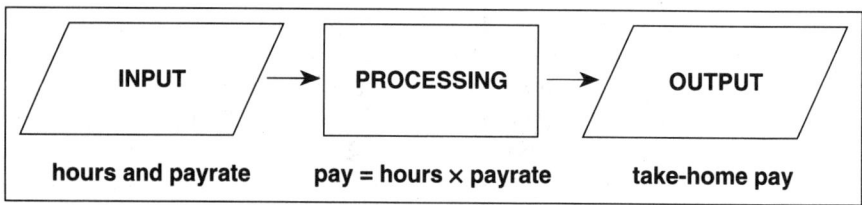

FIGURE 3.1 Payroll Application

```
         GENERAL FORMATS           DATA TYPES            LENGTH
--1--------10----16------------------------------------------

    Label      DS    H        Numeric halfword      2 bytes
    Label      DS    F        Numeric fullword      4 bytes
    Label      DS    D        Numeric doubleword    8 bytes
    Label      DS    CLn      Character string      n bytes
    Label      DS    XLn      Hexadecimal string    n bytes
```

FIGURE 3.2 Defining Storage Variables

Examples:

```
                                    -LENGTH-
1.  RESULT    DS    F          4 bytes
2.  PAYRATE   DS    H          2 bytes
3.  BIGNUM    DS    D          8 bytes
4.  ADDR      DS    CL20      20 bytes
5.  HEX       DS    XL5        5 bytes
```

For each variable defined in these examples, the number of bytes allocated is either implicitly or explicitly specified by the type and/or length identifier(s) beginning in column 16.

LOAD (L) INSTRUCTION

Format:

```
1--------10----16--------columns
         L    R,S                              R = S
              ←
```

Purpose: To load binary storage constants into the general purpose register. Execution of the load results in the movement of a fullword of data from storage operand (S) to the general purpose register (R). The arrow indicates the direction of the operation, from storage (the source field) to register (the receiving field). Technically speaking, data is not actually moved from one place to another. It is only copied to another location.

Chapter 3: Introduction to Assembler Language

The notation on the right (R = S) indicates that the contents of the storage operand S are copied to the general purpose register operand R.

As a result of the load, the original contents of the register are destroyed. However, the contents of the storage item remain unchanged and may be processed as needed by other instructions in the program.

For the example below, BEFORE and AFTER refer to the contents of the operands before and after execution of the load.

Example:

```
         L      5,MIDTERM                    R5    |  MIDTERM
         :                                         ----------
         :                           BEFORE: ????????  | 0000002D
MIDTERM  DC     F'45'                AFTER:  0000002D | 0000002D
```

During the load, the fullword binary constant (shown above in hexadecimal) located at MIDTERM is copied to register 5. The original contents of the register—shown as question marks to indicate they are unknown—are destroyed and replaced with 0000002D. Of course, the contents of MIDTERM remain unchanged. Note that in decimal form register 5 equals 45, or simply, R5 = 45.

LOAD REGISTER (LR) INSTRUCTION

Format:

```
1--------10----16--------columns
         LR    R1,R2                         R1 = R2
                ←
```

Purpose: To load binary constants from one register to another. Load Register copies a fullword of data from the general purpose register operand (R2) to the register operand (R1). The arrow indicates the direction of the operation, from right (source register) to left (receiving register).

The notation (R1 = R2) indicates that the contents of the second register operand are copied to the first. Hence, the original contents stored at R1 are replaced, and R2 remains unchanged.

Example:

```
LR      7,4                             R7       |    R4
  :                             ─────────────────┼──────────
  :                     BEFORE: ???????  |  000000AE
  :                     AFTER:  000000AE |  000000AE
```

During execution, the contents of register 4 are copied to register 7, replacing the original value stored there. Both registers now hold the same value. Note that in decimal form R7 = 174.

ADD (A) INSTRUCTION

Format:

```
1--------10----16--------columns
         A     R,S                              R = R + S
               ←
```

Purpose: To add binary constants. The Add statement computes the sum of the fullword value located at storage operand (S) and the value stored at the general purpose register operand (R). The arrow indicates that the sum is computed and placed in the register operand. The resulting sum replaces the original value of the register, while the contents of storage remain unchanged.

Example:

```
         A      7,NUM                      R7      |    NUM
                :                    ──────────────┼──────────
                :          BEFORE:  00000009  |  0000004F
                :          AFTER:   00000058  |  0000004F
NUM      DC     F'79'
```

During the addition, the binary value stored at NUM (0000004F) is added to the contents of register 7 (00000009). The sum then replaces the original contents of the register, while the value stored at NUM remains the same.

Chapter 3: Introduction to Assembler Language

This example shows the before and after conditions. As an illustration, let's show the addition process in a slightly different manner:

```
A       7,NUM ─────────► R7  =     R7    +    NUM

        (decimal)        R7  =      9    +     79    =      88
        (hexadecimal)    R7  = 00000009  + 0000004F  = 00000058
```

ADD REGISTER (AR) INSTRUCTION

Format:

```
1--------10----16--------columns
         AR   R1,R2                         R1 = R1 + R2
              ←
```

Purpose: To add binary constants stored in registers. Add Register computes the sum of the two general purpose registers, R1 and R2. The contents of the second register operand (R2) are added to the contents of the first (R1). The resulting sum replaces the original value of R1, while the contents of R2 remain unaltered.

Example:

```
AR      5,9                            R5         |    R9
   :                                 ─────────────┼───────────
   :                         BEFORE: 00000AF0     | 000001DC
   :                         AFTER:  00000CCC     | 000001DC
```

At run time, the binary value stored at register 9 (000001DC) is added to the contents of register 5 (00000AF0). The resulting sum replaces the original contents of register 5 and the value stored at register 9 remains unchanged. Note that in decimal R5 = 2800 + 476, or R5 = 3276.

```
AR      5,9 ─────────► R5  =     R5    +    R9

        (decimal)      R5  =    2800   +    476    =    3276
        (hexadecimal)  R5  = 00000AF0  + 000001DC  = 00000CCC
```

SUBTRACT (S) INSTRUCTION

Format:

```
1--------10----16--------columns
        S     R,S                         R = R - S
              ←
```

Purpose: To subtract binary constants. The Subtract statement computes the difference between the value stored at the general purpose register operand (R) and the fullword value located at the storage operand (S). The arrow indicates the direction of the operation. According to the notation (R = R - S), the difference replaces the original value of the register. The contents of the storage area remain unchanged.

Example:

```
        S       3,PAYMENT                 R3       | PAYMENT
                :                         ─────────┼─────────
                :                BEFORE:  00000064 | 00000014
                :                AFTER:   00000050 | 00000014
PAYMENT DC      F'20'
```

During execution, the binary constant stored at PAYMENT is subtracted from the contents of register 3. The difference (00000050) replaces the original contents of register 3 and the fullword located at PAYMENT remains unchanged. Note that in decimal R3 = 100 − 20, or R3 = 80:

```
S     3,PAYMENT ─────→ R3  =      R3       -   PAYMENT

        (decimal)      R3  =      100      -      20     =    80
        (hexadecimal)  R3  =   00000064    -   00000014  = 00000050
```

SUBTRACT REGISTER (SR) INSTRUCTION

Format:

```
1--------10----16--------columns
        SR    R1,R2                       R1 = R1 - R2
              ←
```

Purpose: To subtract binary constants stored in registers. Subtract Register computes the difference between the two general purpose registers, R1 and R2. The contents of the second register operand (R2) are subtracted from the contents of the first (R1). The resulting difference replaces the original value of R1, while the contents of R2 remain unaltered.

Example:

```
SR     6,10
 :
 :
 :
```

	R6	R10
BEFORE:	00000100	000000A0
AFTER:	00000060	000000A0

During the subtraction process, the binary value stored at register 10 is subtracted from the contents of register 6. The difference replaces the original contents of register 6 and the contents of register 10 remains unchanged. Note that in decimal R6 = 256 − 160, or R6 = 96.

```
S      6,10 ⟶  R6  =  R6  -  R10

       (decimal)      R6 =  256      -  160      =  96
       (hexadecimal)  R6 =  00000100 -  000000A0 =  00000060
```

STORE REGISTER (ST) INSTRUCTION

Format:

```
1--------10----16--------columns
         ST    R,S                              S = R
               →
```

Purpose: To store binary constants in program variables. Store Register does the opposite of Load. It moves data from the general purpose register (R) to the storage area (S). Notice the direction of the arrow. The contents of the register operand are copied to the fullword storage operand. The original value of the storage item is replaced, while the contents of the register operand remain unaltered.

Example:

```
        ST      4,ANSWER                    R4       |  ANSWER
                :                   ─────────────────┼──────────
                :           BEFORE: 000001C3 |  ????????
                :           AFTER:  000001C3 |  000001C3
ANSWER  DS      F
```

At run time, the fullword contents of register 4 are copied to the storage item `ANSWER`. The previous contents of `ANSWER` are replaced with 000001C3, while the value stored at register 4 remains unchanged. Note that in decimal `ANSWER = 451`.

PARTIAL DUMP (PDUMP) MACRO

Format:

```
1--------10----16--------columns
         PDUMP S1,S2                        print partial dump
```

Purpose: To print registers and contents of partial storage. Partial Dump produces a printed listing or dump of the program from the first operand (`S1`) up to, but not including, the second operand (`S2`).

Partial Dump provides a "snapshot" of memory at the time the dump is taken. Multiple dumps may be placed at any point to monitor changes in the program from one dump to the next. This can be helpful during the debugging process.

The partial dump below represents a simplified version of the mainframe PDUMP statement. Note that the contents of the registers and data items are shown in hexadecimal. A full dump on the mainframe would provide an extensive printout of main memory including registers, program statements, and storage.

NOTE: PDUMP is a macro; a macro is a single statement that represents a series of stored Assembler instructions. During the translation process, Assembler replaces the macro with the stored commands. Essentially, the program runs as if the inserted statements were actually part of the original source code.

Chapter 3: Introduction to Assembler Language

Example:

```
                :
        PDUMP   PACKAGES,INCOME
                :
PACKAGES  DC    F'36'
FEE       DC    F'10'
HOURS     DC    F'8'
INCOME    DS    F
                :
```

The dump produces the output shown in Fig. 3.3. Note that the contents of PACKAGES through HOURS are printed, while INCOME is not printed. If we wanted to include INCOME, we would simply change the PDUMP statement to: PDUMP PACKAGES,INCOME+4.

The contents of the registers are printed across the page in groups of four, while the names of the program variables and their contents are listed down the page. A dump can provide a programmer with a great deal of information when looking for errors in a program.

The fourth line from the end of the partial dump—DT LABEL VALUE—can be understood with the following legend:

```
PDUMP    CHAP3B      IBM System/370 ASSEMBLER for the Microcomputer
                        Copyright (c) 1994 by David M. Collopy

REG 0 - 3:    000003FF      000005B2      0000000E      000007B3
REG 4 - 7:    FFFFFFFF      0000006C      00000000      0000002D
REG 8 - B:    0000002D      FFFFFFFF      00000041      0000174B
REG C - F:    00000644      0000028F      0000051C      00001AE0

DT LABEL      VALUE

B  PACKAGES   24
B  FEE        A
B  HOURS      8
```

FIGURE 3.3 Partial Dump (Packages through Hours)

DT = data type:
- B for binary
- D for decimal
- H for hexadecimal

LABEL = name of the constant or variable

VALUE = the hexadecimal value of the storage item

The last three lines of the partial dump show the contents of the storage items in hexadecimal:

```
B    PACKAGES    24
B    FEE         A
B    HOURS       8
```

END-OF-JOB (EOJ) STATEMENT

Format:

```
1--------10----16--------columns
         EOJ
```

Purpose: To mark the end of the program instructions. The End-of-Job statement signals the end of the executable statements. Normally, any or all statements coded after the EOJ are used to define program storage variables (DCs and DSs), input and output data items, and/or file and record descriptors.

Example:

```
CHAP3A    CSECT
            :
          executable statements
            :
          EOJ
            :
          data and file descriptors
            :
          END    CHAP3A
```

END STATEMENT

Format:

```
1--------10----16--------columns
         END    Label
```

Purpose: To mark the end of the program. END signals the physical end of the program and tells Assembler to begin executing the program commands. The Label field is required and refers to the program name specified in the control section. The control section (CSECT) marks the beginning of the program. The End statement is the last physical statement in the program.

Example:

```
CHAP3A    CSECT
            :
            :
            :
          END    CHAP3A
```

SAMPLE PROGRAM CHAP3A

Sample program CHAP3A computes the total amount due for the account of Stuart Hall when he has a balance of $45.00 and charges an additional $42.00 to his bank credit card (Fig. 3.4). CHAP 3A's program dump is shown in Fig. 3.5.

Program Data:

DC statements are used to define data for the balance due and the charged amount.

Processing Functions:

Total amount due = balance + charges

Store total in AMTDUE

Program Output (Dump):

Dump the registers, constants, and variables

Locate the total amount due in the dump

Pseudocode Logic Design:

START
Load amount due
Compute total amount due
Store total amount due
Dump registers and variables
END

Sample Program CHAP3A

```
 1  * ------------------- TOTAL CHARGES -----------------------
 2  *   Compute total credit card charges and perform a PDUMP.
 3  *
 4  *         PROGRAM-ID: CHAP3A
 5  *         PROGRAMMER: David M. Collopy
 6  *         RUN DATE:   mm/dd/yy
 7  ***************************************************************
 8  CHAP3A   CSECT                               (system
 9           PRINT NOGEN                         use and
10           BALR  2,0                           general
11           USING *,2                           housekeeping)
12           L     5,BALANCE             load balance into R5
13           A     5,CHARGES             add charges to balance
14           ST    5,AMTDUE              store total in AMTDUE
15           PDUMP BALANCE,AMTDUE+4      dump the program
16           EOJ                         end of job
17  ***************************************************************
18  *                  DATA DEFINITIONS
19  *--------------------------------------------------------------
20  BALANCE  DC    F'45'                          balance due
21  CHARGES  DC    F'42'                          amount charged
22  AMTDUE   DS    F                              total amount due
23           END   CHAP3A
```

FIGURE 3.4 Sample program CHAP3A: Compute the total credit card charges made by Stuart Hall.

```
PDUMP    CHAP3A      IBM System/370 ASSEMBLER for the Microcomputer
                        Copyright (c) 1994 by David M. Collopy

REG 0 - 3:    000003FF      000005B2      0000000E      000007B3
REG 4 - 7:    FFFFFFFF      00000057  ◄── 0000002C      000022B8
REG 8 - B:    0000002D      FFFFFFFF      00000041      0000174B
REG C - F:    00000644      0000028F      0000051C      00001AE0
DT LABEL      VALUE

B  BALANCE    2D
B  CHARGES    2A
B  AMTDUE     57   ◄─────────────────────── 87 in decimal
```

FIGURE 3.5 Program Dump for CHAP3A

DISSECTION OF SAMPLE PROGRAM CHAP3A

Note the first seven lines of the program in Fig. 3.4. An asterisk in column 1 indicates that the line is a comment. Line comments are neither processed nor translated into machine code by assembler.

Now look at the CSECT and EOJ statements; they mark the beginning and end of the executable instructions, respectively. Note also that the CSECT and END statements include the name of the program. This is required for the DOS version of assembler.

The next three lines (PRINT, BALR, and USING) represent general housekeeping functions that suppress system messages, establish initial base register addressability, and maintain the instruction location counter, respectively. We will not examine these three functions in further detail.

Let's examine the program beginning at line 12.

```
12           L      5,BALANCE
```

The above statement means: Move (load) a copy of the binary constant stored at BALANCE to register 5.

```
13           A      5,CHARGES
```

The above statement means: Add the amount charged to the current balance due (stored in register 5) and place the resulting total in the register operand.

```
14           ST     5,AMTDUE
```

The above statement means: Move (store) a copy of the total amount due located in register 5 to the fullword variable AMTDUE.

```
15           PDUMP  BALANCE,AMTDUE+4
```

The above statement means: Dump the registers and the storage items BALANCE through AMTDUE. Since we have not yet learned how to print the output, we will rely on the dump as a means of verifying that the program processed the data as expected.

In looking over the dump, we see that the program did produce the correct result. The binary contents of register 5 (00000057) are equal to 87 in decimal. Hence, the sum of the balance and charge equals a total of $87.

MULTIPLY (M) INSTRUCTION

Format:

```
1--------10----16--------columns
        M    R,S                              R = R × S
             ←
```

Purpose: To multiply binary constants. The Multiply statement computes the product of the binary fullword located at the storage operand (S) and the value stored at the general purpose register operand (R).

When the contents of two fullwords are multiplied, the resulting product (R × S) may not fit into one 4-byte register. Because of this, binary multiplication requires the use of an even/odd consecutive pair of registers. Examples of even/odd pairs include R4/R5, R6/R7, and R8/R9.

Before the Multiply statement is executed, the multiplicand is loaded into the odd register of the even/odd pair. Assembler requires that the even register of the pair be specified as the first operand. During execution, the contents of the odd register are multiplied by the contents of the storage operand, the multiplier (Fig. 3.6).

According to Fig. 3.6, the multiplicand is replaced with the product, which normally occupies the odd register of the even/odd register pair. However, if the product is too large for the odd register, it overflows to the even register. In either case, the leftmost byte of the even register holds the sign of the product.

R (even/odd R)		R (even/odd R)		S (storage)
product	=	multiplicand	×	multiplier
300	=	10	×	30

FIGURE 3.6 Binary Multiplication

Example:

```
        L      7,TEN
               :
               :                       EVEN/ODD PAIR
               :                       R6        R7        THIRTY
               :           BEFORE:  ???????? 0000000A  0000001E
        M      6,THIRTY    AFTER:   00000000 0000012C  0000001E
               :
               :
TEN     DC     F'10'       0000000A (multiplicand)
THIRTY  DC     F'30'       0000001E (multiplier)
```

The multiplicand is loaded into register 7, the odd register of the even/odd pair. Note that for multiplication we specify register 6, the even register of the even/odd register pair, as the first operand. The resulting product 10 × 30 is computed and stored in register 7, the odd register of the even/odd register pair. The sign of the product (0) propagates across the even register, and the contents of THIRTY (the multiplier) remain unchanged. Note that in decimal R7 = 10 × 30, or R7 = 300.

```
M       6,THIRTY ──▶ R7   =    R7   ×   THIRTY
─────────────────────────────────────────────────────
                     R6   =    ?
        BEFORE:      R7   =    10   ×   30 ◀── multiplier
                              ▲_____ multiplicand
─────────────────────────────────────────────────────
        AFTER:       R6   =    0
                     R7   =    300 ◀── product
```

MULTIPLY REGISTER (MR) INSTRUCTION

Format:

```
1--------10----16--------columns
         MR    R1,R2                              R1 = R1 × R2
               ←
```

Multiply Register (MR) Instruction

Purpose: To multiply binary constants stored in registers. The Multiply Register statement computes the product of two general purpose register operands, R1 and R2. This instruction also uses an even/odd register pair and requires that the first register operand (R1) be specified as the even register of the even/odd pair.

During execution, the first operand, R1 (the multiplicand), is multiplied by the second register operand, R2 (the multiplier). The resulting product is then stored in the odd register of the even/odd pair. If the product is too large, it occupies both the even and odd registers of the even/odd pair.

Example:

```
        L       5,TEN
        L       6,THIRTY
                :                       EVEN/OD PAIR
                :                       R4         R5         R6
                :       BEFORE:  ???????  0000000A   0000001E
        MR      4,6     AFTER:   00000000 0000012C   0000001E
                :
                :
TEN     DC      F'10'   0000000A  (multiplicand)
THIRTY  DC      F'30'   0000001E  (multiplier)
```

First the multiplicand is loaded into the odd register (R5) of the even/odd pair and the multiplier is loaded into register 6. Note that the multiplier may be loaded into either an even or odd register, since it has no register-pair requirement.

Once the product has been computed, it is stored in register 5, the odd register. The sign of the product propagates across the even register (R4) of the pair. Note that in decimal R5 = 10 × 30, or R5 = 300.

```
    MR      4,6  ──▶  R5  =   R5  ×  R6
    ─────────────────────────────────────────
                      R4  =   ?
            BEFORE:   R5  =   10  ×  30 ◀── multiplier
                              ▲────── multiplicand
    ─────────────────────────────────────────
            AFTER:    R4  =   0
                      R5  =   300 ◀── product
```

DIVIDE (D) INSTRUCTION

Format:

```
1--------10----16--------columns
        D    R,S                              R = R ÷ S
             ←
```

Purpose: To divide binary constants. Division also requires the use of an even/odd register pair; the even register must be specified as the first operand.

Before executing the Divide statement, there are two things that should be done. First, load the dividend into the odd register of the even/odd pair. Second, clear the contents of the even register by multiplying the register pair by one. In effect, this action clears any value stored there by propagating the sign of the dividend across the even register.

If we neglect to clear the even register and it contains a value other than zero, then the dividend would not be equal to the value we placed there. Instead, it would represent a much larger value.

During execution, the value of the even/odd register pair, R (the dividend) is divided by the contents of the storage operand, S (the divisor). The quotient is then placed in the odd register of the pair, while the remainder is stored in the even register (Fig. 3.7). The value of the divisor in the storage operand remains unchanged.

According to Figure 3.8, the sign of the quotient is determined algebraically and is derived from the signs of the dividend and the divisor. However, the sign of the remainder is always equal to that of the dividend.

(even R)		(odd R)		R (even/odd R)		S (storage)
remainder	+	quotient	=	dividend	÷	divisor
2	+	4	=	30	÷	7

FIGURE 3.7 Binary Division (R÷S)

Divide (D) Instruction

```
REMAINDER  +  QUOTIENT  =  DIVIDEND  ÷  DIVISOR
   +2           +4           +30          +7
   -2           -4           -30          +7
   +2           -4           +30          -7
   -2           +4           -30          -7
```

FIGURE 3.8 Division Sign Table

Example:

```
                                   EVEN/ODD PAIR
                                   R8         R9
          L    9,THIRTY   BEFORE:  ????????   0000001E
          M    8,ONE      AFTER:   00000000   0000001E
               :
               :                   R8         R9         SEVEN
               :          BEFORE:  00000000   0000001E   00000007
          D    8,SEVEN    AFTER:   00000002   00000004   00000007
               :                       ↑          ↑
               :                       |          └── quotient
                                       └─────────────── remainder
ONE       DC   F'1'       00000001
THIRTY    DC   F'30'      0000001E  (dividend)
SEVEN     DC   F'7'       00000007  (divisor)
```

In the example, the dividend (30) is loaded into register 9, the odd register of the even/odd pair. Then the even register is cleared by multiplying the dividend by one, and the sign of the dividend propagates across register 8. After executing the divide, the remainder and quotient are computed and stored in registers 8 and 9, respectively.

Note the decimal result of the division: R9 = 30 ÷ 7, or R9 = 4 (quotient) and R8 = 2 (remainder).

```
D    8,SEVEN ──→ R9   =   R9   ÷   SEVEN
─────────────────────────────────────────────────
                 R8   =   0
        BEFORE:  R9   =   30   ÷   7 ←── divisor
                          ↑
                          └── dividend
─────────────────────────────────────────────────
        AFTER:   R8   =   2  ←── remainder
                 R9   =   4  ←── quotient
```

DIVIDE REGISTER (DR) INSTRUCTION

Format:

```
1--------10----16--------columns
         DR   R1,R2                               R1 = R1 ÷ R2
              ←
```

Purpose: To divide the contents of two registers. The Divide Register statement computes the quotient and remainder for the two general purpose register operands, R1 and R2.

There are three things we should remember to do prior to coding the DR instruction: First, load the dividend into the odd register of the even/odd register pair, R1. Second, clear the even register and set the sign by multiplying the dividend by one. And third, load the divisor into the second register operand, R2.

During the execution of the program, the contents of the register pair, R1 (the dividend), are divided by the contents of R2 (the divisor). The remainder and quotient are then placed in the even and odd registers, respectively, of the register pair (Fig. 3.9).

Example:

```
         L    10,SEVEN
         :                         EVEN/ODD PAIR
         :                    R8           R9           R10
         L    9,THIRTY        ????????     0000001E     00000007
         M    8,ONE           00000000     0000001E     00000007
         :
         :                    R8           R9           R10
         :            BEFORE: 00000000     0000001E     00000007
         DR   8,10    AFTER:  00000002     00000004     00000007
         :                        ▲            ▲___ quotient
         :                        |_____ remainder
         :
ONE      DC   F'1'    00000001
THIRTY   DC   F'30'   0000001E  (dividend)
SEVEN    DC   F'7'    00000007  (divisor)
```

In this example, the divisor (7) is loaded into register 10, and the dividend (30) is loaded into register 9, the odd register of the even/odd pair. The

				R1		R2
(even R)		(odd R)		(even/odd R)		(register)
remainder	+	quotient	=	dividend	÷	divisor
2	+	4	=	30	÷	7

FIGURE 3.9 Binary Division (R1÷R2)

dividend is multiplied by one to force the sign across the even register. Following the divide, the remainder and quotient are computed and stored in registers 8 and 9, respectively. Note the decimal result of the division: R9 = 30 ÷ 7, or R9 = 4 (quotient) and R8 = 2 (remainder).

```
DR      8,10    ──────▶  R9  =  R9  ÷  R10

                         R8  =  0
         BEFORE:         R9  =  30  ÷  7  ◀────── divisor
                              ▲_____ dividend

         AFTER:          R8  =  2  ◀────── remainder
                         R9  =  4  ◀────── quotient
```

SAMPLE PROGRAM CHAP3B

Marie Osborne works for EnTour Delivery Service, which delivers parcels to local area businesses. We want to write a program to compute the hourly income generated by Marie if she delivers thirty-six packages during an eight-hour shift and EnTour charges $10 per delivery. We will then dump the registers and program variables to verify our output. Sample program CHAP3B is shown in Fig. 3.10; the program's output is shown in Fig. 3.11.

Program data:
> DC statements are used to define data for deliveries made, hours worked, and the delivery charge.

Processing functions:
> Income = charge × deliveries
> Hourly income = income ÷ hours worked

Chapter 3: Introduction to Assembler Language

Program output (Dump):
  Print the dump and locate the hourly income.

Pseudocode logic design:
  START
  Load deliveries
  Compute delivery income
  Compute hourly income
  Store hourly income
  Dump registers and variables
  END

```
 1  * -------------------- DELIVERY INCOME --------------------
 2  *  Compute the hourly income generated by Marie Osborne.
 3  *
 4  *          PROGRAM-ID: CHAP3B
 5  *          PROGRAMMER: David M. Collopy
 6  *          RUN DATE:   mm/dd/yy
 7  **************************************************************
 8  CHAP3B    CSECT                                   (system
 9            PRINT NOGEN                             use and
10            BALR  2,0                               general
11            USING *,2                               housekeeping)
12            L     7,PACKAGES                        load deliveries
13            M     6,FEE                             total income
14            D     6,HOURS                           hourly income
15            ST    7,INCOME                          store in INCOME
16            PDUMP PACKAGES,INCOME+4                 dump program
17            EOJ                                     end of job
18  **************************************************************
19  *                DATA DEFINITIONS
20  *-------------------------------------------------------------
21  PACKAGES  DC    F'36'                             deliveries made
22  FEE       DC    F'10'                             charge per delivery
23  HOURS     DC    F'8'                              constant 8
24  INCOME    DS    F                                 hourly income
25            END   CHAP3B
```

FIGURE 3.10 Sample Program CHAP3B: Compute the hourly income generated by Marie Osborne during an eight-hour shift for EnTour Delivery Service.

```
PDUMP    CHAP3B       IBM System/370 ASSEMBLER for the Microcomputer
                          Copyright (c) 1994 by David M. Collopy

REG 0 - 3:   000003FF      000005B2      0000000E      000007B3
REG 4 - 7:   FFFFFFFF      0000006C      00000000      0000002D
REG 8 - B:   0000002D      FFFFFFFF      00000041      0000174B
REG C - F:   00000644      0000028F      0000051C      00001AE0
DT LABEL     VALUE

B PACKAGES   24
B FEE        A
B HOURS      8
B INCOME     2D
```

FIGURE 3.11 Program Dump for CHAP3B

DISSECTION OF SAMPLE PROGRAM CHAP3B

We will not dissect lines 1–11, which are program comments and general housekeeping commands. Instead, we will begin with line number 12.

```
12        L        7,PACKAGES
```

The above statement means: Load the number of deliveries made (36) into register 7, the odd register of the even/odd pair.

```
13        M        6,FEE
```

The above statement means: Multiply the number of delivered packages stored in register 7 by the delivery fee ($10) to determine the daily income.

```
14        D        6,HOURS
```

The above statement means: Divide the income stored in register 7 by 8, and place the hourly income in register 7.

```
15        ST       7,INCOME
```

The above statement means: Move (store) a copy of the hourly income located at register 7 to INCOME.

```
         16              PDUMP PACKAGES,INCOME+4
```

The above statement means: Dump the contents of the general purpose registers and the program storage variables `PACKAGES` through `INCOME+4`.

By inspection, we see that register 7 and `INCOME` both contain a hexadecimal 2D (decimal 45). Since $(36 \times 10) \div 8 = 45$, we know that the program produced the correct result.

KEY REVIEW TERMS

Define the following:

AR instruction	ST instruction	SR instruction
DC statement	alphanumeric	fixed-point binary
L instruction	constant	operations
MR instruction	PDUMP instruction	D instruction
numeric constant	output	EOJ macro
A instruction	halfword constant	DS statement
input	boundary alignment	constant
even/odd register	END statement	variable
pair	S instruction	LR instruction
fullword constant	M instruction	CSECT statement
storage area	macro	DR instruction

REVIEW EXERCISES

Show the contents of storage after each DC statement has been assembled.

```
                                         Storage
*1.  FIRST    DC    F'100'       FIRST:_____
 2.  TYPE     DC    X'C8C5E7'    TYPE:_____
*3.  HALF     DC    H'25'        HALF:_____
*4.  LARGE    DC    F'1765'      LARGE:_____
*5.  MINUS    DC    F'-46'       MINUS:_____
*6.  NEG      DC    H'-198'      NEG:_____
*7.  STRING   DC    C'HELLO'     STRING:_____
```

Review Exercises

				Storage
8.	MESG1	DC	C'DIVIDE'	MESG1:_____
*9.	MESG2	DC	CL4'HI'	MESG2:_____
10.	NOTE1	DC	CL10'ASSEMBLER LANG'	

NOTE1:_____

Code DC statements that correspond to the following hexadecimal storage values. (Assume X-data types were not used.)

		Storage
*11.	WHAT: FF17	_____
12.	GUESS: 00000098	_____
*13.	WHO: FFFFFF3E	_____
*14.	TRYIT: FFFFF10A	_____
*15.	NOTE2: C4C1E3C160C9D5	_____
16.	NOTE3: F5F96C40D6C6C6	_____
*17.	ANS: 0000AE5D	_____
18.	CODE: D55CC15CE25CC840F4F0F7F7	_____
*19.	NUM: FFFF	_____
20.	NUMX: 00015A0C	_____

Show the contents of the registers and/or storage items after each of the following instructions has been executed. For these exercises, assume the following initial values.

```
    R5:0000000C       VAL2  DC  F'14'     STOR2 DS  F
    R6:00000000       VAL3  DC  F'2'      NUM1  DC  F'95'
    R7:00000048       OUT   DS  F         NUM2  DC  F'50'
    R8:FFFFFFF3       STOR1 DS  F         NUM3  DC  F'120'
VAL1 DC  F'10'        R10:00000006        NBR   DC  F'-63'
```

*21. L   6,VAL2   L   5,NUM2
           R6:_____   R5:_____
*22. LR 7,5   LR 6,5
           R7:_____   R6:_____

Chapter 3: Introduction to Assembler Language

*23. A   6,NUM3   A   7,VAL1
        R6:_____   R7:_____
*24. AR 10,7   AR 7,8
        R10:_____   R7:_____
*25. S   7,VAL1   L   6,NUM1
        R7:_____   S   6,NUM2
                                        R6:_____
*26. SR 5,7   SR 7,8
        R5:_____   R7:_____
*27. ST 8,STOR2   L   6,NUM2
        R8:_____   S   6,NUM1
                                   ST 6,OUT
                                        R6:_____
*28. M   6,NUM3   M   6,NBR
        R7:_____   R7:_____
*29. MR 6,5   MR 6,8
        R7:_____   ST 7,STOR1
                                        STOR1:_____
*30. D   6,VAL1   D   6,VAL3
        R6:_____   R6:_____
        R7:_____   R7:_____
*31. DR 6,10   DR 6,8
        R6:_____   R6:_____
        R7:_____   R7:_____

PROGRAMMING EXERCISES

Instructions: For each exercise, design the pseudocode and write the Assembler program to produce the output specified. Model your program after the sample programs presented in this chapter. Verify your output.

NOTE: Refer to Appendix A and B for details of entering and running programs using PC 370 Assembler.

Programming Exercises

1. Fuel consumption: Write a program to project the yearly fuel consumption for the Williams family automobile, given the consumption rates of 135 and 125 gallons for the first and second quarters, respectively.

    Program data:

    Define the consumption rates, RATE1 and RATE2, in the program with DC statements.

    Processing functions:

    Yearly consumption = 2 × (RATE1 + RATE2)

    Dump the registers, constants, and program variables

    Program output (Dump):

    Store the result in register 9 and TOTFUEL. Locate the projected yearly consumption rate in the dump.

2. Algebra problem: Write a program to solve the quadratic equation: $(3X^2 - 7X + 2) \div Y$, where $X = 20$ and $Y = 3$.

    Program data:

    Define variables X and Y with DC statements.

    Processing functions:

    Result = $(3X^2 - 7X + 2) \div Y$.

    Dump the program registers and variables.

    Program output (Dump):

    Store the result in register 3 and ANSWER. Locate the result in the dump.

3. Space travel: Assume space travel (speed) is measured in zentrons. By definition, ten zentrons equal 235 feet per second. A space shuttle is traveling at the rate of 940 feet per second. Write a program to show the speed of the shuttle in zentrons.

    Program data:

    Define the data internally with DC statements.

    Processing functions:

    Result = (10 × 940) ÷ 235

    Dump the contents of the program.

    Program output (Dump):

    Store the result in ZENTRONS. In the dump, locate the speed of the space shuttle.

4. Investments: Dave Nelson invested $500 in Rydex stock. He expects his investment to double each year over a three-year period. Write a program to compute the total value of his investment at the end of the third year, assuming his speculations are correct.

   Program data:

   Define the data in the program with DC statements.

   Processing functions:

   Total value = $2^3 \times$ investment

   Dump the program registers and variables

   Program output (Dump):

   Store total value in VALUE and locate the result in the register dump.

5. Perimeter: Code an Assembler program to compute the perimeter of a rectangle, given a length of 36 feet and a width of 25.

   Program data:

   Use DC statements to define the length and width of the rectangle.

   Processing functions:

   Perimeter = 2 × (length + width)

   Dump the program.

   Program output (Dump):

   Store the perimeter in register 7 and RESULT. Locate the perimeter in the register dump.

6. Rent: Mr. Donahue, the principal of Nicholas Junior High School, rents the school gym to a local karate club for $23 per hour and to an aerobics class for $17 per hour. Compute the total weekly income earned by the school when the karate club and the aerobics class rent the gym 3 hours and 5 hours per week, respectively.

   Program data:

   Define the data with DC statements.

   Processing functions:

   Karate rent = 3 × $23

   Aerobics rent = 5 × $17

   Total rent = karate rent + aerobics rent

   Dump the program

Program output (Dump):

Store total rent income in RENT. Locate the rental income in the register dump.

7. Payroll: Write an Assembler program to compute the net pay for Mary Dushinski.

    Program data:

    Use DC statements to define the following source data:

HOURLY PAYRATE	HOURS WORKED	FICA TAX	FWT TAX	STATE TAX	CITY TAX	MISC
$7	38	$21	$40	$16	$4	$37

    Processing functions:

    Gross pay = payrate × hours

    Deductions = sum of taxes and miscellaneous

    Net pay = gross pay − deductions

    Dump the program

    Program output (Dump):

    Store the result in NETPAY and locate the hexadecimal equivalent in the register dump.

8. Tuition: Calculate the total tuition revenue earned by Woodview Business School over a one-year period. Also compute the cost associated with attending Woodview for one year.

    Program data:

    Use DC statements to define the program data.

AVERAGE QUARTERLY STUDENT ENROLLMENT	AVERAGE STUDENT CREDIT HOURS	COST PER CREDIT HOUR
250	14	$42

    Processing functions:

    Quarterly revenue = 250 × 14 × 42

    Yearly revenue = 3 × quarterly revenue

    Cost = yearly revenue ÷ enrollment

    Dump the contents of the program

Program output (Dump):

Store quarterly revenue in QREVENU, yearly revenue in YREVENU, and cost in YCOST. Locate the values for all three items in the register dump. Can all three items be found in the dump of your program? If not, why?

9. Inventory: Write a program to compute the potential profit which may be earned from the inventory items shown below.

Program data:

Define the source data internally with DC statements.

ITEM#	QUANTITY	COST	SELLING PRICE
12355	100	$50	$80
27883	125	$33	$62
31940	214	$12	$37
47502	139	$27	$49

Processing functions:

Item profit = quantity (price − cost)

Potential profit = sum of item profit

Dump the program

Program output (Dump):

Store potential profit in PROFIT and locate the hexadecimal equivalent in the register dump.

10. Grades: Compute the class average for the midterm and final exams.

Program data:

Define the data shown below with DC statements.

| Midterm: | 85, 70, 69, 90, 70, 57, 63, 45, 92, 79 |
| Final: | 72, 93, 90, 70, 80, 88, 75, 79, 81, 81 |

Processing functions:

Midterm average = (sum of midterm scores) ÷ 10

Final average = (sum of final scores) ÷ 10

Dump the program

Program output (Dump):

Store the midterm average in MIDTERM and the final average in FINAL. Locate both in the register dump.

4 FILES, MODULAR STRUCTURE, AND PRINTING OUTPUT

OVERVIEW

Learning Objectives
Files and Records
Defining Files in Assembler
Open (OPEN) Macro
Close (CLOSE) Macro
Preparing Data for Output
Convert to Decimal (CVD) Instruction
Unpack (UNPK) Instruction
Move Zone (MVZ) Instruction
Move Immediate (MVI) Instruction
Get (GET) Macro
Put (PUT) Macro
Equate (EQU) Statement
Sample Program CHAP4A
Move Character (MVC) Instruction
Edit (ED) Instruction
   Editing Patterns
Modular Structured Programming
Branch and Link (BAL) Instruction
Branch Register (BR) Instruction
Sample Program CHAP4B
Additional Sample Programs: CHAP4C and CHAP4D
Key Review Terms
Review Exercises
Programming Exercises

Chapter 4: Files, Modular Structure, and Printing Output

LEARNING OBJECTIVES

After reading this chapter and completing the exercises, the reader should be able to:

- explain why names are assigned to independent segments of code.
- assign symbolic names to general purpose registers.
- define program files using DTF macros.
- convert and prepare binary data for printer output.
- use edit and DC/DS statements to format and print program output.
- use BAL and BR statements to break a program into logically related segments.
- discuss the concepts and benefits of modular structured programming.
- write Assembler programs using top-down design and modular, structured programming techniques.

FILES AND RECORDS

From Chapter 1, we saw that data is organized to facilitate processing by the computer. As a review, the hierarchical organization of data presented in Chapter 1 is repeated here.

database   A set of integrated files. A database represents a central repository of information that may be retrieved and processed by multiple applications within an organization. For example, a customer database could provide information for the following applications: collecting accounts receivable, taking inventory, paying accounts payable, and recording sales-staff performance. Information in the customer database is related to sales. When a sale is made, the database is updated to record the items sold. For example, a credit sale could affect the database in several ways: A charge is made to the customer's account; an employee is given credit for the sale; the inventory on record is reduced; and an order is placed to replenish the stock sold.

file   A finite set of related records that pertain to a specific application. In the example of an organization that has a staff of 263 employees, the payroll file would consist of 263 records—one for each employee.

record	A set of related data items or fields. For instance, a payroll record would consist of all the fields necessary for computing the payroll for a given employee.
field	A set of character positions grouped together to form a single unit of information. For the payroll application, a field might include any one of the following items for each employee—number, name, payrate, hours worked, and deductions.
character	A single alphabetic, numeric, or special character entered at the keyboard.

DEFINING FILES IN ASSEMBLER

Assembler accesses files through special Input/Output Control System (IOCS) routines that are part of the computer's operating system access method. DOS and OS represent operating systems that use slightly different IOCS routines to link input/output files to the program. Files are defined in DOS with the DEFINE THE FILE (DTF) macro and in OS with the DATA CONTROL BLOCK (DCB) macro.

Figure 4.1 shows two DTFs that identify the parameters used to define input and output files in DOS. Figure 4.2 shows the DCBs for setting up input and output files in OS. For the remainder of this text, we will use DOS specifications for defining program files. Check with your instructor or

```
1--------10----16------------ - - - - ----------------------72
IPTFILE   DTFCD DEVADDR=SYSIPT,IOAREA1=IPTBUFF,DEVICE=2501,   X
               WORKA=YES,EOFADDR=EXIT

PRINTER   DTFPR DEVADDR=SYSLST,IOAREA1=PRTBUFF,DEVICE=1403,   X
               WORKA=YES,CTLCHR=YES,BLKSIZE=80

DTFxx: Define the file type.
     DTFCD - card file
     DTFCN - console typewriter unit
     DTFDU - floppy disk file
     DTFIS - indexed sequential disk file
     DTFMT - magnetic tape file
     DTFPR - printer file
     DTFSD - sequential disk file
```

FIGURE 4.1 Basic DOS Input/Output File Definition

supervisor for the appropriate file control statements for your particular computer system environment.

In Fig. 4.1, the following codes and terms are used:

DEVADDR Device address is required and specifies a symbolic name for the input/output device used to read/write the file. SYSIPT and SYSLST are normally used to specify the standard input and output devices, respectively.

IOAREA1 Input/output area 1 is required and specifies the I/O buffer reserved in memory for the input/output record. The buffer must be capable of holding the data transferred to and from the input/output devices. IPTBUFF and PRTBUFF are programmer-supplied names that specify the input and output buffers, respectively.

DEVICE DEVICE specifies the system unit number for the input/output hardware device used to read/write data. Unit numbers 2501 and 1403 specify the input and output devices, respectively.

WORKA YES for work area instructs Assembler to reserve a separate work area in memory for the input/output record. The GET and PUT commands, which read and write records from and to the file, must specify the name of the work area.

EOFADDR End-of-file address applies to the input file and specifies where the program branches when the end of the file is reached. EXIT is a programmer-supplied label that specifies where processing should continue upon reaching the end of the file.

CTLCHR Control character applies to printer output, and YES indicates that the first position of the output record is used to specify the carriage control character. The valid control characters are:

blank	single space before printing
0	double space before printing
-	triple space before printing
+	suppress line spacing before printing
1	skip to the top of the next page

BLKSIZE Block size specifies the length in bytes of one physical block. Records grouped into blocks are called physical records and BLKSIZE refers to the total number of bytes required to hold one physical record.

Defining Files in Assembler

```
1--------10----16------------ - - - - ----------------------72
IPTFILE   DCB   DDNAME=IPTFILE,MACRF=GM,DSORG=PS,            X
                EODAD=EXIT,LRECL=80,BLKSIZE=80

PRINTER   DCB   DDNAME=PRINTER,MACRF=PM,DSORG=PS,            X
                LRECL=80,BLKSIZE=80
```

FIGURE 4.2 Basic OS Input/Output File Definition

In Fig. 4.2, the following codes and terms are used:

DDNAME   Data-definition name assigns a symbolic name to an actual input/output device.

MACRF   Macro form specifies the input/output macros used by Assembler to access the program files. GM indicates the input will be read using the GET macro and the contents of the input will be moved to the work area designated by the GET macro. For example, GET IPTFILE,IPTRECD will read a record from IPTFILE and store the data in the IPTRECD work area. PM indicates that data will be moved from the work area specified to the output file with the PUT macro. For example, PUT PRINTER,OUTRECD will write the contents of the OUTRECD work area to the PRINTER FILE.

DSORG   Data-set organization specifies the organizational mode of the file. PS indicates the file records are physically stored or written sequentially.

EODAD   End-of-data address applies to input files only and specifies where the program branches when the end of file is detected. At the end of a file, control branches to the statement labeled EXIT.

LRECL   Logical-record length specifies the length in bytes of one actual record.

BLKSIZE   Block size specifies the length in bytes of one physical record. A physical record may contain one or more logical records. LRECL and BLKSIZE often show the same length.

OPEN MACRO

Format:

```
1--------10----16--------columns
         OPEN  F1,F2,etc.              activate file
```

Purpose: To open program files. All files must be opened before the program accesses them. The open macro activates the files and informs the operating system that GET and PUT calls will be made to the named files. We may use one open macro to open all files at once, as long as the file operands are separated by commas.

Examples:

1. `OPEN  PRINTER`
2. `OPEN  DATAFILE,PRTFILE`

Example 1 opens one file (PRINTER), while Example 2 opens two files (DATAFILE and PRTFILE).

CLOSE MACRO

Format:

```
1--------10----16--------columns
         CLOSE F1,F2,etc.              release file
```

Purpose: To close program files. All files must be closed prior to exiting the program. The close macro releases the files and informs the operating system that calls will no longer be made to the named files. We may use a single close statement to close all files at the same time, as long as multiple file operands are separated by commas.

Examples:

1. `CLOSE  INFILE,OUTFILE`
2. `CLOSE  MAST,TRAN,UPDTFILE`

Example 1 closes two files (INFILE and OUTFILE) and Example 2 closes three files (MAST, TRAN, and UPDTFILE).

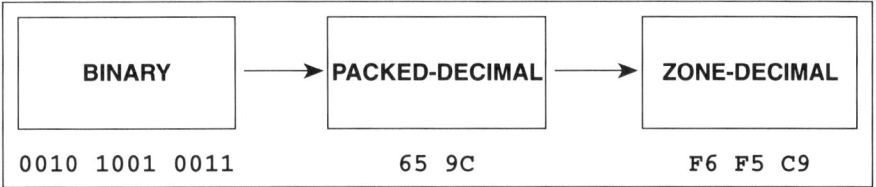

FIGURE 4.3 Conversion Process

PREPARING DATA FOR OUTPUT

The next three instructions (CVD, UNPK, and MVZ) are primarily used to convert and prepare binary data for output. During the conversion process, Assembler requires that the binary value stored in a register be converted to an intermediate format. Actually the binary value is converted to packed-decimal, which is then converted to zone-decimal. Packed-decimal stores data by packing two digits per byte. Note the byte configurations shown in Fig. 4.3 for binary, packed-decimal, and zone-decimal formats. Bear in mind that the spaces between the bytes are not part of the actual data; they are included so that the data are easier to read.

According to Fig. 4.3, Assembler converts the binary value 001010010011 to a packed-decimal 659C, where C represents the sign of the positive integer. D is used to represent negative integers. Then the packed-decimal value is converted to a zone-decimal F6F5C9. Keep this conversion process in mind as you read the rest of this chapter.

CONVERT TO DECIMAL (CVD) INSTRUCTION

Format:

```
1--------10----16--------columns
      CVD   R,S                     data conversion
            →
```

Purpose: To convert binary constants to packed-decimal. The binary constant stored at register operand (R) is converted to packed-decimal and placed in storage operand (S). Storage operand S must be defined as a doubleword.

Example:

```
CVD     3,PKFLD                    R3       |    PKFLD
                    BEFORE:   000005B2   |  ??????????????
                    AFTER:    000005B2   |  000000000001458C
```

During execution of the CVD, the binary constant stored at register 3 is converted to packed-decimal and placed in PKFLD, replacing PKFLD's previous contents.

UNPACK (UNPK) INSTRUCTION

Format:

```
1--------10----16--------columns
        UNPK    S1,S2                       data conversion
                 ←
```

Purpose: To convert packed-decimal constants to zone-decimal. The packed-decimal constant stored at the second operand (S2) is converted to zone-decimal and is placed in the first operand (S1). S2 must be defined as packed-decimal, and S1 must be defined as zone-decimal.

Example:

```
        UNPK    ZDFLD,PKFLD              ZDFLD    |   PKFLD
                          BEFORE:     ????????   |  0001238C
                          AFTER:      F1F2F3C8   |  0001238C
                                           ↑___ sign
```

During the conversion process, the decimal constant stored at PKFLD is unpacked and placed in ZDFLD. Note that the sign (C) occupies the zone portion of the rightmost byte.

We now have a small problem. What do you think will happen if we were to print the contents of ZDFLD? It will not print "1234." Instead, it will print: "123H." The error occurs because C8 represents the character H, not the character 8. Before the computer can print the 8 in the output, the zone portion of the sign byte must be changed from C to F. As you may recall, F8 is the equivalent for the character 8.

Move Zone (MVZ) Instruction

As we shall see in the next section, the Move Zone statement will be used to take care of this problem. But for now, note that UNPK only unpacks the decimal digits; it does not change the zone bits of the sign byte.

MOVE ZONE (MVZ) INSTRUCTION

Format:

```
1--------10----16---------columns
         MVZ    S1,S2                    change zone bits
                ←
```

Purpose: To change zone bits. Move Zone copies the zone bits from the second storage operand (S2) to the zone bits of the first operand (S1). However, the sending and receiving fields may be the same. By definition, both operands must be defined as zone-decimal.

Examples:

			(receiving)	(sending)
1.	MVZ	ZDFLD+3(1),ZDFLD	ZDFLD	ZDFLD
		BEFORE:	F1F2F3C4	F1F2F3C4
		AFTER:	F1F2F3F4	F1F2F3F4
2.	MVZ	THERE+3(1),HERE	THERE	HERE
		BEFORE:	F0F6F5C5	F1F9F7F1
		AFTER:	F0F6F5F5	F1F9F7F1

Both examples replace the sign bits of the first operand with the zone bits of the first byte of the second operand. The first example uses the same variable for the sending and receiving operands, whereas the second example uses different variables.

Let's take a closer look at the first example, since it represents the most popular form.

```
            bytes ⟶  0  1  2  3

ZDFLD BEFORE:        F1 F2 F3 C4
                              ↑
                     └────────┘
ZDFLD AFTER:         F1 F2 F3 F4
```

According to the illustration, the zone bits of the first byte (F) are copied to the zone bits of the last byte, replacing C with F. The value enclosed within parentheses specifies the number of zone bits to replace—in this example, only one zone bit is replaced.

In summary, preparing decimal data for output involves the two-step process of unpacking and moving zone.

MOVE IMMEDIATE (MVI) INSTRUCTION

Format:

```
1--------10----16---------columns
         MVI   S,C'I'                              S = I
               ←
```

Purpose: To move a single character. MVI moves the 1-byte character enclosed within single quotes, as defined by the immediate operand (I), to the storage operand (S). As a result of the move, the immediate character replaces the single character specified in the receiving item.

Example:

```
1.            MVI   PRTCTL,C'0'           PRTCTL
                                          _____
                                 BEFORE:  ??
                                 AFTER:   F0

2.            MVI   NETPAY,C'$'           NETPAY
                :                         _____
                :                BEFORE:  F0F4F9F2
                :                AFTER:   5BF4F9F2
    NETPAY    DC    CL4
```

For Example 1, zero is moved to the print-control operand PRTCTL. During the move in Example 2, a dollar sign (5B) is moved to the first byte of the four-byte operand NETPAY. If NETPAY were printed, the output would be $492. Hence MVI may be used to apply minor editing to the output.

GET (GET) MACRO

Format:

```
1--------10----16-------------columns
         GET    F,S                      input function
                →
```

Purpose: To read records from the input file. The Get macro reads a record from the file specified by the first operand (F) and places it in the storage operand (S). GET also checks for the end-of-file condition and then sends control to the program statement with the label specified by the EOFADDR operand of the input file DTF.

Example:

```
GET    INFILE,INRECORD
```

During the input process, the computer transfers one record from the input device assigned to INFILE and stores the contents of the record in the work area INRECORD. The work area must be large enough to hold the complete record.

PUT (PUT) MACRO

Format:

```
1--------10----16-----------columns
         PUT    F,S                      output function
                ←
```

Purpose: To write records to the output file. The Put macro writes the record from storage operand (S) to the output device specified by the file operand (F).

Example:

```
PUT    PRTFILE,PRTRECD
```

During the output process, the computer transfers the contents of PRTRECD to the output device assigned to PRTFILE. The work area (PRTRECD) must be large enough to hold the complete output record.

EQUATE (EQU) STATEMENT

Format 1:

```
1--------10----16--------columns
Label     EQU   *                       Label = location
```

Purpose: To assign a name to a location in the program. The Equate statement can be used to document the program by giving a name to either a location or a section of code. It can also be used to provide a reference point during the execution of a branch command. We will discuss basic branching concepts later in this chapter. Note that this particular form of Equate requires an asterisk in column 16.

The notation on the right (Label = location) indicates that the label assigns a symbolic name to the next executable statement.

Each label should be unique and self-documenting. A label should clearly identify the function performed by the statement or segment it represents.

Example:

```
PROCESS   EQU    *   - - CALCULATIONS - -
          L      5,PACKAGES           load deliveries
          M      4,FEE                compute total income
          D      4,HOURS              compute hourly income
```

According to the example, the symbolic name PROCESS is assigned to the load, which is the first statement in the calculations segment. An alternate way of labeling or specifying a block of code is shown in Fig. 4.4. In this book, we will use the latter method to identify a module or segment of code. Regardless of which method is used, it is important to realize that programs can be divided into logically related segments that help organize, document,

```
*---------------------------------------------------
*                 COMPUTE HOURLY INCOME
*---------------------------------------------------
PROCESS   L      5,PACKAGES           load deliveries
          M      4,FEE                compute total income
          D      4,HOURS              compute hourly income
```

FIGURE 4.4 Calculations Module

and produce programs that are more reliable and easier to read. This approach to designing and writing programs is called modular structured programming.

Format 2:

```
1--------10----16--------columns
Label    EQU   R                    Label = register
```

Purpose: To assign a name to a register. This format equates a symbolic name to a register. The label is used to document the purpose or contents of the register. One advantage to such labeling is that it helps a programmer remember the contents of each register. For example, it is easier to remember the contents of a register labeled NETPAY than one labeled register 9.

By itself, a register number bears little (if any) meaning or relationship to its contents. However, a label, such as NETPAY, assigns a specific purpose to the register. According to Example 1 below, the labels PAYRATE, HOURS, and TAXPAID are used to assign names to registers 4, 6, and 7, respectively. Ordinarily, we will not use this form of the Equate statement. Instead, we will document the purpose of a register by coding a brief explanation at the end of the line of the instruction itself.

Example 2 shows how to attach the prefix "R" to the numeric specification of a register. Some programmers may prefer "R5" to "5" when specifying register operands. Although this option of the Equate statement is a reasonable one, we will continue to code only the register numbers.

Examples:

```
1.        PAYRATE   EQU   4
          HOURS     EQU   6
          TAXPAID   EQU   7

2.        R5        EQU   5
```

SAMPLE PROGRAM CHAP4A

The program shown in Fig. 4.5 was introduced in Chapter 3; we present it here to illustrate how to organize the program code into logically related segments and how to print the output produced by the program. Sample program CHAP4A computes the hourly income generated by Marie Osborne during her eight-hour shift at EnTour Delivery Service.

Program data:
> DC statements are used to define the data required by the program: delivery charge, hours worked, and deliveries made.

Processing functions:
> Income = charge × deliveries
>
> Hourly income = income ÷ hours worked

Program output (Printer):
> Print hourly income.

Pseudocode logic design:
> START
> Load deliveries
> Compute delivery income
> Compute hourly income
> Print hourly income
> END

DISSECTION OF SAMPLE PROGRAM CHAP4A

The program code for CHAP4A is shown in Fig. 4.5; the program's output is shown in Fig. 4.6. Notice how dashed lines, section headings, and labels are used to divide the program code into individual segments. Each segment performs a specific task. Clearly all arithmetic operations are logically related and, consequently, have been grouped together under COMPUTE HOURLY INCOME. Similarly, the instructions that print the hourly income have been grouped together under PRINT HOURLY INCOME.

Also note the asterisks in column 1 for lines 28, 35, and 46. We follow this convention to highlight certain statements, so that they are easier to find.

Organizing the statements into logically related sections makes the program easier to read and understand. Let's now discuss the processing and output performed by the program, and take a look at the detail line (DTLLINE) defined in the data section of the program.

```
C O M P U T E    H O U R L Y    I N C O M E:
   14  *-----------------------------------------------
   15  *                   COMPUTE HOURLY INCOME
   16  *-----------------------------------------------
   17 PROCESS   L      5,PACKAGES
```

The above statement means: Load the number of packages delivered during the eight-hour period into register number 5.

Sample Program CHAP4A

```
 1 *  ------------------- DELIVERY INCOME --------------------
 2 *    Compute and print the hourly income generated by Marie
 3 *    Osborne.
 4 *
 5 *            PROGRAM-ID: CHAP4A
 6 *            PROGRAMMER: David M. Collopy
 7 *            RUN DATE:   mm/dd/yy
 8 ***************************************************************
 9 CHAP4A   CSECT                                       (system
10          PRINT NOGEN                                 use and
11          BALR  2,0                                   general
12          USING *,2                              housekeeping)
13          OPEN  PRINTER                            open file
14 *--------------------------------------------------------------
15 *              COMPUTE HOURLY INCOME
16 *--------------------------------------------------------------
17 PROCESS  L     5,PACKAGES                      load deliveries
18          M     4,FEE                              daily income
19          D     4,HOURS                           hourly income
20 *--------------------------------------------------------------
21 *              PRINT HOURLY INCOME
22 *--------------------------------------------------------------
23 PRTOUT   CVD   5,DBLWORD                       convert income...
24          UNPK  INCOME,DBLWORD                  ...to zone-decimal
25          MVZ   INCOME+1(1),INCOME                 replace sign
26          MVI   CCD,C'0'                          double space...
27          PUT   PRINTER,DTLLINE                 ...and print output
28 *
29          CLOSE PRINTER                             close file
30          EOJ                                       end of job
31 ***************************************************************
32 *              I/O FILE DEFINITIONS
33 *--------------------------------------------------------------
34 PRINTER  DTFPR DEVADDR=SYSLST,IOAREA1=PRTBUFF,DEVICE=1403,     X
                 CTLCHR=YES,WORKA=YES,BLKSIZE=80
35 *
36 PRTBUFF  DS    CL80                          printer record buffer
```

FIGURE 4.5 Sample Program CHAP4A: Compute and print the hourly income produced by Marie Osborne during an eight-hour shift for EnTour Delivery Service.

```
37 *---------------------------------------------------------------
38 *                   RECORD/DATA DEFINITIONS
39 *---------------------------------------------------------------
40 DTLLINE   DS    0CL80                         DETAIL LINE
41 CCD       DS    CL1' '                    carriage control
42           DC    CL18'HOURLY INCOME IS $'     line message
43 INCOME    DS    CL2                          hourly income
44           DC    CL3'.00'                              cents
45           DC    CL56' '                              unused
46 *
47 PACKAGES  DC    F'36'                       deliveries made
48 FEE       DC    F'10'                    charge per delivery
49 HOURS     DC    F'8'                         hours worked
50 DBLWORD   DS    D                                work area
51           END   CHAP4A
```

FIGURE 4.5 (cont.)

```
              HOURLY INCOME IS $45.00
```

FIGURE 4.6 Program Output for CHAP4A

```
    18            M      4,FEE
```

The above statement means: Multiply the number of packages delivered (stored in register 5) by the delivery charge, and place the product—the daily income—in register 5.

```
    19            D      4,HOURS
```

The above statement means: Divide the daily income stored in register 5 by 8 and replace the contents of register 5 with the quotient—the hourly income.

PRINT HOURLY INCOME:

```
    20 *---------------------------------------------------------------
    21 *                     PRINT HOURLY INCOME
    22 *---------------------------------------------------------------
    23 PRTOUT    CVD    5,DBLWORD
```

The above statement means: Convert the binary value stored in register 5 to packed-decimal and place the result in the `DBLWORD` operand. `DBLWORD` is used as a temporary work area to hold the data during the conversion process.

```
24            UNPK    INCOME,DBLWORD
```

The above statement means: Unpack the decimal value stored in `DBLWORD`, convert it to zone-decimal, and place the result in `INCOME`.

```
25            MVZ     INCOME+1(1),INCOME
```

The above statement means: Replace the sign portion of the right-most byte of income with `F` by moving a copy of the zone portion of the left-most byte of `INCOME`.

```
26            MVI     CCD,C'0'
```

The above statement means: Move zero to carriage control to double space the detail line. Carriage control is used to set-up line spacing for data written to the printer. Note `CCD` stands for carriage control (`CC`) for the detail (`D`) line.

```
27            PUT     PRINTER,DTLLINE
```

The above statement means: Print the detail line (`DTLLINE`) to the printer. Note the output shown in Fig. 4.6. The program performed as expected and produced the correct result.

R E C O R D / D A T A   D E F I N I T I O N

```
40 DTLLINE    DS      0CL80
```

The above statement means: Define a record (`DTLLINE`) and allocate 80 bytes of storage for it. A zero in column 16 indicates that the next 80 bytes will be used to hold the record, which will be subdivided into fields.

```
41 CCD        DS      CL1
```

The above statement means: Define a labeled field (`CCD`) and allocate 1 byte of storage for it. Normally the first byte of each output record is used for carriage control purposes.

```
42              DC      CL18'HOURLY INCOME IS $'
```

The above statement means: Define an unlabeled field and allocate 18 bytes of storage for it. Initialize the field to the character string enclosed within single quotes. Data fields are not required to have labels.

```
43 INCOME       DS      CL2
```

The above statement means: Allocate 2 bytes of storage for the field labeled INCOME.

```
44              DS      CL3'.00'
```

The above statement means: Allocate 3 bytes of storage for the unlabeled field and initialize it to the character string enclosed within single quotes. This field is used to attach cents to the dollar value ultimately stored in INCOME.

```
45              DC      CL56'  '
```

The above statement means: Allocate 56 bytes of storage to an unlabeled field and initialize it to spaces.

MOVE CHARACTER (MVC) INSTRUCTION

Format:

```
1--------10----16---------columns
         MVC    S1,S2                          S1 = S2
                ←
```

Purpose: To move non-numeric data. Execution of the Move Character statement results in the movement of data from the second storage (S2) operand to the first (S1). The length of S1 dictates the number of bytes that are moved. The arrow indicates the direction of the operation.

As a result of the move, the original contents of storage operand S1 are destroyed and the data stored at S2 remains unchanged. Data is not physically moved, but copied from one location to another.

Example:

```
              MVC    CODE,STATE              CODE    |    STATE
                :                   BEFORE:  ??????  |  D5C5E640E8D6D9D2
                :                   AFTER:   D5C5E6  |  D5C5E640E8D6D9D2
CODE          DS     CL3
STATE         DC     CL8'NEW YORK'
```

During the move, the character string D5C5E6 is copied from STATE to CODE. Since the length of the receiving operand is 3, only the first 3 bytes are moved to CODE. After the move, the data stored at STATE remains intact, whereas the contents of CODE have been replaced.

EDIT (ED) INSTRUCTION

We edit printer output to improve its readability. For example, numeric data for a sales report is easier to read when leading zeros are suppressed and commas and decimal points are inserted as needed. Adding such improvements is part of the editing process and requires the edit command.

Format:

```
1--------10----16-------------columns
         ED    S1,S2                        S1 = S2
               ←
```

Purpose: To edit printer output. ED unpacks the data stored at S2, edits it according to the edit pattern stored in S1, and places the zone-decimal result in the first operand. The actual edit pattern is defined with a DC statement. The length of S1 determines the number of bytes that participate in the edit. S1 and S2 must be defined as zone-decimal and packed-decimal, respectively. The arrow indicates the direction of the operation.

As a result of the edit, the contents of S2 remain unchanged, whereas the contents of S1 hold the edited result.

EDITING PATTERNS

Before we show an actual example of the edit instruction, let's pause to see how an edit pattern, or edit mask, is created. An edit pattern consists of a series of special editing characters coded in hexadecimal that allows us to

Hex Edit Code	Purpose
40	Blank fill character: Use spaces to replace leading zeros.
20	Selection character: Print the digit from the sending item.
21	Significant start character: Force the printing of the digits to the right of the significant start character (zeros or otherwise).
5C	Asterisk fill character: Use asterisks to replace leading zeros.
4B	Decimal point insert: Insert a decimal point at the location specified.
6B	Comma insert: Insert a comma at the location specified.

TABLE 4.1 Editing Characters

suppress leading zeros and insert various editing characters, such as asterisks, commas, and decimal points. A list of editing characters is shown in Table 4.1.

Let's illustrate the above concepts with some examples. Note that each pattern must begin with a fill character and always contains one editing character for each digit in the packed field. Note also that b is used to indicate the presence of a blank space in the result.

PACKED DATA	EDIT PATTERN	PRINTED RESULT
	0 0 0 0 0	
00000C	X'402020202020'	bbbbbb
	0 0 0 4 5	
00045C	X'402020202020'	bbbb45

- 40   Replace each leading zero with a blank space. (The fill character must be attached to the front of the pattern.)
- 20   Print the digit if other than zero.

PACKED DATA	EDIT PATTERN	PRINTED RESULT
	0 0 0 4 5	
00045C	X'402020212020'	bbbb45
00045C	X'402021202020'	bbb045

Editr (ED) Instruction   109

21 Stop replacing leading zeros with spaces and start printing the digit that is present in the data.

PACKED DATA	EDIT PATTERN	PRINTED RESULT
00045C	0 0 0 4 5 X'5C2021202020'	***045

5C Replace each leading zero with an asterisk. Note that 21 stops the asterisk replacement and causes the digits (including zeros) to the right of the significant start character to print.

PACKED DATA	EDIT PATTERN	PRINTED RESULT
05963C	X'402020214B2020'	bb59.63
05963C	X'4020204B202020'	bb5.963

4B Insert a decimal point in the result. This edit code may be used with other editing characters.

PACKED DATA	EDIT PATTERN	PRINTED RESULT
0023456C	0 0 , 2 3 4 . 5 6 X'4021206B2020204B2020'	bb0,234.56
0023456C	X'4020206B2020214B2020'	bbbb234.56

6B Insert a comma in the result. This edit code may be used with other editing characters. Comma insertion is replaced with the fill character when the digit on the left is nonsignificant.

PACKED DATA	EDIT PATTERN	PRINTED RESULT
0129876C	0 1 , 2 9 8 . 7 6 X'4020206B2020204B2020'	bb1,298.76
0047500C	0 0 , 4 7 5 . 0 0 X'4020206B2020214B2020'	bbbb475.00
0047500C	X'5C20206B2020214B2020'	****475.00

Let's look at an example of the Edit statement (Fig. 4.7). First, MVC is used to move a copy of the pattern to the output area, PRTDATA. This

```
             :
         MVC   PRTDATA,PATRN
         ED    PRTDATA,PACKNUM
             :
             :
PRTDATA  DS    CL7    ...assume PRTDATA is part of the output
             :
PACKNUM  DS    PL3    ...assume 27025C was placed in PACKNUM
                             by the program
             :
PATRN    DC    XL7'402020204B2020'
             :
```

FIGURE 4.7 Example of the Edit Statement

preserves the pattern for later use. If we moved data directly to the pattern, it would be destroyed and would not be available for future use.

During execution of the edit, the packed-decimal value stored at PACKNUM is unpacked and edited according to the pattern shown. Hence, the value 27025C is edited as b270.25.

MODULAR STRUCTURED PROGRAMMING

Real-world applications often involve pages upon pages of program code and logic. Even now, at our level, it is becoming obvious that we need a better way to organize and manage program logic.

The purpose of modular structured programming is to provide a methodology for managing the programming task. This method allows the programmer to divide a large application into a finite number of self-contained modules. In this way, a large program becomes a series of smaller, logically related modules that can be developed and tested individually. It is much easier to program one module at a time than to undertake an entire project all at once.

A module is a group of logically related instructions (or block of code) that performs a single task. The modules are assembled to form the completed program.

Consider, as an example, a program that reads input, performs calculations, and prints output. These activities represent three distinct processing functions. For the sake of simplifying the logic and controlling the program, it is better to create three modules, one for reading the input, one for performing the calculations, and one for printing the output.

This technique facilitates program management and error control. For example, if a payroll program produces an incorrect result for net pay, we can examine the calculations module directly and correct any errors. Similarly, we would examine the output module to fix errors related to printing pay checks.

Modular programming simplifies the debugging process and saves time, since errors can be traced more readily. Modular programs are also easier to design and read.

BRANCH AND LINK (BAL) INSTRUCTION

Format:

```
1--------10----16--------columns
        BAL    R,L                      control transfer
```

Purpose: To transfer and return program control. Branch and Link causes an unconditional branch, or jump, to the program statement that has a label field that matches the one coded in the label operand (L). Before the branch occurs, the address of the next sequential instruction is loaded into the register operand (R).

An unconditional branch sends control directly to the statement in the program specified by the label operand.

Example:

```
                :
14 FIRST    BAL    8,PROCESS
15 SECOND   BAL    9,OUTPUT
                :
                :
```

For the first BAL on line 14, control stops executing the instructions sequentially and jumps, or branches, to the statement in the program labeled PROCESS. But before the branch is actually taken, the address of the next instruction (line 15) is loaded into register 8.

After loading the address of the next sequential instruction into register 9, the second BAL causes an unconditional branch to the statement with the label OUTPUT.

Chapter 4: Files, Modular Structure, and Printing Output

Normally, Branch and Link is used in conjunction with the Branch Register statement to set up a jump to and return from a module. We will see in the next section how this instruction works.

BRANCH REGISTER (BR) INSTRUCTION

Format:

```
1--------10----16--------columns
        BR    R                        control transfer
```

Purpose: To transfer the program control. Branch Register causes an unconditional branch, or jump, to the address of the statement stored in the register operand (R). This instruction is frequently used to exit a lower-level module and return to the sending, or calling, statement.

Example:

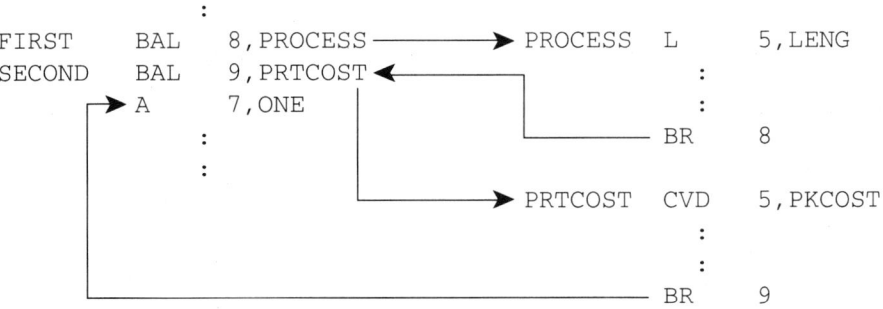

The first BAL loads the address of the second BAL into register 8 and then branches to the PROCESS module. From there, the instructions are executed sequentially, until the BR is encountered. Processing control then returns to the address specified in register 8, the second BAL in the MAINLINE module. In this case, MAINLINE is the calling module.

Once back, the second BAL sends control to the PRTCOST module. Upon completing the processing there, control returns to the Add statement in MAINLINE.

Note how the BAL and BR statements work together to branch to and return from the modules. We use BAL to send control to a module, and we use BR to return to the calling module.

SAMPLE PROGRAM CHAP4B

In Sample Program CHAP4B (Fig. 4.8) we continue to compute the hourly income for Marie Osborne. We have changed some minor specifications to demonstrate the application of mainline control and the editing process: The delivery charge has been changed to include cents ($10.00), and the program utilizes an edit mask to format the output for hourly income.

```
 1  * -------------------- DELIVERY INCOME ----------------------
 2  * Compute the hourly income generated by Marie Osborne. This
 3  * program demonstrates mainline processing and editing.
 4  *
 5  *              PROGRAM-ID: CHAP4B
 6  *              PROGRAMMER: David M. Collopy
 7  *              RUN DATE:   mm/dd/yy
 8  **************************************************************
 9  CHAP4B    CSECT                                       (system
10            PRINT NOGEN                                 use and
11            BALR  2,0                                   general
12            USING *,2                               housekeeping)
13            OPEN  PRINTER                             open file
14  *-------------------------------------------------------------
15  *              MAINLINE CONTROL
16  *-------------------------------------------------------------
17  MAINLINE  BAL   8,PROCESS                compute hourly income
18            BAL   9,PRTOUT                   print hourly income
19            B     EXIT                            process exit
20  *-------------------------------------------------------------
21  *              COMPUTE HOURLY INCOME
22  *-------------------------------------------------------------
23  PROCESS   L     5,PACKAGES                  load deliveries: 36
24            M     4,FEE                     daily income: 10.00 × 36
25            D     4,HOURS                   hourly income: 360.00 ÷ 8
26            BR    8                             return to mainline
```

FIGURE 4.8 Sample Program CHAP4B: This revised version of CHAP4A illustrates the application of the mainline control module and editing.

114 Chapter 4: Files, Modular Structure, and Printing Output

```
27   *-----------------------------------------------------------------
28   *                 PRINT HOURLY INCOME
29   *-----------------------------------------------------------------
30   PRTOUT    CVD    5,DBLWORD                       convert income
31             MVC    INCOME,PATRN            move pattern to output
32             ED     INCOME,DBLWORD+5              yields: bb45.00
33             MVI    CCD,C'0'                       double space...
34             PUT    PRINTER,DTLLINE        ...and print detail line
35             BR     9                           return to mainline
36   *
37   EXIT      CLOSE  PRINTER                            close file
38             EOJ                                      end of job
39   ******************************************************************
40   *                 I/O FILE DEFINITIONS
41   *-----------------------------------------------------------------
42   PRINTER   DTFPR  DEVADDR=SYSLST,IOAREA1=PRTBUFF,DEVICE=1403,     X
                      CTLCHR=YES,WORKA=YES,BLKSIZE=80
43   *
44   PRTBUFF   DS     CL80                      printer record buffer
45   *-----------------------------------------------------------------
46   *                 RECORD/DATA DEFINITIONS
47   *-----------------------------------------------------------------
48   DTLLINE   DS     0CL80                      D E T A I L   L I N E
49   CCD       DS     CL1                           carriage control
50             DC     CL19'HOURLY INCOME IS: $'         line message
51   INCOME    DS     CL7                             hourly income
52             DC     CL53' '                                unused
53   *
54   PACKAGES  DC     F'36'                         deliveries made
55   FEE       DC     F'1000'            ($10.00) delivery charge
56   HOURS     DC     F'8'                            hours worked
57   *                       0 4 5 . 0 0   →  bb45.00
58   PATRN     DC     XL7'402020214B2020'             edit pattern
59   DBLWORD   DS     D                                   work area
60             END    CHAP4B
```

FIGURE 4.8 (cont.)

```
           HOURLY INCOME IS: $  45.00
```

FIGURE 4.9 Program Output for CHAP4B

DISSECTION OF SAMPLE PROGRAM CHAP4B

Sample program CHAP4B contains three modules: one for controlling the functions performed by the program, one for processing the data, and one for printing the output.

The functions performed by sample program CHAP4B are the same as those performed by sample program CHAP4A. However, we have added the `MAINLINE` module. It is placed at the top of the program and is executed prior to the other modules.

Take a look at the `MAINLINE`. It controls the overall processing performed by the program, dictating the order in which the other modules are executed.

This particular coding structure, or arrangement of modules, from high-level control logic to low-level control logic, is commonly referred to as top-down design. Top-down programming refers to a programming technique that develops the high-level control logic first and then proceeds downward, level-by-level, to the detailed processing steps of the program.

```
M A I N L I N E    C O N T R O L:

   17 MAINLINE BAL    8,PROCESS
```

The above statement means: Store the address of the next executable statement in register 8 and branch to `PROCESS` to compute the hourly income.

```
   18           BAL    9,PRTOUT
```

The above statement means: Store the address of the next executable instruction in register 9 and branch to the `PRTOUT` module.

```
   19           B      EXIT
```

The above statement means: Branch to `EXIT`, close the printer file, and terminate processing.

```
C O M P U T E    H O U R L Y    I N C O M E:

   23 PROCESS   L      5,PACKAGES
```

The above statement means: Load the number of packages delivered during the day. Hence, 36 is loaded into register 5.

```
24              M       4,FEE
```

The above statement means: Compute the daily income by multiplying 36 by 1000. (The delivery fee is $10.00, or 1000 cents.) 36 × 1000 = 36,000. Since we are performing fixed-point binary arithmetic, we do not include a decimal point. Decimal-point alignment should be tracked by the programmer and then used to build the edit mask.

```
25              D       4,HOURS
```

The above statement means: Compute the hourly income by dividing the daily income by the number of hours required to produce it: 36,000 ÷ 8 = 4500. Once again, we do not include a decimal point in our calculations, although we continue to track its position (45.00).

```
26              BR      8
```

The above statement means: Return to the address of the statement stored in register 8. In this case, control branches to the mainline beginning with line number 18.

```
P R I N T    H O U R L Y    I N C O M E:

30 PRTOUT      CVD     5,DBLWORD
```

The above statement means: Convert the register value to packed decimal and store it in DBLWORD (000000000004500C). If we skip the first five bytes of leading zeros, we see that the actual result occupies the right-most three bytes of DBLWORD (04500C).

```
31             MVC     INCOME,PATRN
```

The above statement means: Move a copy of the edit pattern (PATRN) to INCOME, an output field defined by the detail line.

```
32             ED      INCOME,DBLWORD+5
```

The above statement means: Move a copy of the packed-decimal value stored at DBLWORD+5 (04500C) to the edit pattern stored at INCOME and perform the editing specified; INCOME contains bb45.00.

```
33              MVI    CCD,C'0'
34              PUT    PRINTER,DTLLINE
```

The above statements mean: Set up carriage control for double spacing and print the detail line.

```
35              BR     9
```

The above statement means: Branch to the address of the statement stored in register 9; control returns to line 19 of the MAINLINE module.

ADDITIONAL SAMPLE PROGRAMS: CHAP4C AND CHAP4D

To further illustrate the concepts of top-down design and modular structure programming, let's look at the Assembler code for a simple stock market investment application. Sample program CHAP4C (Fig. 4.10) organizes the code into processing segments; the output for this program is shown in Fig. 4.11. Sample program CHAP4D (Fig. 4.12) illustrates the use of top-down design strategy; the output for this program is shown in Fig. 4.13. The functional specifications for both programs follow.

Function:

Compute and print the average return gained from the following stock market investments: RoTron ($150.00), Pentek ($100.00), Winslow ($80.00), and Vaxcom ($70.00).

Program data:

Use DC statements to define the investment earnings for RoTron, Pentek, Winslow, and Vaxcom.

Processing functions:

Total gain = sum of investment earnings

Average gain = Total gain ÷ 4

Program output (Printer):

Print the average investment gain

Pseudocode logic design:

START
Compute total investment gain
Compute average investment gain
Print average investment gain
END

Chapter 4: Files, Modular Structure, and Printing Output

```
 1 *------------------ STOCK MARKET RETURN -------------------
 2 * Compute and print the average gain earned from investments.
 3 * The program code is organized into logical segments.
 4 *
 5 *              PROGRAM-ID:  CHAP4C
 6 *              PROGRAMMER:  David M. Collopy
 7 *              RUN DATE:    mm/dd/yy
 8 **************************************************************
 9 CHAP4C    CSECT                                      (system
10           PRINT NOGEN                                use and
11           BALR  2,0                                  general
12           USING *,2                              housekeeping)
13           OPEN  PRINTER                            open file
14 *--------------------------------------------------------------
15 *                  COMPUTE AVERAGE GAIN
16 *--------------------------------------------------------------
17 PROCESS   L     9,ROTRON                   load gain for RoTron
18           A     9,PENTEK                   add gain for Pentek
19           A     9,WINSLOW                  add gain for Winslow
20           A     9,VAXCOM                   add gain for Vaxcom
21           M     8,ONE                      clear even register
22           D     8,FOUR                     compute average gain
23 *--------------------------------------------------------------
24 *                  PRINT AVERAGE GAIN
25 *--------------------------------------------------------------
26 PRTAVG    CVD   9,DBLWORD                   convert avg gain...
27           UNPK  AVG,DBLWORD                 ...to zone-decimal
28           MVZ   AVG+2(1),AVG                       replace sign
29           MVI   CCD,C'0'                          double space...
30           PUT   PRINTER,DTLLINE          ...and print detail line
31 *
32           CLOSE PRINTER                             close file
33           EOJ                                       end of job
34 **************************************************************
35 *                  I/O FILE DEFINITIONS
36 *--------------------------------------------------------------
37 PRINTER   DTFPR DEVADDR=SYSLST,IOAREA1=PRTBUFF,DEVICE=1403,    X
                  CTLCHR=YES,WORKA=YES,BLKSIZE=80
38 *
39 PRTBUFF   DS    CL80                         printer file buffer
```

FIGURE 4.10 Sample Program CHAP4C: Compute and print the average return gained from stock market investments.

Additional Sample Programs: CHAP4C and CHAP4D

```
40  *----------------------------------------------------------
41  *                  RECORD/DATA DEFINITIONS
42  *----------------------------------------------------------
43  DTLLINE   DS    0CL80                       DETAIL  LINE
44  CCD       DS    CL1                         carriage control
45            DC    CL26'AVERAGE INVESTMENT GAIN: $'   line mesg
46  AVG       DS    CL3                         average gain
47            DC    CL3'.00'                    cents
48            DC    CL47' '                     unused
49  *
50  ROTRON    DC    F'150'                      RoTron earnings
51  PENTEK    DC    F'100'                      Pentek earnings
52  WINSLOW   DC    F'80'                       Winslow earnings
53  VAXCOM    DC    F'70'                       Vaxcom earnings
54  DBLWORD   DS    D                           work area
55  ONE       DC    F'1'                        constant 1
56  FOUR      DC    F'4'                        constant 4
57            END   CHAP4C
```

FIGURE 4.10 (cont.)

```
                AVERAGE INVESTMENT GAIN: $100.00
```

FIGURE 4.11 Program Output for CHAP4C

```
 1  *------------------ STOCK MARKET RETURN -------------------
 2  * Compute and print the average gain earned from investments.
 3  * This program demonstrates mainline control and editing.
 4  *
 5  *           PROGRAM-ID:  CHAP4D
 6  *           PROGRAMMER:  David M. Collopy
 7  *           RUN DATE:    mm/dd/yy
 8  **************************************************************
 9  CHAP4D    CSECT                                       (system
10            PRINT NOGEN                                 use and
11            BALR  2,0                                   general
12            USING *,2                                   housekeeping)
13            OPEN  PRINTER                               open file
```

FIGURE 4.12 Sample Program CHAP4D: Stock market investment program rewritten using top-down modular structure and editing.

```
14   *------------------------------------------------------------
15   *                 MAINLINE CONTROL
16   *------------------------------------------------------------
17           BAL    10,PROCESS              compute average gain
18           BAL    10,PRTAVG                 print average gain
19           B      EXIT                          process exit
20   *------------------------------------------------------------
21   *                 COMPUTE AVERAGE GAIN
22   *------------------------------------------------------------
23   PROCESS L      9,ROTRON         load gain for RoTron: 150.00
24           A      9,PENTEK         add gain for Pentek: 100.00
25           A      9,WINSLOW        add gain for Winslow: 80.00
26           A      9,VAXCOM          add gain for Vaxcom: 70.00
27           M      8,ONE                  clear even register
28           D      8,FOUR                average gain: 100.00
29           BR     10                      return to mainline
30   *------------------------------------------------------------
31   *                 PRINT AVERAGE GAIN
32   *------------------------------------------------------------
33   PRTAVG  CVD    9,DBLWORD              convert average gain
34           MVC    AVG,EDMASK          move pattern to output
35           ED     AVG,DBLWORD+5             yields: b100.00
36           MVI    AVG,C'$'                  yields: $100.00
37           MVI    CCD,C'0'                   double space...
38           PUT    PRINTER,DTLLINE     ...and print detail line
39           BR     10                      return to mainline
40   *
41   EXIT    CLOSE  PRINTER                         close file
42           EOJ                                   end of job
43   *************************************************************
44   *                 I/O FILE DEFINITIONS
45   *------------------------------------------------------------
46   PRINTER DTFPR  DEVADDR=SYSLST,IOAREA1=PRTBUFF,DEVICE=1403,   X
                    CTLCHR=YES,WORKA=YES,BLKSIZE=80
47   *
48   PRTBUFF DS     CL80                    printer file record
```

FIGURE 4.12 (cont.)

Additional Sample Programs: CHAP4C and CHAP4D

```
49  *------------------------------------------------------------
50  *                  RECORD/DATA DEFINITIONS
51  *------------------------------------------------------------
52  DTLLINE   DS    0CL80                             DETAIL  LINE
53  CCD       DS    CL1                                carriage control
54            DC    CL25'AVERAGE INVESTMENT GAIN:  '      line mesg
55  AVG       DS    CL7                                 average gain
56            DC    CL47' '                                  unused
57  *
58  ROTRON    DC    F'15000'           ($150.00)   RoTron earnings
59  PENTEK    DC    F'10000'           ($100.00)   Pentek earnings
60  WINSLOW   DC    F'8000'             ($80.00)  Winslow earnings
61  VAXCOM    DC    F'7000'             ($70.00)   Vaxcom earnings
62  *                   1 0 0 . 0 0  →   b100.00
63  EDMASK    DC    XL7'402020214B2020'                   edit mask
64  DBLWORD   DS    D                                     work area
65  ONE       DC    F'1'                                 constant 1
66  FOUR      DC    F'4'                                 constant 4
67            END   CHAP4D
```

FIGURE 4.12 (cont.)

```
              AVERAGE INVESTMENT GAIN: $100.00
```

FIGURE 4.13 Program Output for CHAP4D

NOTE: Consider the statement on line 36 of sample program CHAP4D:

```
        36              MVI    AVG,C'$'
```

As a result of the edit, AVG contains the zone-decimal string b100.00. Next, the MVI on line 36 is used to move a dollar sign to the left-most byte of AVG, yielding the final string $100.00.

KEY REVIEW TERMS

Define the following:

record	MVZ instruction	logical end
module	IOCS	unconditional branch
line spacing	database	top-down design
DTF macro	carriage control	GET/PUT
modular programming	CVD instruction	BR instruction
	DCB macro	MVI instruction
OPEN/CLOSE	MVC instruction	field
ED instruction	mainline module	UNPK instruction
physical end	EQU statement	edit mask
file	BAL instruction	

REVIEW EXERCISES

*1. Use EQU statements to document the program and assign names to the segments that perform the following functions: read the input, process the data, print a detail line, and compute a total.

*2. Code EQU statements to assign labels to registers 5, 7, 8, and 9, which are used to store credit hours, textbook expenses, change order fee, and tuition, respectively.

*3. Code DS statements to define an 80-column output record that contains the following fields:

column 1	carriage control
columns 7–10	item number
columns 12–34	item description
columns 36–38	quantity on hand
columns 40–42	unit price

*4. Code a DTF that will allow us to print the contents of the output record described in Exercise 3. Use BUFFOUT for input/output area 1.

*5. Given that SCORE is stored in register 9, write statements to convert and prepare SCORE for printing. Assume OSCORE is a three-position field defined by the detail line.

*6. Code DC/DS statements to define TESTOUT as an 80-byte output area that contains the message, "YOUR SCORE FOR TEST-1 IS " in columns 20–44 and SCORE in columns 45–47. Triple space the output.

Review Exercises — Answers

7. Card input DTF and work area

```
CARDIN   DTFCD DEVADDR=SYSIPT,IOAREA1=INBUFF,BLKSIZE=80,           X
               EOFADDR=EOJ,TYPEFLE=INPUT,DEVICE=2540,WORKA=YES
INBUFF   DS    CL80

WORKAREA DS    0CL80
EMPNO    DS    CL5           columns 1–5
EMPNAME  DS    CL31          columns 6–36
DEPTNO   DS    CL2           columns 37–38
         DS    CL1           column 39
JOBTITLE DS    CL20          columns 40–59
         DS    CL5           columns 60–64
YEARS    DS    CL2           columns 65–66
         DS    CL14          columns 67–80
```

Instruction results

#	Instruction	Operand	Storage
*8.	MVZ VAL+3(1),VAL+2	VAL	F1F0F2F3
*9.	UNPK FLD,NET	FLD	F0F0F2C0
*10.	MVI ACE,C'*'	ACE	5CF6F5D9
*11.	CVD 10,NUM	NUM	0000115D
12.	MVZ ACE+3(1),ACE	ACE	F0F6F5F9
13.	CVD 5,STOR	STOR	0000423C
14.	UNPK VAL,STOR	VAL	F0F0F4D5
15.	CVD 8,PAC	PAC	00588C
16.	UNPK ACE,NUM	ACE	F0F0F2C9
17.	MVZ VAL+3(1),FLD+1	VAL	F1F0F2F3

Edit patterns / results

#	Packed Data	Edit Pattern	Printed Results
18.	00018C	X'402020212020'	bbb018
19.	0123456C	X'5C20206B2020204B2020'	**1,234.56
20.	0000213C	X'4020212020204B2020'	bbb002.13

124 Chapter 4: Files, Modular Structure, and Printing Output

	Packed Data	Edit Pattern	Printed Results
21.	00213C	_____	bbb213
22.	0001775C	_____	bbb01,775

*23. For the skeletal code shown, fill in the branching statements (BAL or BR) for lines a, b, c, and d, such that MODULE1 is processed after MODULE2.

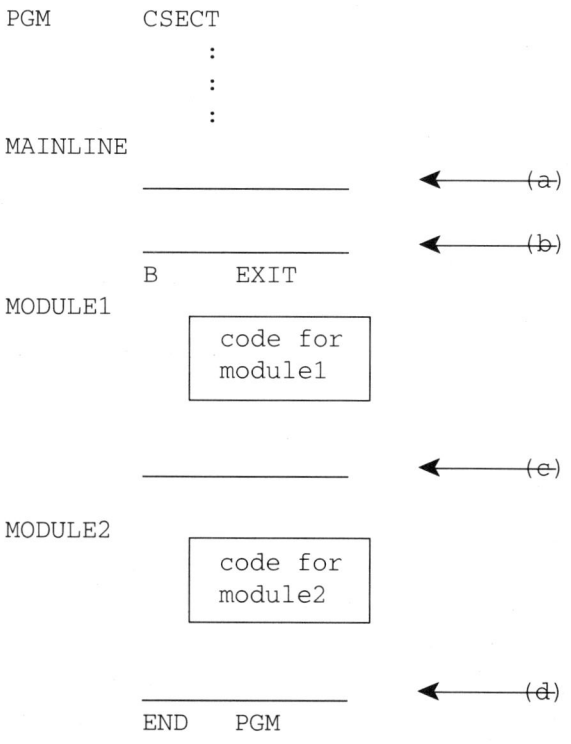

*24. Assume we have the following four modules: MAINLINE, MODULE1, MODULE2, and MODULE3. Sketch the skeletal code for the program and show the branch statements (BAL and BR) required if the modules are to be processed in the order given:

    a. MODULE2 is executed from the MAINLINE first.
    b. MODULE3 is executed from within MODULE2.
    c. MODULE1 is executed from the MAINLINE after MODULE2.

Use the method shown in Exercise 23 to sketch the program code.

PROGRAMMING EXERCISES

Instructions: For each exercise, design the pseudocode and write the modular structured program to produce the output. Model your program after the sample programs presented in this chapter. Verify your output.

1. Average sales: Dylan Walsh works part-time selling NULIFE health food. Compute his average sales over the past three-day period given he sold $60.00, $100.00, and $80.00 worth of merchandise.

   Program data:
   Use DC statements to define the sales.

   Processing functions:
   Total sales = sum of sales
   Average sales = total sales ÷ 3

   Program output (Printer):
   Average sales. Print the following output:

   ```
   Dylan Walsh averaged $999.99 in sales.
   ```

   (*Note:* 9s are used to indicate where to print the result.)

2. Rectangular volume: Calculate and print the combined volume of two rectangles.

   Program data:
   Use DC statements to define the height, length, and width of the rectangles.

	Height	Length	Width
Rectangle 1:	10	20	30
Rectangle 2:	17	10	23

   Processing functions:
   Volume1 = height1 × length1 × width1
   Volume2 = height2 × length2 × width2
   Combined volume = volume1 + volume2

   Program output (Printer):
   Combined volume. Print the following output:

   ```
   The combined rectangular volume equals: 9999.
   ```

3. Sales pay: Calculate and print the take home pay for Darren Stevens, an automobile sales representative at Perfecto Auto.

Program data:

    Define the following source data with DC statements.

Base rate	Bonus pay	Deductions
$200	$150	$75

Processing functions:

    Gross pay = base + bonus

    Net pay = gross − deductions

Program output (Printer):

    Total weekly pay. Print the following output:

```
Take home pay for Darren Stevens = $999.99.
```

4. PTA cookie sale: Write a program to compute and print the total profit derived from a PTA-sponsored cookie sale.

    Program data:

        Use DC statements to define the source data.

Boxes sold	Cost per box	Selling price
1457	$1	$3

    Processing functions:

        Income = boxes × price

        Expense = boxes × cost

        Profit = income − expense

    Program output (Printer):

        Total profit. Print the following output:

```
PTA cookie sale made $9,999.99 in profit.
```

5. Aerobics profit: Amy McIntire operates an aerobics business on a part-time basis. Write a program to compute her yearly net profit given the following monthly data.

    Program data:

        Define the data with DC statements.

Members	Monthly Fees	Rent	Insurance	Advertising
25	$19	$120	$45	$59

    Processing functions:

        Monthly income = members × fees

        Monthly expenses = rent + insurance + advertising

        Monthly net profit = income − expenses

        Yearly net profit = 12 × monthly net profit

Program output (Printer):

Total profit. Print the following output:

```
Amy earns $9,999.99 teaching aerobics.
```

6. Net worth: Compute Clark Fowler's total net worth using the following estimates for what he owns and what he owes.

    Program data:

    Use DC statements to define the data.

Owns:	Savings	Auto	Furniture	Tools	Clothes
	$3,000	$6,000	$2,500	$1,000	$275
Owes:	Auto	Charge Cards			
	$2,500	$1,959			

    Processing functions:

    Total owned = sum of items owned

    Total owed = sum of items owed

    Net worth = total owned − total owed

    Program output (Printer):

    Print the following output:

    ```
    Clark Fowler has a net worth of $9,999.99.
    ```

7. Modify the Assembler program in Exercise 6 to compute your net worth.

8. Accounts payable: Write a program to compute the total amount payable to Pannatek Supply Company.

    Program data:

    Use DC statements to define the purchase order data.

P.O. Number	Vendor	Date	Quantity	Cost	Shipping Charges
A12346	Pannatek	(date)	175	$5.00	$12.00

    Processing functions:

    Amount due = (quantity × cost) − shipping

    Program output (Printer):

    Print the following output:

    ```
    PO-NUM     VENDOR       DATE      AMOUNT DUE
    ------     ----------   ------    ----------
    A12346     Pannatek     (date)    $999.99
    ```

5 | READING DATA AND PERFORMING LOOPS

OVERVIEW

Learning Objectives
Iteration and Loop Processing
Branch on Count (BCT) Instruction
Sample Program CHAP5A
Assigning Data to the Input File
Reading Data
Pack (PACK) Instruction
Convert to Binary (CVB) Instruction
Reading a File and Processing Totals
   Sample Program CHAP5B
   Sample Program CHAP5C
Tracking the General Purpose Registers
Structured Programming
   Programming Guidelines
Key Review Terms
Review Exercises
Programming Exercises

LEARNING OBJECTIVES

After reading this chapter and completing the exercises, the reader should be able to:

- understand the concepts of iteration and loop processing.
- set up counter-controlled loops using the BCT statement.
- read and assign data to the program using GET and DTF macros.
- code MVC statements to move character string data from one operand to another.
- format output and accumulate report totals.
- use top-down design and modular structure to write Assembler programs to print simple reports.
- discuss the advantages of modular structured programming and explain why programming guidelines are necessary.
- describe the technique used to assign and track program registers.

ITERATION AND LOOP PROCESSING

Iteration is an important part of programming. A program can be set up to process more than one record. As an example, consider sample program CHAP4B, which computes the hourly income for Marie Osborne, an employee of EnTour Delivery Service. Suppose we now want to compute hourly incomes for six employees. Can we do this without changing the DC statements and running the program six times?

We could code DC statements for six different sets of variables (NUMPKG1, NUMPKG2,...NUMPKG6, and HOURS1, HOURS2,... HOURS6) and then code six independent segments to compute and print the hourly income for each employee. Although this method would work, it isn't very efficient. What if there were fifty employees? We would have to recode the program fifty times. Fortunately there is a better way.

What we want the computer to do is to execute the program once, but repeat, or loop through, the instructions until all the data has been processed.

By definition, a loop is a set of instructions that is processed repeatedly until a given condition has been met. In other words, the condition tells the computer how many times to repeat the statements in the loop. In our example, the condition would tell the computer to repeat the statements until the program has computed the hourly incomes for all six employees.

Chapter 5: Reading Data and Performing Loops

Additionally, the body of a loop represents the set of instructions that is executed a specified number of times by the computer. The term "iteration" refers to the process of repeating a series of instructions a specific number of times.

Every loop has an entrance point and an exit point that enclose the body of the loop and control the iteration process. In the sample program in Fig. 5.1, we will see how to use a trailing decision to test for the occurrence of a specific condition to determine whether to repeat or exit the loop. A trailing decision performs the condition test at the end of the loop; a leading decision performs the condition test at the beginning of the loop.

BRANCH ON COUNT (BCT) INSTRUCTION

Format:

```
1--------10----16--------columns
         BCT   R,L                        control transfer
```

Purpose: To set up a counter-controlled loop. The Branch on Count instruction is frequently used to control the number of times the body of a loop is executed. Each time the BCT is encountered, the value of the loop counter register (R) is reduced by one and tested for zero. If the value of the counter is not zero, then control branches to the statement specified by the label operand (L). But if the counter equals zero, then control exits the loop and continues processing with the first statement after the BCT.

Examples:

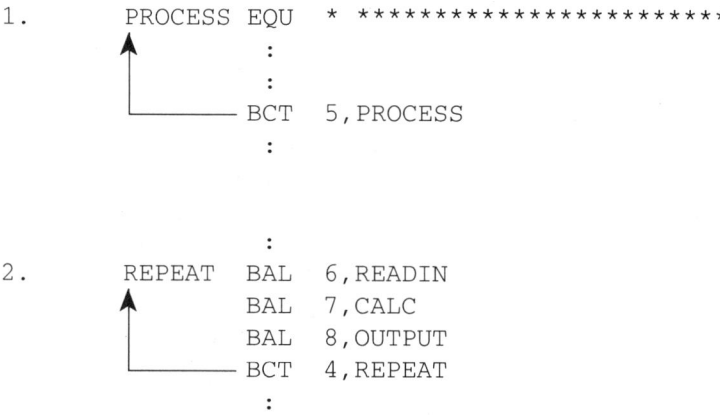

In the first example, assume register 5 (the count register) is initialized to 20. On the first pass through the loop, the BCT statement reduces the count by one and compares 19 to zero. Since count is not equal to zero, control branches to the statement labeled PROCESS. For each subsequent pass, count is reduced by one and compared to zero. Ultimately, count will equal zero, and the loop will terminate. Hence, the body of the loop will execute twenty times, once for each iteration.

Now look at the second example. The body of the loop consists of three BALs and one BCT statement. Let's assume register 4 equals 16. Accordingly, each of the three modules, READIN, CALC, and OUTPUT, will execute sixteen times before control exits the loop. Example 2 illustrates how to use a loop to control the major processing functions performed by the program.

In both examples, the BCT was used to set up a counter-controlled loop to process a series of instructions a certain number of times. Obviously, Branch on Count is a powerful tool that gives the Assembler programmer the ability to code applications involving repetitive tasks.

SAMPLE PROGRAM CHAP5A

The sample program in Fig. 5.1 computes and prints the square of the integers 1–10. Figure 5.2 shows the program's output. The following specifications apply:

Program data:
    The integers 1–10 are generated internally by the program.

Processing functions:
    Generate the integer
    Square = integer × integer

Program output (Printer):
    Print the integer and its square

Pseudocode logic design:
```
START
Open print file
Initialize integer to 1
LOOP until count = 0
    Save integer                    (Note how a loop
    Compute square                  is set up in pseudocode)
    Increment integer
    Print integer and square
End LOOP
Close print file
END
```

```
 1  * --------------- SQUARE INTEGERS 1 THROUGH 10 ---------------
 2  * This program demonstrates use of a counter-controlled loop
 3  *
 4  *              PROGRAM-ID: CHAP5A
 5  *              PROGRAMMER: David M. Collopy
 6  *              RUN DATE:   mm/dd/yy
 7  ****************************************************************
 8  CHAP5A    CSECT                                          (system
 9            PRINT NOGEN                                    use and
10            BALR  2,0                                      general
11            USING *,2                                housekeeping)
12            OPEN  PRINTER                              open file
13  *---------------------------------------------------------------
14  *              MAINLINE CONTROL
15  *---------------------------------------------------------------
16  MAINLINE  BAL   10,SETUP                         program setup
17            BAL   10,PROCESS              detail processing loop
18            B     EXIT                              process exit
19  *---------------------------------------------------------------
20  *              PROGRAM SET UP
21  *---------------------------------------------------------------
22  SETUP     L     4,TEN                      set loop counter to 10
23            L     7,ONE                         set integer to 1
24            MVI   CCB,C'1'                   advance to new page...
25            PUT   PRINTER,BLKLINE           ...and print blank line
26            BR    10                           return to mainline
27  *---------------------------------------------------------------
28  *              DETAIL PROCESSING LOOP
29  *---------------------------------------------------------------
30  PROCESS   ST    7,SAVINT                           save integer
31            CVD   7,PKINT                  convert integer to PD
32            MR    6,7                              compute square
33            CVD   7,PKSQR                  convert square to PD
34            L     7,SAVINT                            load integer
35            A     7,ONE                          add 1 to integer
36            BAL   9,OUTPUT                       print detail line
37            BCT   4,PROCESS              if R4 not 0, repeat process
38            BR    10                           return to mainline
```

FIGURE 5.1 Sample Program CHAP5A: Compute and print the square of the integers 1–10.

```
39 *-----------------------------------------------------------------
40 *                 PRINT DETAIL LINE
41 *-----------------------------------------------------------------
42 OUTPUT    MVI   CCD,C' '                         single space
43          UNPK  INTEGER,PKINT            convert integer to ZD
44          MVZ   INTEGER+1(1),INTEGER              replace sign
45          UNPK  SQUARE,PKSQR             convert integer to ZD
46          MVZ   SQUARE+2(1),SQUARE                replace sign
47          PUT   PRINTER,DTLLINE              print detail line
48          BR    9                            return to process
49 *
50 EXIT     CLOSE PRINTER                              close file
51          EOJ                                        end of job
52 *****************************************************************
53 *                 I/O FILES DEFINITIONS
54 *-----------------------------------------------------------------
55 PRINTER  DTFPR DEVADDR=SYSLST,IOAREA1=PRTBUFF,DEVICE=1403,     X
                 CTLCHR=YES,WORKA=YES,BLKSIZE=80
56 *
57 PRTBUFF  DS    CL80                      printer record buffer
58 *-----------------------------------------------------------------
59 *                 RECORD/DATA DEFINITIONS
60 *-----------------------------------------------------------------
61 DTLLINE  DS    0CL80                   D E T A I L   L I N E
62 CCD      DS    CL1                           carriage control
63          DC    CL14'THE SQUARE OF '              line message
64 INTEGER  DS    CL2                                    integer
65          DC    CL4' IS '                         line message
66 SQUARE   DS    CL3                            integer squared
67          DC    CL56' '                                 unused
68 *
69 BLKLINE  DS    0CL80                   B L A N K   L I N E
70 CCB      DS    CL1                           carriage control
71          DC    CL79' '                                 spaces
72 *
73 ONE      DC    F'1'                       integer lower limit
74 TEN      DC    F'10'                      integer upper limit
75 SAVINT   DS    F                                 save integer
76 PKINT    DS    D                              packed integer
77 PKSQR    DS    D                               packed square
78          END   CHAP5A
```

FIGURE 5.1 (cont.)

```
THE SQUARE OF 01 IS 001
THE SQUARE OF 02 IS 004
THE SQUARE OF 03 IS 009
THE SQUARE OF 04 IS 016
THE SQUARE OF 05 IS 025
THE SQUARE OF 06 IS 036
THE SQUARE OF 07 IS 049
THE SQUARE OF 08 IS 064
THE SQUARE OF 09 IS 081
THE SQUARE OF 10 IS 100
```

FIGURE 5.2 Program Output for CHAP5A

DISSECTION OF SAMPLE PROGRAM CHAP5A

Let's look at the program code (Fig. 5.1) and output (Fig. 5.2). Note the processing performed by the mainline. It executes a call to two subordinate modules, SETUP and PROCESS, before terminating the program.

M A I N L I N E   C O N T R O L:

```
16 MAINLINE BAL    10,SETUP
```

The above statement means: Store the address of the next statement in register 10 and branch to SETUP to perform the program initialization.

```
17           BAL    10,PROCESS
```

The above statement means: Store the address of the instruction on line 18 in register 10 and branch to PROCESS to perform the detail processing.

```
18           B      EXIT
```

The above statement means: Branch to line 50, close the printer file, and exit the program.

P R O G R A M   S E T U P:

```
22 SETUP     L      4,TEN
```

The above statement means: Load ten into register 4. Register 4 holds the control counter for the BCT. Since we are squaring the integers 1–10, the counter is set to ten.

       23   L   7,ONE

The above statement means: Initialize register 7 to one to begin processing. One represents the value of the first integer to be squared.

       24   MVI   CCB,C'1'

The above statement means: Move one to carriage control to advance to the top of the next page.

       25   PUT   PRINTER,BLKLINE

The above statement means: Advance to the top of the next page and print a blank line. The output work area (BLKLINE) has been initialized to spaces in order to print a blank line.

       26   BR   10

The above statement means: Branch register causes a jump to the address of the instruction stored in register 10. In this case, processing continues with the statement on line 17.

D E T A I L   P R O C E S S I N G   L O O P

   30 PROCESS   ST   7,SAVINT

The above statement means: Copy the integer stored in register 7 to SAVINT. Since register 7 is used to hold the integer and its square, we must copy the integer to a save area so it will not be lost. (We need the integer for later processing.)

       31   CVD   7,PKINT

The above statement means: Convert the binary value stored in register 7 to packed-decimal and place the result in PKINT.

       32   MR   6,7

The above statement means: Multiply the integer stored in register 7 by itself and store the resulting square in register 7: R7 = R7 × R7.

```
33              CVD    7,PKSQR
```

The above statement means: Convert the square stored in register 7 to zone-decimal and place the result in PKSQR.

```
34              L      7,SAVINT
```

The above statement means: Load the integer stored in SAVINT into register 7.

```
35              A      7,ONE
```

The above statement means: Add one to the contents of register 7. The value of the integer is incremented before entering the loop again.

```
36              BAL    10,OUTPUT
```

The above statement means: Store the address of the BCT on line 37 in register 10 and branch to OUTPUT to print the detail line.

Note that the program calculations and output are under the direct control of the processing loop and are executed exactly ten times, once for each integer 1–10.

```
37              BCT    4,PROCESS
```

Branch on Count automatically decrements the value of the counter stored in register 4 by one and compares the result to zero. When the counter equals zero, control exits the loop and continues processing with the statement on line 38. Otherwise, the above statement instructs control to branch back to the statement labeled PROCESS (line 30) and execute the body of loop again.

```
38              BR     10
```

The above statement means: Return to the address of the instruction stored in register 10. Control returns to the statement beginning on line 18.

PRINT DETAIL LINE:

```
42 OUTPUT      MVI    CCD,C' '
```

The above statement means: Move space to carriage control to single-space the detail line.

```
43            UNPK    INTEGER,PKINT
44            MVZ     INTEGER+1(1),INTEGER
45            UNPK    SQUARE,PKSQR
46            MVZ     SQUARE+2(1),SQUARE
47            PUT     PRINTER,DTLLINE
48            BR      9
```

Statements 43–46 prepare the output for the printer by converting the integer and its square from packed-decimal to zone-decimal and replacing the sign bits with F.

The Put macro on line 47 prints the output on the printer by transmitting the data stored at DTLLINE to the printer. Control then returns to the MAINLINE beginning at line 19.

ASSIGNING DATA TO THE INPUT FILE

Earlier in this chapter, we expanded the income computations performed by a previous program to handle multiple records. We further stipulated that the program should run only once, but repeat the body of the loop six times, once for each employee. We learned how to set up the loop, but we have not yet learned how to define data for multiple records.

According to a previous definition, a record is a collection of logically related fields. For example, data for the income program would require two fields, one for the number of packages delivered and one for the hours worked. Therefore, each employee would require one record with two fields; six employees would require a total of six records.

What we need now is some way of assigning data to the program. Assembler's DOS method for assigning data is shown in Fig. 5.3; Assembler's OS method for assigning data is shown in Fig. 5.4. Ask your instructor or supervisor for the job control statements required by your installation (see Appendix B).

Figure 5.3 shows the job control statements required to assemble, link, and execute an Assembler program under DOS. Job Control Language (JCL) is used to communicate with the operating system. Programmers use JCL to issue commands to the operating system to perform a variety of activities ranging from executing jobs and accessing files to managing system resources.

A job can be defined as one program or a system of programs that represent a single unit of work. For our purposes, a job consists of one complete program and all related files.

```
// JOB jobname                    ...signals start of job
// OPTION LINK                    ...requires the linkage editor
// EXEC ASSEMBLY                  ...execute assembler
(insert program statements here)
/*                                ...signals end of program
// EXEC LNKEDT                    ...link I/O and object modules
// EXEC                           ...execute load module
Barker    1005
Ditmar    1278     (program
Tanner    1134             data)
Wilcox    1410
/*                                ...signals end of data
/&                                ...signals end of job
```

FIGURE 5.3 Job Control Statements for DOS

```
// jobname JOB (password), programmer   ...signals start of job
// EXEC ASMFCLG                  ...execute assembler, link, and go
// ASM.SYSIN   DD *              ...program follows
(insert program statements here)
/*                               ...signals end of program
//GO.SYSPRINT DD SYSOUT=A        ...print all output on printer
//GO.SYSIN    DD *               ...data follows
(insert program data here)
/*                               ...signals end of data
//                               ...signals end of job
```

FIGURE 5.4 Job Control Statements for OS

Note where the program statements and file data are placed in Fig. 5.3. Data for sample program CHAP5B were used to illustrate the JCL statements.

Figure 5.4 shows the job-control statements required to assemble, link, and execute an Assembler program under OS.

READING DATA

Assigning data to the program can be as simple as coding the correct Get macro. However, there is a relationship among a number of factors that we should clarify at this point.

Defining an input file and reading data involves the following five-step process:

1. Define the input file and assign it to the appropriate input device. For example, the following DTF defines the input card file (IPTFILE) and assigns it to the card reader (DEVICE=2501).

```
IPTFILE    DTFCD  DEVADDR=SYSIPT,IOAREA1=IPTBUFF,DEVICE=2501,    X
                  WORKA=YES,EOFADDR=TOMAIN

IPTBUFF    DS     CL80                  input file buffer
```

When a record is read from the input file stream, it is placed in the temporary input buffer (holding area) IPTBUFF.

2. Assign a name to the input work area and define the format (field names and field lengths) of the record. The 0 in column 16 specifies that IPTRECD is a record that has been subdivided into fields: a 10-byte name field, a 4-byte sales field, and a 66-byte filler to pad the record length to 80 bytes. The filler doesn't have a label because data is not stored there. Note the input fields have been declared as characters. As we learned in Chapter 2, all data enters the computer as character strings.

```
IPTRECD    DS     0CL80   Work area/record name and length
INAME      DS     CL10    Name field
ISALES     DS     CL4     Sales field
           DS     CL66    Filler or pad
```

3. Before a record can be retrieved from the input file, the file must be activated or opened. The following Open statement performs the necessary activities and prepares the input file for the read operation.

```
OPEN    IPTFILE
```

4. In Assembler, the Get macro is used to read data from the input file. According to the following statement, a record is retrieved from the input (IPTFILE) file and placed in the work area (IPTRECD) reserved for the input record. In other words, data is transmitted from the input file and is placed in the INAME and ISALES fields of the IPTRECD record.

```
GET IPTFILE,IPTRECD
```

5. After processing has been completed, the input file is closed.

```
CLOSE   IPTFILE
```

The Close macro releases (deactivates) the file and informs the Input/Output Control Systems that no more calls will be made to the file.

PACK INSTRUCTION

Format:

```
1--------10----16--------columns
         PACK   S1,S2                    data conversion
                ←
```

Purpose: To convert zone-decimal constants to packed-decimal. The contents of the second operand (S2) are converted from zone-decimal to packed-decimal and placed in the first operand (S1). Syntax requires that the first operand be defined as a packed-decimal field and the second as zone-decimal.

Although neither operand has a specific length requirement, S1 is normally defined as a doubleword. Since the Pack statement is often used in combination with the Convert to Binary instruction, which requires an 8-byte operand, S1 is defined as a doubleword.

Example:

```
         PACK   DBLWORD,ZDFLD       DBLWORD              ZDFLD
           :                        ───────────────────  ────────
           :                BEFORE: ??????????????????   F1F2F3F4
           :                AFTER:  000000000001234C     F1F2F3F4
DBLWORD  DS     D
```

During the conversion process, the contents of the ZDFLD operand are packed two digits per byte and stored in the receiving operand DBLWORD. Note that the right-most byte of DBLWORD holds the sign of the decimal constant.

CONVERT TO BINARY (CVB) INSTRUCTION

Format:

```
1--------10----16--------columns
         CVB    R,S                     data conversion
                ←
```

Purpose: To convert packed-decimal constants to binary. The decimal constant stored at the second operand (S) is converted to binary and placed in the register operand (R). Assembler requires that the storage operand (S) be defined as a doubleword.

Example:

```
          CVB     7,DBLWORD          R7       |    DBLWORD
            :
            :              BEFORE: ????????   | 000000000001458C
            :              AFTER:  000005B2   | 000000000001458C
DBLWORD   DS      D
```

During the conversion, the decimal constant stored at the sending operand DBLWORD is converted to binary and placed in register 7, the receiving operand.

READING A FILE AND PROCESSING TOTALS

Sample programs CHAP5B and CHAP5C are presented here to illustrate how Assembler reads data and assigns values to the input variables. Both programs accumulate totals that are printed at the end of the report.

SAMPLE PROGRAM CHAP5B

Sample program CHAP5B (Fig. 5.5) reads a monthly sales file, processes the data, and produces a printed listing of the sales activity for the past month. Monthly sales are totalled and the result is printed at the end of the report. The output for sample program CHAP5B is shown in Fig. 5.6.

```
1   * ------------------ MONTHLY SALES REPORT ------------------
2   *      This program illustrates how to read a file and
3   *      accumulate a report total.
4   *
5   *            PROGRAM-ID: CHAP5B
6   *            PROGRAMMER: David M. Collopy
7   *            RUN DATE:   mm/dd/yy
8   ****************************************************************
9   CHAP5B    CSECT                                    (system
10            PRINT NOGEN                              use and
11            BALR  2,0                                general
12            USING *,2                                housekeeping)
13            OPEN  IPTFILE,PRINTER                    open files
14  *---------------------------------------------------------------
15  *                MAINLINE CONTROL
16  *---------------------------------------------------------------
17  MAINLINE  BAL   10,SETUP                           program setup
18            BAL   10,HEADING                         print heading line
19            BAL   10,PROCESS                         detail processing loop
20            BAL   10,TOTAL                           print total line
21            B     EXIT                               close files and stop
22  *---------------------------------------------------------------
23  *                PROGRAM SET UP
24  *---------------------------------------------------------------
25  SETUP     SR    5,5                                set total sales to 0
26            BR    10                                 return to mainline
27  *---------------------------------------------------------------
28  *                PRINT HEADING LINE
29  *---------------------------------------------------------------
30  HEADING   MVI   CCH,C'1'                           advance to new page...
31            PUT   PRINTER,HDGLINE                    ...and print heading line
32            MVI   CCB,C' '                           single space...
33            PUT   PRINTER,BLKLINE                    ...and print blank line
34            BR    10                                 return to mainline
```

FIGURE 5.5 Sample Program CHAP5B: This program reads input, computes total monthly sales, and prints a line for each record processed. Monthly sales are totalled and the result is printed at the end of the report.

```
35  *-----------------------------------------------------------
36  *              DETAIL PROCESSING LOOP
37  *-----------------------------------------------------------
38  PROCESS  GET    IPTFILE,IPTRECD              read record
39           PACK   DBLWORD,ISALES               convert sales...
40           CVB    7,DBLWORD                        ...to binary
41           AR     5,7                          add to total sales
42           MVC    ONAME,INAME                  move input to output
43           MVC    OSALES,ISALES                move input to output
44           MVI    CCD,C' '                         single space...
45           PUT    PRINTER,DTLLINE              ...print detail line
46           B      PROCESS                      loop until out of data
47  EOD      BR     10                           return to mainline
48  *-----------------------------------------------------------
49  *              PRINT TOTAL LINE
50  *-----------------------------------------------------------
51  TOTAL    MVI    CCT,C'0'                     double space output
52           CVD    5,DBLWORD                    convert total sales...
53           UNPK   TOTSALES,DBLWORD                 ...to zone-decimal
54           MVZ    TOTSALES+3(1),TOTSALES       replace sign
55           PUT    PRINTER,TOTLINE              print total line
56           BR     10                           return to mainline
57  *
58  EXIT     CLOSE  IPTFILE,PRINTER              close files
59           EOJ                                 end of job
60  **************************************************************
61  *              I/O FILE DEFINITIONS
62  *-----------------------------------------------------------
63  IPTFILE  DTFCD  DEVADDR=SYSIPT,IOAREA1=IPTBUFF,DEVICE=2501,   X
                   WORKA=YES,EOFADDR=EOD
64  PRINTER  DTFPR  DEVADDR=SYSLST,IOAREA1=PRTBUFF,DEVICE=1403,   X
                   CTLCHR=YES,WORKA=YES,BLKSIZE=80
65  *
66  IPTBUFF  DS     CL80                         input file buffer
67  PRTBUFF  DS     CL80                         printer file buffer
```

FIGURE 5.5 (cont.)

```
 68  *----------------------------------------------------------------
 69  *                   RECORD/DATA DEFINITIONS
 70  *----------------------------------------------------------------
 71  IPTRECD   DS    0CL80                     I N P U T   R E C O R D
 72  INAME     DS    CL10        (01 - 10)       salesperson's name
 73  ISALES    DS    CL4         (11 - 14)          monthly sales
 74            DS    CL66        (15 - 80)                 unused
 75  *
 76  HDGLINE   DS    0CL80                     H E A D I N G   L I N E
 77  CCH       DS    CL1                           carriage control
 78            DC    CL21'SALESPERSON      SALES'       line message
 79            DC    CL58' '                                  unused
 80  *
 81  DTLLINE   DS    0CL80                     D E T A I L   L I N E
 82  CCD       DS    CL1         (01 - 01)       carriage control
 83  ONAME     DS    CL10        (02 - 11)       salesperson's name
 84            DC    CL5' '      (12 - 16)                 unused
 85  OSALES    DS    CL4         (17 - 20)          monthly sales
 86            DC    CL3'.00'    (21 - 23)                  cents
 87            DC    CL57' '     (24 - 80)                 unused
 88  *
 89  TOTLINE   DS    0CL80                     T O T A L   L I N E
 90  CCT       DS    CL1                           carriage control
 91            DC    CL15'TOTAL SALES:'                line message
 92  TOTSALES  DS    CL4                       total monthly sales
 93            DC    CL3'.00'                                cents
 94            DC    CL57' '                                unused
 95  *
 96  BLKLINE   DS    0CL80                     B L A N K   L I N E
 97  CCB       DS    CL1                           carriage control
 98            DC    CL79' '                                 spaces
 99  *
100  DBLWORD   DS    D                           temporary storage
101            END   CHAP5B
```

FIGURE 5.5 (cont.)

```
SALESPERSON        SALES

Barker             1005.00
Ditmar             1278.00
Tanner             1134.00
Wilcox             1410.00

TOTAL SALES:       4827.00
```

FIGURE 5.6 Program Output for CHAP5B

The following specifications apply to sample program CHAP5B:

Input data:

The values enclosed within parentheses specify the column positions of the data.

(01–10)   Salesperson's name
(11–14)   Monthly sales

Processing functions:

Read data

Accumulate total monthly sales

Program output (Sales Report):

```
SALESPERSON        SALES

Barker             1005.00
Ditmar             1278.00
Tanner             1134.00
Wilcox             1410.00

TOTAL SALES:       4827.00
```

Pseudocode logic design:
    START
    Open files
    Initialize registers
    Print report headings

LOOP until end of data
   Read name and sales
   Accumulate total sales
   Print name and sales
End LOOP
Print total sales
Close files
END

DISSECTION OF SAMPLE PROGRAM CHAP5B

Note the Open statement. Two files are required by the program, one for the input (`IPTFILE`) and one for the output (`PRINTER`). Sales records are read from the input file and include the following data: salesperson (`INAME`) and monthly sales (`ISALES`). The output is written to the printer.

Take a look at the `MAINLINE`. It controls the processing performed by the other modules. `MAINLINE` calls (or sends control to) the modules in the order shown in Table 5.1.

First, control branches to `SETUP` to initialize register 5. When control returns to `MAINLINE`, it is then sent to the `HEADINGS` module to print the heading line.

Upon the second return, control branches to `PROCESS`. This is the point in the program where the loop reads the input and processes the data.

The third return sends control to `TOTAL` to print the total monthly sales. On the fourth return, control encounters the branch to `EXIT` where the files are closed and the processing terminated.

P R O G R A M   S E T   U P:

Register 5 is set to zero by subtracting the value stored there from itself: R5 = R5–R5. Register 5 is used to accumulate the total monthly sales. Control then returns to the `MAINLINE` beginning at line 18.

Processing order	Lower-level modules
1	SETUP
2	HEADING
3	PROCESS
4	TOTAL

TABLE 5.1 Module Processing Table

PRINT HEADING LINE:

```
30 HEADING    MVI    CCH,C'1'
31            PUT    PRINTER,HDGLINE
```

The above statements mean: Move one to the carriage control field of the heading line. The Put macro advances the printer to the top of the next page and prints the heading. HDGLINE defines the following three output fields:

```
HDGLINE   DS   0CL80
CCTL1     DS   CL1
          DC   CL21'SALESPERSON      SALES'
          DC   CL58' '
```

The heading line defines an 80-byte record that contains a 1-byte carriage control field, a 21-byte column heading, and a 58-byte filler. The filler has been initialized to spaces and is used to pad the record to 80 bytes.

```
32            MVI    CCB,C' '
33            PUT    PRINTER,BLKLINE
34            BR     10
```

The above statements mean: A blank space is moved to carriage control, which causes the printer to single space and print a blank line. The blank line is used to separate the heading line from the body of the report. Control then returns to MAINLINE beginning at line 19. BLKLINE defines the following two output fields:

```
BLKLINE   DS   0CL80
CCB       DS   CL1
          DC   CL79' '
```

BLKLINE contains a 1-byte carriage control field and a 79-byte filler.

DETAIL PROCESSING LOOP:

```
38 PROCESS   GET    IPTFILE,IPTRECD
```

The above statement means: Get (read) a record from the input file (IPTFILE) and move the contents to the IPTRECD work area. IPTRECD defines an input record with three data fields:

```
IPTRECD      DS      0CL80
INAME        DS      CL10    (01-10)
ISALES       DS      CL4     (11-14)
             DS      CL66    (15-80)
```

The input work area defines an 80-byte record that contains a 10-byte name field, a 4-byte sales field, and a 66-byte filler. The values enclosed within parentheses represent the relative column positions or location of the fields in the record.

```
39           PACK    DBLWORD,ISALES
40           CVB     7,DBLWORD
```

The above statements mean: Convert the character data stored at ISALES to packed-decimal and place the result in the DBLWORD operand. Now convert the packed-decimal value to binary and store it in register 7.

These two statements are coded together and are used to convert the input to binary.

```
41           AR      5,7
```

The above statement means: Add the contents of register 7 to the value stored at register 5 and place the resulting sum in register 7. Register 5 is used to accumulate total monthly sales.

```
42           MVC     ONAME,INAME
43           MVC     OSALES,ISALES
```

The above statements mean: Move the salesperson's name and sales total from the input to the output. The I/O prefixes are used to differentiate between input and output data items. We use this convention to help clarify the program code.

```
44           MVI     CCD,C' '
45           PUT     PRINTER,DTLLINE
```

The above statements mean: Move a blank space to the carriage control field of the detail line to set up single spacing for the output. The Put macro advances the printer one line and prints the detail line.

```
DTLLINE   DS    0CL80       (Detail Line)
CCD       DS    CL1
ONAME     DS    CL10
          DC    CL5' '
OSALES    DS    CL4
          DC    CL3'.00'
          DC    CL57' '
```

DTLLINE defines an 80-byte record that contains a 1-byte carriage control field, a 10-byte name field, a 5-byte filler, a 4-byte sales field, a 3-byte cents field, and a 57-byte filler.

```
46              B     PROCESS
47  EOD         BR    10
```

The above statements mean: If there is more data, then branch to PROCESS and repeat the loop. But if there is no more data, then exit the loop and branch to EOD, where EOD represents the label assigned to the EOFADDR operand in the input DTF (line 63). In other words, when the program detects the end of the data, control exits the loop, branches to EOD, and returns to the MAINLINE beginning at line 20.

PRINT TOTAL LINE:

```
51  TOTAL       MVI   CCT,C'0'
52              CVD   5,DBLWORD
53              UNPK  TOTSALES,DBLWORD
54              MVZ   TOTSALES+3(1),TOTSALES
55              PUT   PRINTER,TOTLINE
56              BR    10
```

The above statements mean: Move zero to carriage control to set up double spacing. A blank line is used to separate the total line from the last detail line.

Convert total sales to zone-decimal and replace the sign bits with the character F. Print the total line and return to the MAINLINE beginning at line

21. `TOTLINE` defines the following four output fields:

```
TOTLINE     DS      0CL80
CCT         DS      CL1
            DC      CL15'TOTAL SALES:'
TOTSALES    DS      CL4
            DC      CL3'.00'
            DC      CL57' '
```

`TOTLINE` defines an 80-byte record that contains a 1-byte carriage control field, a 15-byte line message, a 4-byte total sales field, a 3-byte cents field, and a 57-byte filler.

Look at the second field. Note the character string `TOTAL SALES:` is 12 bytes long. When 12 bytes are moved to a 15-byte field, the remaining 3 bytes are padded with spaces. The 3-byte filler is used to align total sales under the sales column.

SAMPLE PROGRAM CHAP5C

Sample program CHAP5C (Figure 5.7) reads a payroll file, processes the data, and prints a payroll report. A detail line is printed for each record that includes an employee name, hours worked, payrate, and gross pay. Gross pay is totalled and averaged, and both results are printed at the end of the report. The output for sample program CHAP5C is shown in Fig. 5.8.

The following specifications apply to sample program CHAP5C:

Input data:

    (01–10) Employee name

    (11–12) Hours worked

    (13–13) Payrate

Processing functions:

    Gross pay = hours × payrate

    Accumulate total gross pay

    Accumulate employee count

    Average gross pay = total gross pay ÷ employee count

Program output (Payroll Report):

```
EMPLOYEE          HOURS          PAYRATE        GROSS PAY

Bradshaw           30             4.00           120.00
Cummings           20             6.00           120.00
Frecker            40             4.00           160.00
Kessler            40             6.00           240.00
Toronto            30             4.00           120.00
Williams           40             5.00           200.00

TOTAL GROSS PAY:                                 960.00
AVERAGE GROSS PAY:                               160.00
```

Pseudocode logic design:
>START
>Open files
>Initialize total pay
>Print column heading line
>LOOP until end of data
>>Read a record
>>Compute pay
>>Accumulate total pay
>>Print detail line
>
>End LOOP
>Print total pay
>Compute average pay
>Print average pay
>Close files
>END

DISSECTION OF SAMPLE PROGRAM CHAP5C

Since the MAINLINE, SETUP, and HEADING of the payroll program are similar in concept to those in sample program CHAP5B, we will skip them and begin our discussion with the DETAIL module. If you need to review MAINLINE,

```
 1  * ---------------- SIMPLE PAYROLL REPORT -----------------
 2  *  This program reads a payroll file, processes the data, and
 3  *  prints a payroll report.
 4  *
 5  *             PROGRAM-ID: CHAP5C
 6  *             PROGRAMMER: David M. Collopy
 7  *             RUN DATE:   mm/dd/yy
 8  ****************************************************************
 9  CHAP5C    CSECT                                       (system
10            PRINT NOGEN                                 use and
11            BALR  2,0                                   general
12            USING *,2                                   housekeeping)
13            OPEN  IPTFILE,PRINTER                       open I/O files
14  *---------------------------------------------------------------
15  *                   MAINLINE CONTROL
16  *---------------------------------------------------------------
17  MAINLINE  BAL   10,SETUP                              program setup
18            BAL   10,HEADING                            print heading
19            BAL   10,DETAIL                             detail processing loop
20            BAL   10,TOTALS                             print totals
21            B     EXIT                                  process exit
22  *---------------------------------------------------------------
23  *                   PROGRAM SET UP
24  *---------------------------------------------------------------
25  SETUP     SR    7,7                                   set total pay to 0
26            SR    11,11                                 set employee count to 0
27            BR    10                                    return to mainline
28  *---------------------------------------------------------------
29  *                   PRINT HEADING
30  *---------------------------------------------------------------
31  HEADING   MVI   CCH,C'1'                              advance to new page...
32            PUT   PRINTER,HDGLINE                       ...and print heading
33            MVI   CCB,C' '                              single space...
34            PUT   PRINTER,BLKLINE                       ...and print blank line
35            BR    10                                    return to mainline
```

FIGURE 5.7 Sample Program CHAP5C: A simple payroll program to calculate gross pay and print a payroll report. Gross pay is totalled and averaged.

```
36   *-----------------------------------------------------------------
37   *              DETAIL PROCESSING LOOP
38   *-----------------------------------------------------------------
39   DETAIL   BAL    9,GETDATA                       get data
40            BAL    9,PROCESS                compute gross pay
41            BAL    9,OUTPUT                 print detail line
42            B      DETAIL                         repeat loop
43   EOD      BR     10                       return to mainline
44   *-----------------------------------------------------------------
45   *              GET DATA
46   *-----------------------------------------------------------------
47   GETDATA  GET    IPTFILE,IPTRECD                read record
48            A      11,ONE                       add 1 to count
49            PACK   DBLWORD,IHOURS              convert hours...
50            CVB    5,DBLWORD                       ...to binary
51            PACK   DBLWORD,IPAYRATE           convert payrate...
52            CVB    6,DBLWORD                       ...to binary
53            BR     9                          return to detail
54   *-----------------------------------------------------------------
55   *              COMPUTE GROSS PAY
56   *-----------------------------------------------------------------
57   PROCESS  MR     4,6                             compute pay
58            AR     7,5                     add pay to total pay
59            BR     9                          return to detail
60   *-----------------------------------------------------------------
61   *              PRINT DETAIL LINE
62   *-----------------------------------------------------------------
63   OUTPUT   MVI    CCD,C' '                 single space output
64            CVD    5,DBLWORD                       convert pay...
65            MVC    OEMPNAME,IEMPNAME        move input to output
66            MVC    OHOURS,IHOURS            move input to output
67            MVC    OPAYRATE,IPAYRATE        move input to output
68            UNPK   OPAY,DBLWORD                ...to zone-decimal
69            MVZ    OPAY+2(1),OPAY                  replace sign
70            PUT    PRINTER,DTLLINE          print detail line
71            BR     9                          return to detail
```

FIGURE 5.7 (cont.)

154 Chapter 5: Reading Data and Performing Loops

```
 72 *----------------------------------------------------------------
 73 *                 PRINT TOTALS
 74 *----------------------------------------------------------------
 75 TOTALS    MVI    CCT1,C'0'              double space output
 76           CVD    7,DBLWORD              convert total pay...
 77           UNPK   TOTPAY,DBLWORD         ...to zone-decimal
 78           MVZ    TOTPAY+2(1),TOTPAY     replace sign
 79           PUT    PRINTER,TOTLINE1       print total line-1
 80           SR     6,6                    set register to 0
 81           DR     6,11                   compute average pay
 82           MVI    CCT2,C' '              single space output
 83           CVD    7,DBLWORD              convert average pay...
 84           UNPK   AVGPAY,DBLWORD         ...to zone-decimal
 85           MVZ    AVGPAY+2(1),AVGPAY     replace sign
 86           PUT    PRINTER,TOTLINE2       print total line-2
 87           BR     10                     return to mainline
 88 *
 89 EXIT      CLOSE  IPTFILE,PRINTER              close files
 90           EOJ                                 end of job
 91 ****************************************************************
 92 *                 I/O FILE DEFINITIONS
 93 *----------------------------------------------------------------
 94 IPTFILE   DTFCD  DEVADDR=SYSIPT,IOAREA1=IPTBUFF,DEVICE=2501,    X
                    WORKA=YES,EOFADDR=EOD
 95 PRINTER   DTFPR  DEVADDR=SYSLST,IOAREA1=PRTBUFF,DEVICE=1403,    X
                    CTLCHR=YES,WORKA=YES,BLKSIZE=80
 96 *
 97 IPTBUFF   DS     CL80                   input file buffer
 98 PRTBUFF   DS     CL80                   printer file buffer
 99 *----------------------------------------------------------------
100 *                 RECORD/DATA DEFINITIONS
101 *----------------------------------------------------------------
102 IPTRECD   DS     0CL80              I N P U T   R E C O R D
103 IEMPNAME  DS     CL10     (01 - 10)         employee name
104 IHOURS    DS     CL2      (11 - 12)         hours worked
105 IPAYRATE  DS     CL1      (13 - 13)         payrate per hour
106           DS     CL67     (14 - 80)                  unused
107 *
108 HDGLINE   DS     0CL80              H E A D I N G   L I N E
109 CCH       DS     CL1                       carriage control
```

FIGURE 5.7 (cont.)

Reading a File and Processing Totals

```
110            DC    CL28'EMPLOYEE       HOURS'            line mesg
111            DC    CL51'PAYRATE        GROSS PAY'        line mesg
112 *
113 DTLLINE    DS    0CL80                          D E T A I L   L I N E
114 CCD        DS    CL1                                carriage control
115 OEMPNAME   DS    CL10                                 employee name
116            DC    CL7' '                                     unused
117 OHOURS     DS    CL2                                   hours worked
118            DC    CL9' '                                     unused
119 OPAYRATE   DS    CL1                                payrate per hour
120            DC    CL3'.00'                                    cents
121            DC    CL11' '                                    unused
122 OPAY       DS    CL3                                      gross pay
123            DC    CL3'.00'                                    cents
124            DC    CL30' '                                    unused
125 *
126 TOTLINE1   DS    0CL80                          T O T A L   L I N E - 1
127 CCT1       DS    CL1                                carriage control
128            DC    CL16'TOTAL GROSS PAY:'            line message
129            DC    CL28' '                                    unused
130 TOTPAY     DS    CL3                                total gross pay
131            DC    CL3'.00'                                    cents
132            DC    CL29' '                                    unused
133 *
134 TOTLINE2   DS    0CL80                          T O T A L   L I N E - 2
135 CCT2       DS    CL1                                carriage control
136            DC    CL18'AVERAGE GROSS PAY:'          line message
137            DC    CL26' '                                    unused
138 AVGPAY     DS    CL3                              average gross pay
139            DC    CL3'.00'                                    cents
140            DC    CL29' '                                    unused
141 *
142 BLKLINE    DS    0CL80                          B L A N K   L I N E
143 CCB        DS    CL1                                carriage control
144            DC    CL79' '                                    unused
145 *
146 DBLWORD    DS    D                                temporary storage
147 ONE        DC    F'1'                                   constant 1
148            END   CHAP5C
```

FIGURE 5.7 (cont.)

```
EMPLOYEE            HOURS         PAYRATE         GROSS PAY

Bradshaw             30            4.00            120.00
Cummings             20            6.00            120.00
Frecker              40            4.00            160.00
Kessler              40            6.00            240.00
Toronto              30            4.00            120.00
Williams             40            5.00            200.00

TOTAL GROSS PAY:                                   960.00
AVERAGE GROSS PAY:                                 160.00
```

FIGURE 5.8 Program Output for CHAP5C

SETUP, and HEADING, refer to the dissection of sample program CHAP5B.

DETAIL PROCESSING LOOP:

```
39  DETAIL     BAL    9,GETDATA
40             BAL    9,PROCESS
41             BAL    9,OUTPUT
42             B      DETAIL
43  EOD        BR     10
```

The DETAIL module consists of a loop that controls the processing performed by the submodules shown: a record is read (GETDATA), the input is processed (PROCESS), and the detail line is printed (OUTPUT). Each module is executed once for every record read. At the end of the file, control exits the loop and branches to the label (EOD) specified by the EOFADDR of the DTF.

GET DATA:

For each record read, the contents of IHOURS and IPAYRATE are converted to binary and placed in registers 5 and 6, respectively.

COMPUTE GROSS PAY:

```
56  PROCESS    MR     4,6
57             AR     7,5
58             BR     9
```

The above statements mean: Multiply the contents of register 5 (hours worked) by the value stored at register 6 (payrate) and place the resulting product (pay) in register 5.

Now add the contents of register 5 (pay) to the value stored in register 7 (total pay) and return to the DETAIL module.

PRINT DETAIL LINE:

The OUTPUT module converts pay to zone-decimal and prints the detail line containing employee name, hours worked, payrate, and pay.

PRINT TOTALS:

After the data has been processed, control branches to process total pay: Total pay is converted to zone-decimal and moved to the output work area. The total line is printed, and register 6 is cleared. Then average pay is computed: Average pay is converted to zone-decimal, moved to the output work area, and the average line is printed. Finally, control returns to the MAINLINE to perform the exit procedures.

TRACKING THE GENERAL PURPOSE REGISTERS

Student programmers often have trouble remembering the connections between specific registers and their data. If you find yourself in a similar situation, try the following: On the left side of a piece of paper, list the register numbers for your program in sequential order. While you are coding the program, write down the data you assign to each register. In this way, you keep a log of each register and its corresponding data.

Let us illustrate this procedure with an example. Figure 5.9 shows the register assignments for sample program CHAP5C. In looking over the list, it's easy to discern those registers that were used (and for what purpose) and those that were not. Look at registers 5 and 7. Both were used twice. Register 5, for example, was first used to hold hours worked. Later, it was used to hold earned pay. Similarly, register 7 was used to hold total pay and average pay. Registers 3, 4, 8, and 12 were not used at all.

```
R0  ─ ┌ system use
R1  ─ │ and general
R2  ─ └ housekeeping

R3  ─
R4  ─
R5  ─ input hours and earned pay
R6  ─ input payrate
R7  ─ total pay and average pay
R8  ─
R9  ─ address to GETDATA, PROCESS and OUTPUT
R10 ─ address to SETUP, HEADING, DETAIL and TOTALS
R11 ─ employee count
R12 ─

R13 ─ ┌ reserved
R14 ─ │ for system
R15 ─ └ use
```

FIGURE 5.9 Register Assignments for Sample Program CHAP5C

STRUCTURED PROGRAMMING

From the previous chapter, we learned that structured programming represents an organized approach to writing programs that emphasizes top-down design and modularity. This approach helps us design and write high-quality programs that are easy to read, understand, and maintain.

Top-down refers to the design strategy that concentrates on designing and coding high-level processing functions first. The intermediate-level functions follow, while low-level functions are coded last.

Of course, modularizing refers to the process of dividing a program into smaller, self-contained modules. In other words, logically related functions are grouped together to perform a single task.

PROGRAMMING GUIDELINES

The following guidelines apply to structured programming:

1. Each module should have one entry point and one exit point. In sample program CHAP5C, notice how the Branch and Link statement issues control to the top of a module, while the Branch Register causes an exit from the bottom.

2. Each module should perform exactly one task. For example, reading data and computing totals are two unrelated tasks. Therefore, you should keep them in separate modules. Do not put unrelated functions together in the same module. Group only logically related statements that belong together.
3. Each program should include the following:
   - meaningful data names (prefix input and output data items with I and O, respectively).
   - remarks and line comments to document the code (explain unusual or complex processing).
   - simple coding structures; avoid complicated processing.
   - line comments to identify the modules.
   - no more than 24 statements per module.

The benefits of structured programming include:

1. maintainability—easier to update and modify
2. development ease—easier to design and code, with fewer errors during the development stage
3. reliability—fewer errors encountered in production
4. clarity—easier to read, particularly by someone unfamiliar with the program
5. debugging simplification—easier to debug
6. documentation—easier to write and maintain

KEY REVIEW TERMS

Define the following:

input file	iteration	BCT instruction
top-down design	structured	modularity
detail line	programming	tracking registers
programming loop	JCL	programming
CVB instruction	trailing decision	guidelines
loop processing	loop counter	body of a loop
leading decision	column heading	program data
report totals	Pack instruction	total line

REVIEW EXERCISES

*1. Code Assembler statements to set up a counter-controlled loop to perform the `READIN`, `PROCESS`, and `OUTPUT` modules 120 times.

2. Write statements to set up a counter-controlled loop to read name, age, and telephone number for ten records. Use GET to read the data and code the DC/DS statements to define the input record.

Show the contents of the general purpose registers after the PACK and CVB statements have been executed. For each, assume the initial values shown below.

```
NETPAY: F4F5F0       AVG:    60F1F3F7F4
ISALES: F1F5F0F0     CRDHRS: F9F9
AMOUNT: F5F3D5       DBLWORD DS D
```

                                                       Registers

```
*3. PACK   DBLWORD,NETPAY
    CVB    9,DBLWORD         R9  _____
*4. PACK   DBLWORD,CRDHRS
    CVB    10,DBLWORD        R10 _____
*5. PACK   DBLWORD,ISALES
    CVB    4,DBLWORD         R4  _____
*6. PACK   DBLWORD,AVG
    CVB    5,DBLWORD         R5  _____
*7. PACK   DBLWORD,AMOUNT
    CVB    7,DBLWORD         R7  _____
```

8. What is the purpose of programming guidelines for structured programming? Are they necessary? Explain your answer.

9. List the benefits of structured programming. Can you think of any other benefits?

PROGRAMMING EXERCISES

Instructions: For each exercise, design the pseudocode and write the modular structured program to produce the output. Model your program after the structure given for sample program CHAP5C. Verify your output.

1. Sum of integers: Code a program to compute and print the sum of the integers 1–50.

    Program data:

    Generate the integers 1–50 within the program.

    Processing functions:

    Accumulate the sum of the integers 1–50.

    Print the integer and its corresponding accumulative sum.

    Program output (Report):

    ```
    SUM OF THE INTEGERS 1 TO 50

    INTEGER         ACCUMULATIVE SUM
    -------         ----------------
       1                  0001
       2                  0003
       3                  0006
       4                  0010
       5                   :
       :                   :
    ```

2. Modify Exercise 1 to compute and print the sum of the odd integers 1–50.

3. Used car sales: Write an Assembler program to print a report showing the daily used car sales for Kay Wymer Ford. Code the input in the columns shown.

Columns	Field names
01–04	Customer number
05–15	Make of car
16–19	Purchase price
22–25	Dealer cost

    Input data:

Customer #	Make	Purchase Price	Dealer Cost
1471	Escort	$5399	$4498
4556	Ranger	3995	3329
6102	Probe	8995	7496
7315	Mustang	7999	6673
9873	Tempo	7995	6662

Processing functions:
    Car profit = purchase price − dealer cost
    Accumulate total car profit
    Count number of sales
    Average profit = total car profit ÷ number of sales

Program output (Sales Report):

```
                       KAY WYMER FORD

              Used Car Sales Report: mm/dd/yy


        CUSTOMER      MAKE       PURCHASE       SALES
         NUMBER      OF CAR        PRICE        PROFIT

          1471       Escort       5399.00       902.00
            :          :             :             :
            :          :             :             :
          9999       X----X       9999.99       999.99


              TOTAL PROFIT:   $99999.99
              AVERAGE PROFIT: $99999.99
```

4. Accounts receivable: Write a program to print a simple Accounts Receivable report. Each record contains the following:

Columns	Field names
10–14	Account number
16–19	Balance due
22–24	Purchases made
27–29	Payments made

Input data:

Account #	Balance	Purchases	Payments
12345	$1000	$500	$000
34751	5125	600	700
43490	2000	000	350
50963	4000	500	200
60798	7000	200	900

Input data: (cont.)

Account #	Balance	Purchases	Payments
70025	$1500	$000	$000
85670	2450	327	890
89845	3000	300	900
90104	7300	610	100

Processing functions:

New balance = previous balance + purchases – payments

Accumulate totals for:

    Previous balances

    Purchases

    Payments

    New Balances

Program output (Accounts Receivable Report):

```
              THE COPLEY-BERMAN STORE
                 Accounts Receivable
                       mm/dd/yy


          CUSTOMER        PREVIOUS            NEW
          NUMBER          BALANCE           BALANCE

           12345          1000.00          1500.00
             :               :                :
             :               :                :
           99999          9999.99          9999.99

          PREVIOUS BALANCES: $99999.99
                  PURCHASES: $99999.99
                   PAYMENTS: $99999.99
              NEW BALANCES: $99999.99
```

5. Inventory: Compute the monthly inventory investment for the Presto Foods Corporation. Format your program data in the following manner:

Columns	Field names
01–04	Item number
06–06	Number of cartons
08–09	Quantity per carton
11–11	Cost per item

Input data:

Item #	Cartons	Quantity/Carton	Cost/Item
1001	5	12	$5
2004	6	12	4
3006	3	24	7
4008	2	10	9
5010	3	30	6

Processing functions:

Item quantity = number of cartons × quantity per carton

Accumulate total quantity = sum of item quantities

Item cost = quantity × cost per item

Accumulate investment = sum of item cost

Program output (Inventory Investment Report):

```
                PRESTO FOODS CORPORATION
                Inventory Investment Report
                         mm/dd/yy


    ITEM                QUANTITY                ITEM
   NUMBER               ON  HAND             INVESTMENT
  ------------------------------------------------------
    1001                   60                   300.00
     :                      :                      :
     :                      :                      :
     :                      :                      :
    9999                   99                   999.99
  ------------------------------------------------------

   TOTAL QUANTITY:        999
   TOTAL INVESTMENT:                          $9999.99
```

6. Sales report: Code a program to compute the profit for the Westfalls Distributing Company and print a weekly sales report for the company. Each sales record consists of the following data:

Columns	Field names
01–20	Sales employee
21–25	Sales
28–32	Cost of sales

Input data:

Sales Employee	Sales	Cost of Sales
Bruce McKenzie	$5129	$3590
Ron Wilcox	8534	5974
Troy Pauquette	12362	8653
Ross Spencer	4125	2887
Loretta Morris	16962	11873
Larry Price	10347	7242
Bethemy Taylor	3790	2655
Randy Walker	12414	8690
Warren Messer	6722	4705
Darla Kramer	8914	6239

Processing functions:

Profit = sales − cost

Accumulate totals for:
  Sales
  Cost of sales
  Profit

Program output (Weekly Sales Report):

```
              WESTFALLS DISTRIBUTING COMPANY
                   Weekly Sales Report
                        mm/dd/yy


      SALESPERSON         SALES         COST OF SALES        PROFIT

      Bruce McKenzie    $05129.00         $03590.00        $01539.00
           :                :                 :                :
           :                :                 :                :
           :                :                 :                :
      X------------X    $99999.99         $99999.99        $99999.99

      TOTALS:          $999999.99        $999999.99       $999999.99
```

Chapter 5: Reading Data and Performing Loops

7. Piece work: Write an Assembler program to create a piece-work report for the Rollbent Manufacturing Company. Format the data as follows:

Columns	Field names
01–20	Employee name
21–24	Product number
25–27	Production quota
28–30	Pieces made

Input data:

Employee Name	Product #	Quota	Pieces
Tim Duffy	A174	100	100
Rob Wells	B001	57	62
Sarah Rodock	H037	125	119
Sonia Bowers	X341	89	70
Brian Ayers	E849	43	43
Scott Beale	R939	72	89
Trisha Morris	C292	39	39
Kirt Jones	F456	55	67
Seth Cossin	T215	112	99
Carrie Ross	Y771	45	43
Pat Willits	B119	75	75
Trevor Miller	D017	60	60

Processing functions:

  Accumulate total quota pieces

  Accumulate total number of pieces made

Program output (Production Report):

```
                ROLLBENT MANUFACTURING COMPANY
                      Production Report
                          mm/dd/yy

       EMPLOYEE NAME           PRODUCT#    QUOTA    PIECES

       Tim Duffy                 A174       100      100
           :                       :         :        :
           :                       :         :        :
           :                       :         :        :
       X-------------X            XXXX       999      999

       TOTALS:                              9999     9999
```

8. Accounts payable: Modify Exercise 8 in Chapter 4 to include file processing. Write a program to read the data from a file and produce an accounts payable report for the Col-Max Manufacturing Company. Each record includes the following:

Columns	Field names
01–06	Purchase order number
07–26	Vendor/supplier name
27–34	Date of purchase order
35–37	Quantity on order
38–39	Cost per each item

Input data:

Purchase Order #	Vendor/Supplier Name	Date	Quantity	Cost
A12346	Pannatek	(date)	20	$6
Q3785E	MicroMarx	(date)	45	4
Y61178	MaxComm	(date)	100	5
T4261A	Estep Inc.	(date)	96	2
P9823K	Pifer-Kaufman	(date)	24	3
B3419C	IntraTell	(date)	48	6
D87260	Priceton	(date)	144	3
Z0297M	Wakefield	(date)	12	10
R9371B	Scottsdale	(date)	36	8
X20610	Bowman-Cerney	(date)	90	2

Processing functions:

Accumulate total number of purchase orders

Accumulate total amount payable

Program output (Accounts Payable):

```
            COL-MAX MANUFACTURING COMPANY
                  Accounts Payable
                     mm/dd/yy
  PURCHASE                                QUANTITY
  ORDER#   VENDOR/SUPPLIER      DATE      ON ORDER      PO TOTAL

  A12346   Pannatek             (date)       20         $0120.00
    :         :                    :          :            :
    :         :                    :          :            :
    :         :                    :          :            :
  XXXXXX   X-------------X      (date)       99         $9999.99

  NUMBER OF POs:                  99
  TOTAL AMOUNT PAYABLE:                                 $99999.99
```

6 COMPARISON AND CONDITIONAL BRANCHING

OVERVIEW

Learning Objectives
Selecting Alternate Processing Paths
Program Flags
Unconditional and Conditional Branching
Condition Codes and Comparison Statements
Branch Statements
Compare Logical Character (CLC) Instruction
Branch on Equal (BE) and Branch on Not Equal (BNE) Instructions
Branch (B) Instruction
Compare (C) Instruction
Branch on High (BH) and Branch on Not High (BNH) Instructions
Sample Program CHAP6A
Compare Logical Immediate (CLI) Instruction
Compare Register (CR) Instruction
Branch on Low (BL) and Branch on Not Low (BNL) Instructions
Branch on Zero (BZ) and Branch on Not Zero (BNZ) Instructions
Branch on Positive (BP) and Branch on Not Positive (BNP) Instructions
Branch on Minus (BM) and Branch on Not Minus (BNM) Instructions
Load and Test Register (LTR) Instruction
   Sample Program CHAP6B
Key Review Terms
Review Exercises
Programming Exercises

LEARNING OBJECTIVES

After reading this chapter and completing the exercises, the reader should be able to:

- write programs that make decisions and perform different functions.
- explain how flags can be used to read input and control the processing of the program.
- code valid combinations of compare and branch.
- discuss how to set and use the internal condition code to perform branching.
- explain the concepts of conditional and unconditional branching.

SELECTING ALTERNATE PROCESSING PATHS

Decision processing is common to most programming applications. Computers can be programmed to do more than repeat the same sequence of instructions over and over again. In this chapter, we will learn how to code decision tests and perform different processing functions.

In Assembler, decisions are made by comparing the values of two operands to see if one is equal to, greater than, or less than the other. Based on the outcome, Assembler branches to the appropriate module or statement and continues processing. In other words, the computer can be programmed to follow a particular course of action depending on the comparative values of two operands.

Consider, for example, the following payroll application that computes overtime pay.

Compare	Module Processed
HOURS ≤ 40	REGULAR PAY
HOURS > 40	OVERTIME

When HOURS are greater than 40, the program branches to the OVERTIME module to compute overtime pay. Otherwise, control branches to REGULAR PAY.

PROGRAM FLAGS

By definition, a flag is a variable that is used in a comparison test to determine which course of action to follow. Although any value can be assigned to a flag, it is common to use T or F to indicate that a given condition is either true or false, respectively. We are not limited to these values; almost any number, letter, or character string may be used.

Program flags are often used to test for the occurrence of a specific condition. To do this, we begin by initializing the flag to a given value (perhaps, NO). During the processing cycle, the program changes the value (perhaps, to YES) if a certain condition is encountered. The program tests the flag to determine what course of action to follow. After completing the action, the program resets the flag to its initial value before repeating the process.

Examples:

1. if MOREDATA = YES
2. if TESTFLAG = T

In the first example, MOREDATA is tested for the occurrence of the character string YES; in the second example, TESTFLAG is checked for the condition T. Although Assembler can test conditions and make decisions, it does not recognize the "if" statement shown in these examples.

UNCONDITIONAL AND CONDITIONAL BRANCHING

There are two types of branch statements used in Assembler: unconditional and conditional. An unconditional branch sends control directly to a specific place in the program. In the following example, the Branch Register command represents an unconditional directive that sends control to the statement in the program corresponding to the address stored in Register 10.

```
1--------10----16--------columns
        BR    10                           unconditional branch
```

A conditional branch is taken only when a certain condition is met. In the following example, Statement 1 specifies a conditional branch to the REGULAR PAY module when HOURS are less than or equal to 40. Otherwise, the branch is not taken and processing falls through to the next instruction. Statement 2 checks HOURS to see if it is greater than 40. When true, control branches to the OVERTIME PAY module and performs the processing specified there. Otherwise, control falls through to execute the next statement.

	Compare	Module Processed
Statement 1:	HOURS ≤ 40	REGULAR PAY
Statement 2:	HOURS > 40	OVERTIME PAY

The comparison and branching instructions presented in this chapter allow the programmer to code both conditional and unconditional branching statements in Assembler.

CONDITION CODES AND COMPARISON STATEMENTS

There are two different types of comparisons: logical and arithmetic (Table 6.1). Logical comparisons compare nonnumeric, or character string, operands using the operation codes Compare Logical Character (CLC) and Compare Logical Immediate (CLI). Arithmetic comparisons compare numeric operands using the operation codes Compare (C), Compare Register (CR), and Compare Packed (CP).

Opcode	Operands		Type
C	R,S	Compare	arithmetic
CR	R1,R2	Compare Register	arithmetic
CLC	S1,S2	Compare Logical Character	logical
CLI	S,I	Compare Logical Immediate	logical
CP	S1,S2	Compare Packed	arithmetic
Examples			
C	5,COUNT	Compare binary values stored at R5 and COUNT	
CR	4,7	Compare binary values stored at R4 and R7	
CLC	EOF,INAME	Compare character strings stored at EOF and INAME	
CLI	FLAG,C'Y'	Compare character stored at FLAG and immediate character Y	
CP	PNUM1,PNUM2	Compare decimal values stored at PNUM1 and PNUM2 (see Chapter 8)	

TABLE 6.1 Comparison Statements

During the comparison of two operands, for example, A and B, only one of three conditions can be true: A is equal to B; A is less than B; or A is greater than B. In order to test the outcome, a special indicator, called a condition code (ccode), is set during the comparison process. Following the compare, the ccode may be tested with any one of several branching instructions to determine which processing path to follow.

For each example, the second operand is compared to the first, and the condition code is set based upon the results. Following the comparison, the status of the condition code may be checked with any one of the following six branching statements.

BE	Branch if operands equal	$A = B$
BNE	Branch if operands not equal	$A \ne B$
BL	Branch if 1st operand low	$A < B$
BNL	Branch if 1st operand not low	$A \not< B$
BH	Branch if 1st operand high	$A > B$
BNH	Branch if 1st operand not high	$A \not> B$

Overall, branch statements perform the same function as if statements. They test for a specific condition and, based upon the outcome, determine which processing path to follow.

BRANCH STATEMENTS

As a rule, a branch statement should be coded immediately after a comparison. Since other instructions also set the condition code, it would be wise to test and branch before the ccode has a chance to change values.

Branch statements perform two functions: They test the condition code for a specific value, and they perform the branch when the ccode and test value match. Otherwise, control falls through and executes the next instruction.

The condition code settings for Assembler's branch statements are shown in Tables 6.2 and 6.3. Note that for each, the branch is taken when the condition code set by the program matches the condition code specified for the branch.

Let's look at some examples that illustrate how to properly use the branch statements.

For our first example, suppose our program just executed a Compare Logical Character (CLC) instruction. According to Table 6.2, any one of the following branches could be used to test the status of the condition code: BE,

			Condition Code
BE	Branch on `EQUAL`	A = B	1000
BNE	Branch on `NOT EQUAL`	A ≠ B	0111
BL	Branch on `LOW`	A < B	0100
BNL	Branch on `NOT LOW`	A ≮ B	1011
BH	Branch on `HIGH`	A > B	0010
BNH	Branch on `NOT HIGH`	A ≯ B	1101

Note: For each comparison (A:B), three condition codes apply: one major and two minor.

Condition	Major	Minor
Equal	BE	BNL, BNH
Low	BL	BNE, BNH
High	BH	BNE, BNL

TABLE 6.2 Compare A:B (The branch statements above are used to test the condition code after it has been set by one of the following comparisons: C, CR, CLC, CLI, and CP.)

			Condition Code
BZ	Branch on `ZERO`	A = 0	1000
BNZ	Branch on `NOT ZERO`	A ≠ 0	0111
BM	Branch on `MINUS`	A < 0	0100
BNM	Branch on `NOT MINUS`	A ≮ 0	1011
BP	Branch on `POSITIVE`	A > 0	0010
BNP	Branch on `NOT POSITIVE`	A ≯ 0	1101

Note: For each comparison (A:0), three condition codes apply: one major and two minor.

Condition	Major	Minor
Zero	BZ	BNM, BNP
Negative	BM	BNZ, BNP
Positive	BP	BNZ, BNM

TABLE 6.3 Arithmetic Operations A:0 (The branch statements above are used to test the condition code after it has been set by one of the following arithmetic statements: A, AR, AP, ZAP, S, SR, SP, and LTR.)

BNE, BL, BNL, BH, and BNH. If we coded any other branch statement at this point, the program would not work.

For our second example, suppose the program executed an Add (A) statement. We could then use any one of the following branch statements to test the condition code: BZ, BNZ, BM, BNM, BP, and BNP.

A programmer must be careful to code the correct branch statement after a comparison or arithmetic operation. Any mismatch will produce an error message and terminate processing.

COMPARE LOGICAL CHARACTER (CLC) INSTRUCTION

Format:

```
1--------10----16--------columns              type A:B
        CLC    S1,S2                    logical compare
```

Purpose: To compare character string data. This instruction logically compares the contents of two nonnumeric, character string operands (S1 and S2) and sets the condition code based upon the results. Both operands may contain a maximum of 255 bytes. Should the length of one operand be shorter than the other, Assembler will pad the shorter operand with spaces (on the right) until it contains an equal number of bytes. As shown in Table 6.4, the Compare Logical Character instruction results in any one of six ccode settings.

	Condition Code	CLC S1 : S2
1.	1000	=
2.	0111	≠
3.	0010	>
4.	1101	≯
5.	0100	<
6.	1011	≮

TABLE 6.4 Logical Condition Code Settings

Example:

```
        :
CLC     EODFLAG,ISNAME      compare and set ccode
        :
```

In this example, the CLC statement compares the contents of the character strings operands `EODFLAG` and `ISNAME`. Depending on the outcome, the condition code may be set to any one of the six values shown in Table 6.2.

BRANCH ON EQUAL (BE) AND BRANCH ON NOT EQUAL (BNE) INSTRUCTIONS

Formats:

```
1--------10----16--------  [ccode]             type A:B
        BE    L           1000       control transfer
        BNE   L           0111
```

Purpose: To test condition codes and branches for matching values. Both test the current value of the condition code and, when there is a match, execute a branch to the statement or module identified by the label operand (L). Otherwise, control falls through to the instruction on the next line.

Examples:

```
           :
1. CLC     FLAG,COUNT         compare and set ccode
   BE      ENDIT              if FLAG = COUNT, branch
           :
           :
2. CLC     MINDUE,PAYMENT     compare and set ccode
   BNE     CHECKIT            if MINDUE ≠ PAYMENT, branch
           :
```

In Example 1, the Branch on Equal instruction checks the condition code set by the CLC. If the contents of `FLAG` and `COUNT` are equal, then control branches to `ENDIT`. If they are not equal, control continues processing with the first instruction after the BE.

Chapter 6: Comparison and Conditional Branching

In Example 2, the CLC compares the payment made to the minimum amount due and sets the condition code. If they are not equal, control branches to CHECKIT. If they are equal, then control drops through the BNE and continues processing with the next instruction.

BRANCH (B) INSTRUCTION

Format:

```
1--------10----16--------columns
        B    L                         control transfer
```

Purpose: To transfer program control. This command represents an unconditional branch to the statement specified by the label operand (L). Since this is an unconditional branch, the current setting of the condition code has no effect on the execution of this statement.

Example:

```
        :
B       NEXTONE         branch
        :
```

Regardless of the current condition code setting, control branches to the statement in the program labeled NEXTONE. In other words, control will simply go to the statement specified by the label operand. This is why the branch command is commonly refered to as a GO TO statement.

COMPARE (C) INSTRUCTION

Format:

```
1--------10----16--------columns              type A:B
        C    R,S                        arithmetic compare
```

Purpose: To compare binary constants. This instruction compares the contents of two binary operands and sets the condition code based upon the results. Each operand must be defined as a fullword, 32-bit binary integer. The contents of the storage operand (S) are compared to the contents of the register operand (R).

	Condition Code	C R : S
1.	1000	=
2.	0111	≠
3.	0010	>
4.	1101	≯
5.	0100	<
6.	1011	≮

TABLE 6.5 Arithmetic Condition Code Settings

The six possible outcomes for the condition code are shown in Table 6.5.

Example:

```
    :
C    7,COUNT      compare and set ccode
BE   ENDIT        if R7 = COUNT, branch
S    5,ONE
    :
```

In this example, the binary value stored at COUNT is compared to the numeric contents of register 7. If they are equal, the condition code is set to 1000 and control branches to ENDIT. On the other hand, if they are not equal, control falls through and executes the subtraction on the next line.

BRANCH ON HIGH (BH) AND BRANCH ON NOT HIGH (BNH) INSTRUCTIONS

Formats:

```
1--------10----16-------- [ccode]           type A:B
        BH    L           0010       control transfer
        BNH   L           1101
```

Purpose: To test condition codes and branches for matching values. Both branch statements check the current value of the condition code and, on a match, transfer control to the statement or module identified by the label operand (L). Otherwise, control falls through to the instruction on the next line.

Example:

```
        :
CLC   IACCT,ACCTNUM        compare and set ccode
BH    NEXTACCT             if IACCT > ACCTNUM, branch
CLC   BALANCE,PAYMENT      compare and set ccode
BNH   REFUND               if BALANCE ≯ PAYMENT, branch
        :
```

Following the first CLC, the condition code is tested for high. If high (0010), control branches to NEXTACCT. Otherwise, control falls through to the second comparison. If the second CLC results in a condition code of not high (1101), then control skips to REFUND. If there is no match, processing continues with the first statement after the BNH.

SAMPLE PROGRAM CHAP6A

Sample program CHAP6A (Fig. 6.1) illustrates an application of the comparison and branching statements. For each input record, the program reads the student's name and credit hours. Then it checks the credit hours to determine the student's academic rank and prints the report shown in Fig. 6.2.

Input data:

(01–10) Student Name	(11–13) Earned Credit Hours
Brown	090
Cariens	150
Ports	044
Williams	045
End	000 (trailer record)

Processing functions:

Read a record.

Determine rank:

Use the input credit hours and the following table values to determine the student's academic rank.

Hours	Rank
1–44	FR—freshman
45–89	SO—sophomore
90–134	JR—junior
135–up	SR—senior

```
 1  *--------------- ACADEMIC RANK REPORT --------------------
 2  *  This program demonstrates use of compare and branch.
 3  *  The input is read until end of file is detected.
 4  *
 5  *
 6  *              PROGRAM-ID: CHAP6A
 7  *              PROGRAMMER: David M. Collopy
 8  *              RUN DATE:   mm/dd/yy
 9  *****************************************************************
10  CHAP6A    CSECT                                           (system
11            PRINT NOGEN                                     use and
12            BALR  2,0                                       general
13            USING *,2                                  housekeeping)
14            OPEN  IPTFILE,PRINTER                        open files
15  *----------------------------------------------------------------
16  *              MAINLINE CONTROL
17  *----------------------------------------------------------------
18  MAINLINE  BAL   9,HEADING                        print heading line
19            BAL   9,DETAIL                     detail processing loop
20            B     EXIT                                   process exit
21  *----------------------------------------------------------------
22  *              PRINT HEADING LINE
23  *----------------------------------------------------------------
24  HEADING   MVI   CCH,C'1'                         advance to new page...
25            PUT   PRINTER,HDGLINE                  ...and print heading
26            MVI   CCB,C' '                              single space...
27            PUT   PRINTER,BLKLINE               ...and print blank line
28            BR    9                                 return to mainline
29  *----------------------------------------------------------------
30  *              DETAIL PROCESSING LOOP
31  *----------------------------------------------------------------
32  DETAIL    BAL   10,GETDATA                                get data
33            CLC   EODFLAG,INAME                         test for EOD
34            BE    LEAVE                         if EOD, leave module
35            BAL   10,PROCESS                            compute rank
36            BAL   10,OUTPUT                        print detail line
37            B     DETAIL                                 repeat loop
38  LEAVE     BR    9                                return to mainline
```

FIGURE 6.1 Sample Program CHAP6A: A program to determine the academic rank of each student and to display the output in the form of a report.

```
39  *----------------------------------------------------------------
40  *                GET DATA
41  *----------------------------------------------------------------
42  GETDATA  GET    IPTFILE,IPTRECD            read record
43           PACK   DBLWORD,IHOURS             convert credit hours...
44           CVB    5,DBLWORD                  ...to binary
45           BR     10                         return to detail
46  *----------------------------------------------------------------
47  *                COMPUTE RANK
48  *----------------------------------------------------------------
49  PROCESS  C      5,SENIOR                   compare hours to 134
50           BH     MOVESR                     if hours > 134, then branch
51           C      5,JUNIOR                   else compare hours to 89
52           BH     MOVEJR                     if hours > 89, then branch
53           C      5,SOPH                     else compare hours to 44
54           BH     MOVESO                     if hours > 44, then branch
55           MVC    ORANK,FR                   else default rank to FR
56           B      RETURN                     skip to RETURN
57  MOVESR   MVC    ORANK,SR                   move SR to rank
58           B      RETURN                     skip to RETURN
59  MOVEJR   MVC    ORANK,JR                   move JR to rank
60           B      RETURN                     skip to RETURN
61  MOVESO   MVC    ORANK,SO                   move SO to rank
62  RETURN   BR     10                         return to detail
63  *----------------------------------------------------------------
64  *                PRINT DETAIL LINE
65  *----------------------------------------------------------------
66  OUTPUT   MVI    CCD,C' '                   single space output
67           MVC    ONAME,INAME                move input to output
68           MVC    OHOURS,IHOURS              move input to output
69           PUT    PRINTER,DTLLINE            print detail line
70           BR     10                         return to detail
71  *
72  EXIT     CLOSE  IPTFILE,PRINTER            close files
73           EOJ                               end of job
74  ****************************************************************
75  *                I/O FILE DEFINITION
76  *----------------------------------------------------------------
77  IPTFILE  DTFCD  DEVADDR=SYSIPT,IOAREA1=IPTBUFF,DEVICE=2501,     X
                   WORKA=YES,EOFADDR=EXIT
```

FIGURE 6.1 (cont.)

```
 78 PRINTER   DTFPR DEVADDR=SYSLST,IOAREA1=PRTBUFF,DEVICE=1403,   X
                   CTLCHR=YES,WORKA=YES,BLKSIZE=80
 79 *
 80 IPTBUFF   DS    CL80                        input file buffer
 81 PRTBUFF   DS    CL80                      printer file buffer
 82 *----------------------------------------------------------------
 83 *                 RECORD/DATA DEFINITIONS
 84 *----------------------------------------------------------------
 85 IPTRECD   DS    0CL80                     I N P U T   R E C O R D
 86 INAME     DS    CL10       (01 - 10)               student name
 87 IHOURS    DS    CL3        (11 - 13)       earned credit hours
 88           DS    CL67                                    unused
 89 *
 90 HDGLINE   DS    0CL80                     H E A D I N G   L I N E
 91 CCH       DS    CL1                               carriage control
 92           DC    CL14'STUDENT'
 93           DC    CL13'HOURS'
 94           DC    CL52'RANK'
 95 *
 96 DTLLINE   DS    0CL80                     D E T A I L   L I N E
 97 CCD       DS    CL1        (01 - 01)             carriage control
 98 ONAME     DS    CL10       (02 - 11)
 99           DC    CL5' '     (12 - 16)
100 OHOURS    DS    CL3        (17 - 19)
101           DC    CL10' '    (20 - 29)
102 ORANK     DS    CL2        (30 - 31)
103           DC    CL49' '    (32 - 80)
104 *
105 BLKLINE   DS    0CL80                     B L A N K   L I N E
106 CCB       DS    CL1                               carriage control
107           DC    CL79' '
108 *
109 EODFLAG   DC    CL3'End'                  end of data indicator
110 SENIOR    DC    F'134'                    junior cut-off point
111 JUNIOR    DC    F'89'                     sophomore cut-off point
112 SOPH      DC    F'44'                     freshman cut-off point
113 FR        DC    CL2'FR'                             freshman code
114 SO        DC    CL2'SO'                            sophomore code
115 JR        DC    CL2'JR'                               junior code
116 SR        DC    CL2'SR'                               senior code
117 DBLWORD   DS    D                          temporary storage area
118           END   CHAP6A
```

FIGURE 6.1 (cont.)

```
              STUDENT          HOURS           RANK

              Brown            090             JR
              Cariens          150             SR
              Ports            044             FR
              Williams         045             SO
```

FIGURE 6.2 Program Output for CHAP6A

Program output (Report):

```
    STUDENT          HOURS           RANK

    Brown            090             JR
    Cariens          150             SR
    Ports            044             FR
    Williams         045             SO
```

Pseudocode logic design:
    START
    Open files
    Print report heading line
    LOOP until end of file
        Read name and credit hours
        Determine rank
        Print name, credit hours, and rank
    End LOOP
    Close files
    END

DISSECTION OF SAMPLE PROGRAM CHAP6A

Most of the program logic in sample program CHAP6A is straightforward; therefore, we will focus on the processing performed by the DETAIL and PROCESS modules.

The DETAIL module consists of a loop that controls the reading of the data and the detailed processing performed by the program.

```
D E T A I L    P R O C E S S I N G    L O O P :

    32 DETAIL    BAL    10,GETDATA
```

The above statement means: Store the address of the next instruction in register 10 and branch to GETDATA to read a record.

```
    33           CLC    EODFLAG,INAME
```

The above statement means: Compare the input name to END, the contents of the EODFLAG, and set the condition code accordingly. Since we are using a trailer record to detect the end of the file, the last record has END coded for the student's name.

```
    34           BE     LEAVE
```

The above statement means: Check the condition code to see if the contents of INAME and EODFLAG are equal. If they are, branch to the statement labeled LEAVE. Otherwise, execute the next command.

```
    35           BAL    10,PROCESS
```

The above statement means: Load the address of the next statement into register 10 and branch to PROCESS to determine rank.

```
    36           BAL    10,OUTPUT
```

The above statement means: Load the address of the next statement into register 10 and branch to OUTPUT to print a line to the report.

```
    37           B      DETAIL
```

The above statement means: Branch to DETAIL and repeat the processing.

```
    38 LEAVE    BR     9
```

The above statement means: Control returns to the mainline at the address specified by register 9, when the end-of-data indicator is detected.

COMPUTE RANK:

```
49   PROCESS  C      5,SENIOR
```

The above statement means: Compare 134, the contents of the SENIOR operand, to the credit hours stored in register 5, and set the condition code. The value 134 represents the cut-off point for a junior. Hence, a student with 134 or more credit hours is ranked as a senior.

```
50            BH     MOVESR
```

If credit hours exceed 134, then the student is a senior and control branches to MOVESR. Otherwise, control executes the next instruction.

```
51            C      5,JUNIOR
```

The above statement means: Compare 89, the cut-off point for sophomores, to the credit hours stored in register 5, and set the condition code. A student with 89 or more credit hours is ranked as a junior.

```
52            BH     MOVEJR
```

If credit hours exceed 89, then the student is a junior and control branches to MOVEJR. Otherwise, control falls through to the next statement.

```
53            C      5,SOPH
54            BH     MOVESO
```

This process of comparing credit hours and branching continues by checking for the freshman cut-off point of 44. If the comparison test is true, the student is ranked as a sophomore. Otherwise, execution continues with the next statement.

```
55            MVC    ORANK,FR
56            B      RETURN
```

If control reaches this point in the program, then a match was not found for a senior, junior, or sophomore. By default, the student is a freshman. Hence, the program moves the 2-byte character string FR to ORANK and branches to RETURN.

```
57 MOVESR    MVC    ORANK,SR
58           B      RETURN
```

For a match on senior, SR is moved to ORANK. Control then branches to the statement at the end of the module labeled RETURN.

```
59 MOVEJR    MVC    ORANK,JR
60           B      RETURN
61 MOVESO    MVC    ORANK,SO
```

For a match on junior, JR is moved to the ORANK operand. For a match on sophomore, SO is moved to the ORANK operand.

```
62 RETURN    BR     10
```

Control returns to the statement in the program that corresponds to the address stored in register 10. Processing terminates and returns to the DETAIL module.

COMPARE LOGICAL IMMEDIATE (CLI) INSTRUCTION

Format:

```
1--------10----16--------columns          type A:B
         CLI    S,C'I'                    logical compare
```

Purpose: To compare two characters. The CLI statement logically compares two 1-byte character string operands (S and I) and sets the condition code based on the results. The immediate byte I, enclosed within single quotes, is compared to the character located at storage operand S.

Example:

```
         :
CLI    EOD,C'Y'      compare and set ccode
BNE    LOOP          if EOD ≠ 'Y', branch
A      5,INCOME      add and set ccode
         :
```

In the example, a comparison is made between the immediate byte Y and the character stored at EOD. If they are not equal, control branches to the statement labeled `LOOP`. Otherwise, control falls through and executes the Add statement.

COMPARE REGISTER (CR) INSTRUCTION

Format:

```
1--------10----16--------columns            type A:B
        CR    R1,R2               arithmetic compare
```

Purpose: To compare register constants. This instruction compares the contents of two binary register operands (`R1` and `R2`) and sets the condition code based on the outcome. The binary value stored at the register operand `R2` is compared to the contents of the register operand `R1`.

Example:

```
        :
CR    7,9          compare and set ccode
BE    EVENOUT      if R7 = R9, branch
BH    TOOMUCH      if R7 > R9, branch
        :
```

The binary constants stored at register operands 7 and 9 are compared and the condition code is set. If the constants are equal, then control branches to the statement in the program labeled `EVENOUT`.

If the constants are not equal, processing falls through to BH, where the condition code is tested for high. If this test is true, then control jumps to the statement labeled `TOOMUCH`. Otherwise, processing continues with the next command.

BRANCH ON LOW (BL) AND BRANCH ON NOT LOW (BNL) INSTRUCTIONS

Formats:

```
1--------10----16-------- [ccode]           type A:B
        BL    L          0100      control transfer
        BNL   L          1011
```

Purpose: To test condition codes and branches for matching values. Either of these statements will cause a branch to the instruction in the program specified by the label operand (L), when the condition code matches the branch test. If the test fails, then control drops to the statement on the next line.

Example:

```
        :
CLC   ONE,TWO         compare and set ccode
BL    ADDNUM          if ONE < TWO, branch
CLC   NUM1,NUM2       compare and set ccode
BNL   SWITCH          if NUM1 ≮ NUM2, branch
        :
```

Following the first CLC, the condition code is tested for low. If low, control branches to ADDNUM. Otherwise, control falls through to the second CLC and compares the contents of NUM1 and NUM2.

The second CLC checks for the not low condition. If true, control skips to the statement in the program labeled SWITCH; otherwise, processing continues with the next instruction.

BRANCH ON ZERO (BZ) AND BRANCH ON NOT ZERO (BNZ) INSTRUCTIONS

Formats:

```
1--------10----16--------    [ccode]         type A:0
        BZ     L              1000       control transfer
        BNZ    L              0111
```

Purpose: To test condition codes and branches for matching values. We may code either of these instructions to check the value of the condition code and, on a match, send control to the statement or module with the label (L). In simpler terms: The branch is taken when the value of the condition code equals either 1000 or 0111.

Chapter 6: Comparison and Conditional Branching

Example:

```
        :
S    4,WITHDRAW    subtract and set ccode
BZ   BROKE         if R4 = 0, branch
S    4,SERVCHRG    subtract and set ccode
BNZ  PROCESS       if R4 ≠ 0, branch
        :
```

The branch to BROKE occurs when the contents of register 4 are equal to zero. Otherwise, control skips to the second Subtract statement. The following BNZ sends control to PROCESS when the binary value of register 4 is not equal to zero.

BRANCH ON POSITIVE (BP) AND BRANCH ON NOT POSITIVE (BNP) INSTRUCTIONS

Formats:

```
1--------10----16-------- [ccode]            type A:0
        BP    L           0010    control transfer
        BNP   L           1101
```

Purpose: To test condition codes and branches for matching values. Depending on the value of the condition code, processing will either continue with the statement labeled L or skip to the next command after the branch.

Example:

```
        :
A    6,NEG75      add and set ccode
BP   SUMMARY      if R6 > 0, branch
S    9,NUM        subtract and set ccode
BNP  LOWPOINT     if R9 ≯ 0, branch
        :
```

Following the Add statement, the condition code is tested for positive. If true, control branches to SUMMARY. Otherwise, processing falls through to the Subtract statement.

After executing the subtraction and resetting the condition code, Assembler checks for not positive. If true, control branches to LOWPOINT.

BRANCH ON MINUS (BM) AND BRANCH ON NOT MINUS (BNM) INSTRUCTIONS

Formats:

```
1--------10----16-------- [ccode]           type A:0
        BM    L           0100      control transfer
        BMP   L           1011
```

Purpose: To test condition codes and branches for matching values. Execution of either the BM or BNM will cause a conditional branch to the statement identified by the label operand (L). Otherwise, control skips the branch and continues processing with the next command.

Example:

```
        :
S       8,AMOUNT    subtract and set ccode
BM      OVERPAID    if R8 < 0, branch
BZ      PAIDUP      if R8 = 0, branch
BNM     SENDBILL    if R8 ≮ 0, branch
        :
```

In the example, Assembler performs the subtraction and sets the condition code. The branch statements that follow check for minus, zero, and not minus conditions respectively. Based upon the outcome of the test, control will branch to one of the following labels: OVERPAID, PAIDUP, or SENDBILL.

LOAD AND TEST REGISTER (LTR) INSTRUCTION

Format:

```
1--------10----16--------columns
        LTR   R1,R2                           type A:0
              ←
```

Purpose: To set the condition code. This instruction loads the binary value stored at the second register operand (R2) into the first register operand (R1). The LTR then compares the contents of R1 to zero and sets the condition code based upon the outcome. Execution of the LTR does not alter the contents of the second register operand R2.

Examples:

```
           :
1.   LTR   4,9        load and set ccode
     BZ    RESET      if R4 = 0, branch
           :


           :
2.   LTR   3,3        load and set ccode
     BM    ADDNUM     if R3 < 0, branch
           :
```

In Example 1, the value stored at register 9 is loaded into register 4 and the condition code is set. The BZ tests for zero and, when it finds a match, sends control to RESET. Otherwise, control falls through to the next statement.

In Example 2, the contents of register 3 are loaded into register 3 and the condition code is set. Here we see that the sending and receiving registers may be the same. Now, the program tests the condition code for minus and, when it finds a match, sends control to ADDNUM.

SAMPLE PROGRAM CHAP6B

Sample program CHAP6B produces a simple accounts receivable report. Each detail line consists of the customer's name, balance due, and the payment made. Total payment is accumulated and printed at the end of the report. Sample program CHAP6B is shown in Fig. 6.3; the program's output is shown in Fig. 6.4.

Input data:

(1–10) Customer	(11–13) Balance Due	(14–16) Payment
Ayers	$500	$200
Fontaine	750	750
Howard	400	420
Ryan	300	175
Walker	563	563
End	000	000 (trailer record)

Processing functions:
    New balance = balance due − payment
    Accumulate a total for the payments made

Program output (Accounts Receivable Report):

```
CUSTOMER       BALANCE      PAYMENT      AMT-DUE      *COMMENTS*
-----------------------------------------------------------------
Ayers          500.00       200.00       300.00
Fontaine       750.00       750.00       000.00       PAID IN FULL
Howard         400.00       420.00       000.00       CREDIT DUE
Ryan           300.00       175.00       125.00
Walker         563.00       563.00       000.00       PAID IN FULL
-----------------------------------------------------------------
TOTAL PAYMENT               2108.00
```

Pseudocode logic design:
    START
    Open files
    Initialize registers
    Print report heading
    LOOP until no more data
       Read name, balance and payment
       Compute new balance
       Print name, old balance, payment and comment
    End LOOP
    Print total payment
    Close files
    END

DISSECTION OF SAMPLE PROGRAM CHAP6B

The program logic used in this program is similar to what we have seen already. Therefore, we will concentrate on the activities performed by the PROCESS module.

COMPUTE NEW BALANCE:

This module performs two major tasks for each customer: It determines the new balance due and accumulates the total payments made.

```
 1 *-------------- ACCOUNTS RECEIVABLE REPORT -----------------
 2 *  This program demonstrates use of the compare and branch.
 3 *  The input is read until the end-of-data indicator is
 4 *  detected.
 5 *
 6 *
 7 *              PROGRAM-ID: CHAP6B
 8 *              PROGRAMMER: David M. Collopy
 9 *              RUN DATE:   mm/dd/yy
10 **************************************************************
11 CHAP6B    CSECT                                       (system
12           PRINT NOGEN                                 use and
13           BALR  2,0                                   general
14           USING *,2                               housekeeping)
15           OPEN  IPTFILE,PRINTER                    open files
16 *-------------------------------------------------------------
17 *                    MAINLINE CONTROL
18 *-------------------------------------------------------------
19 MAINLINE  BAL   10,SETUP                         program setup
20           BAL   10,HEADINGS                   print heading line
21           BAL   10,DETAIL                  detail processing loop
22           BAL   10,TOTAL                       print total line
23           B     EXIT                              process exit
24 *-------------------------------------------------------------
25 *                    PROGRAM SET UP
26 *-------------------------------------------------------------
27 SETUP     SR    6,6                       set total payments to zero
28           BR    10                             return to mainline
29 *-------------------------------------------------------------
30 *                    PRINT HEADING LINE
31 *-------------------------------------------------------------
32 HEADINGS  MVI   CCH,C'1'                     advance to new page...
33           PUT   PRINTER,HDGLINE                ...and print heading
34           MVI   CCDL,C' '                         single space...
35           PUT   PRINTER,DASHLINE           ...and print dashed line
36           BR    10                             return to mainline
```

FIGURE 6.3 Sample Program CHAP6B: A simple accounts receivable program to compute the new balance due for each customer. The payments made by the customers are accumulated and printed at the end of the report.

```
37 *------------------------------------------------------------
38 *              DETAIL PROCESSING LOOP
39 *------------------------------------------------------------
40 DETAIL   BAL   9,GETDATA                         get data
41          CLC   EODFLAG,INAME                 test for EOD
42          BE    LEAVE                   if EOD, leave module
43          BAL   9,PROCESS                compute new balance
44          BAL   9,OUTPUT                    print detail line
45          B     DETAIL                            repeat loop
46 LEAVE    BR    10                         return to mainline
47 *------------------------------------------------------------
48 *              GET DATA
49 *------------------------------------------------------------
50 GETDATA  GET   IPTFILE,IPTRECD                   read record
51          PACK  DBLWORD,IBALANCE             convert balance...
52          CVB   7,DBLWORD                         ...to binary
53          PACK  DBLWORD,IPAYMENT             convert payment...
54          CVB   8,DBLWORD                         ...to binary
55          BR    9                            return to detail
56 *------------------------------------------------------------
57 *              COMPUTE NEW BALANCE
58 *------------------------------------------------------------
59 PROCESS  MVC   ODUE,ZERO                  set balance due to 0
60          MVC   OCOMMENT,SPACES           set comment to spaces
61          CR    7,8                   compare balance & payment
62          BE    PAIDUP                         if equal, branch
63          BH    AMTDUE                          if high, branch
64          MVC   OCOMMENT,CREDIT           else move credit mesg
65          B     ACCUM                            skip to ACCUM
66 PAIDUP   MVC   OCOMMENT,PAID                  move paid mesg
67          B     ACCUM                            skip to ACCUM
68 AMTDUE   SR    7,8                        compute new balance
69          CVD   7,DBLWORD                 convert new balance...
70          UNPK  ODUE,DBLWORD                 ...to zone-decimal
71          MVZ   ODUE+2(1),ODUE                    replace sign
72 ACCUM    AR    6,8                        add to total payments
73          BR    9                            return to detail
```

FIGURE 6.3 (cont.)

```
 74   *-----------------------------------------------------------------
 75   *                  PRINT DETAIL LINE
 76   *-----------------------------------------------------------------
 77   OUTPUT  MVI    CCD,C' '                     single space output
 78           MVC    ONAME,INAME                  move input to output
 79           MVC    OBALANCE,IBALANCE            move input to output
 80           MVC    OPAYMENT,IPAYMENT            move input to output
 81           PUT    PRINTER,DTLLINE                 print detail line
 82           BR     9                                return to detail
 83   *-----------------------------------------------------------------
 84   *                  PRINT TOTAL LINE
 85   *-----------------------------------------------------------------
 86   TOTAL   MVI    CCDL,C' '                         single space...
 87           PUT    PRINTER,DASHLINE         ...and print dashed line
 88           MVI    CCT,C' '                     single space output
 89           CVD    6,DBLWORD                 convert total payment...
 90           UNPK   TOTPAYMT,DBLWORD              ...to zone-decimal
 91           MVZ    TOTPAYMT+3(1),TOTPAYMT             replace sign
 92           PUT    PRINTER,TOTLINE                 print total line
 93           BR     10                             return to mainline
 94   *
 95   EXIT    CLOSE  IPTFILE,PRINTER                        close files
 96           EOJ                                          end of job
 97   *****************************************************************
 98   *                  I/O FILE DEFINITIONS
 99   *-----------------------------------------------------------------
100   IPTFILE DTFCD  DEVADDR=SYSIPT,IOAREA1=IPTBUFF,DEVICE=2501,      X
                     WORKA=YES,EOFADDR=EXIT
101   PRINTER DTFPR  DEVADDR=SYSLST,IOAREA1=PRTBUFF,DEVICE=1403,      X
                     CTLCHR=YES,WORKA=YES,BLKSIZE=80
102   *
103   IPTBUFF DS     CL80                          input file buffer
104   PRTBUFF DS     CL80                        printer file buffer
```

FIGURE 6.3 (cont.)

Sample Program CHAP6B

```
105 *----------------------------------------------------------------
106 *             RECORD/DATA DEFINITIONS
107 *----------------------------------------------------------------
108 IPTRECD   DS   0CL80                         I N P U T   R E C O R D
109 INAME     DS   CL10       (01 - 10)                    customer name
110 IBALANCE  DS   CL3        (11 - 13)                     balance due
111 IPAYMENT  DS   CL3        (14 - 16)                    payment made
112           DS   CL64                                          unused
113 *
114 HDGLINE   DS   0CL80                         H E A D I N G   L I N E
115 CCH       DS   CL1                                   carriage control
116           DC   CL25'CUSTOMER      BALANCE'
117           DC   CL54'PAYMENT      AMT-DUE       *COMMENTS*'
118 *
119 DASHLINE  DS   0CL80                         D A S H E D   L I N E
120 CCDL      DS   CL1                                   carriage control
121           DC   CL26'--------------------------'
122           DC   CL26'--------------------------'
123           DC   CL27'---------------------------'
124 *
125 DTLLINE   DS   0CL80                         D E T A I L   L I N E
126 CCD       DS   CL1        (01 - 01)                  carriage control
127 ONAME     DS   CL10       (02 - 11)
128           DC   CL3' '     (12 - 14)
129 OBALANCE  DS   CL3        (15 - 17)
130           DC   CL3'.00'   (18 - 20)
131           DC   CL6' '     (21 - 26)
132 OPAYMENT  DS   CL3        (27 - 29)
133           DC   CL3'.00'   (30 - 32)
134           DC   CL6' '     (33 - 38)
135 ODUE      DS   CL3        (39 - 41)
136           DC   CL3'.00'   (42 - 44)
137           DC   CL6' '     (45 - 50)
138 OCOMMENT  DS   CL12       (51 - 62)
139           DC   CL18' '    (63 - 80)
140 *
```

FIGURE 6.3 (cont.)

```
141 TOTLINE   DS    0CL80                         TOTAL LINE
142 CCT       DS    CL1                           carriage control
143           DC    CL24'TOTAL PAYMENTS'
144 TOTPAYMT  DS    CL4
145           DC    CL3'.00'
146           DC    CL48' '
147 *
148 BLKLINE   DS    0CL80                         BLANK LINE
149 CCB       DS    CL1                           carriage control
150           DC    CL79' '
151 *
152 ZERO      DC    CL3'000'
153 SPACES    DC    CL2' '
154 EODFLAG   DC    CL3'End'
155 DBLWORD   DS    D
156 PAID      DC    CL12'PAID IN FULL'
157 CREDIT    DC    CL10'CREDIT DUE'
158           END   CHAP6B
```

FIGURE 6.3 (cont.)

```
CUSTOMER      BALANCE      PAYMENT      AMT-DUE       *COMMENTS*
------------------------------------------------------------------
Ayers         500.00       200.00       300.00
Fontaine      750.00       750.00       000.00        PAID IN FULL
Howard        400.00       420.00       000.00        CREDIT DUE
Ryan          300.00       175.00       125.00
Walker        563.00       563.00       000.00        PAID IN FULL
------------------------------------------------------------------
TOTAL PAYMENTS             2108.00
```

FIGURE 6.4 Program Output for CHAP6B

```
59 PROCESS   MVC    ODUE,ZERO
60           MVC    OCOMMENT,SPACES
```

The amount due and comment fields are initialized to zero and spaces, respectively. Both fields are initialized prior to processing each record.

```
61           CR     7,8
```

The above statement means: Compare the payment made (register 8) to the balance due (register 7) and set the condition code accordingly.

```
62           BE     PAIDUP
```

The above statement means: If payment and balance are equal, branch to `PAIDUP`; otherwise, continue processing with the statement on line 63.

```
63           BH     AMTDUE
```

The above statement means: If balance exceeds payment, then branch to the statement labeled `AMTDUE`; otherwise, execute the next instruction.

```
64           MVC    OCOMMENT,CREDIT
```

At this point, if a match has not been found, then by default the customer overpaid and `CREDIT DUE` is moved to the comment field of the detail line.

```
65           B      ACCUM
```

The above statement means: Branch to the statement labeled `ACCUM`.

```
66 PAIDUP    MVC    OCOMMENT,PAID
67           B      ACCUM
```

The above statements mean: Move `PAID IN FULL` to the comment field and branch to the statement labeled `ACCUM`.

```
68 AMTDUE    SR     7,8
```

The above statement means: Subtract payment from the balance stored in register 7 and place the resulting amount due in register 7.

Chapter 6: Comparison and Conditional Branching

```
69              CVD    7,DBLWORD
```

The above statement means: Convert the amount due stored in register 7 to packed-decimal and place the result in DBLWORD.

```
70              UNPK   ODUE,DBLWORD
```

The above statement means: Unpack the value stored at DBLWORD and convert it to zone-decimal, and place the result at ODUE.

```
71              MVZ    ODUE+2(1),ODUE
```

The above statement means: Replace the sign with the zone character (F) from the left-most byte.

```
72   ACCUM      AR     6,8
```

The above statement means: Add current payment (register 8) to total payments (register 6) and store the resulting sum in register 6. Register 6 is used to accumulate total payments.

```
73              BR     9
```

The above statement means: Return to the DETAIL module beginning at line 44.

KEY REVIEW TERMS

Define the following terms:

comparison statement	BNE instruction	branching statement
numeric comparison	BNL instruction	program flag
CLC instruction	conditional branching	CLI instruction
BH instruction	BNM instruction	LTR instruction
BE instruction	B instruction	BNH instruction
BL instruction	unconditional branching	CR instruction
BNZ instruction	BZ instruction	BP instruction
BM instruction	condition code	BNP instruction
logical comparison		C instruction

REVIEW EXERCISES

For each block of code, indicate the label to which control will branch after the program executes the given compare statement.

*1. ```
    FLAG: C5D5C440   TFLD: D6E4E340
    CLC FLAG,TFLD   CLC TFLD,FLAG
    BH   HIGH   BNL STEP1
    BNL NOTHIGH   BH   STEP2
    BE   EQUAL   BE   STEP3
    B   CHKPOINT   B   ENDALL
    ?_____   ?_____
```

*2. ```
    FLAG: 40D8C5C4        TFLD: 40D5D6E3
    CLC  FLAG,TFLD        CLC  TFLD,FLAG
    BNH  HERE             BNL  LINE10
    BL   THERE            BE   LINE25
    BE   EXIT             BNH  LINE42
    BNL  COMPUTE          BH   LINE90
    B    LOOP             B    LINE5
    ?_____      ?_____
```

*3. ```
    TEST: E7   TEST: D5
    CLI TEST,C'Y'   CLI TEST,C'N'
    BNL ROUTE10   BH   MODULE10
    BE   ROUTE5   BL   MODULE5
    BNH ROUTE8   BNE MODULE8
    B   EXIT   A   5,PAYMT
    ?_____   ?_____
```

*4. ```
    TEST: F1
    CLI  TEST,C'0'        CLI  TEST,C'2'
    BE   ROUTE7           BE   ONE
    BNE  MODULE14         BL   TWO
    BH   LINE33           BNH  THREE
    BL   CALC             B    OUT
    ?_____      ?_____
```

*5.
```
    R3:00000053          R3:00000085
    TEST:00000064        TEST:00000055
    C    3,TEST          C    3,TEST
    BNL  ONE             BL   ONE
    BE   TWO             BNH  TWO
    BL   THREE           BE   THREE
    B    FOUR            S    3,N10
    ?_____     ?_____
```

*6.
```
    R5:00001019          R7:00001010
    CR   5,7             CR   7,5
    BE   EVEN            BNL  SUBMOD
    BL   LOW             BNH  ADD
    BNL  SUBTRACT        BE   EVEN
    B    AGAIN           B    AGAIN
    ?_____     ?_____
```

*7.
```
    R4:00000000          ONE:00000001
    R5:00000064          NUM:0000000A
    A    5,NUM           S    4,NUM
    S    4,NUM           M    4,ONE
    BP   PATH10          A    5,ONE
    BM   PATH20          BP   LINE10
    BZ   PATH30          BNP  LINE20
    ?_____     BNZ  LINE30
                         ?_____
```

*8.
```
    R8:00000000          NBR:0000000F
    R9:00000034          NUM:FFFFFFF4
    ONE:00000001         S    9,9
    A    8,NBR           M    8,NUM
    M    8,ONE           A    9,NBR
    D    8,NUM           BM   STMT1
    BP   ROUTINE7        BP   STMT2
    BZ   ROUTINE3        BZ   STMT3
    BM   ROUTINE1        ?_____
    BNM  ROUTINE6
    ?_____
```

*9. R6:00000000   NUM:0000000B
     R7:00000016   NBR:FFFFFFF5
     A   7,NUM   M   6,NBR
     LTR 7,7   S   7,NUM
     BZ   LINE10   LTR 6,7
     BM   LINE30   BP   PASS6
     BNP LINE50   BM   PASS5
     B   LINE70   BZ   PASS2
     ?_____   ?_____

Assume each of the following LTR statements has been executed. For the data given, list all condition codes (major and minor) that apply. Circle the major condition code.

R4:0000003A   R5:FFFFFFF7   R6:000000EC   R7:00000000

*10. LTR 4,4 _____
 11. LTR 6,5 _____
*12. LTR 5,6 _____
*13. LTR 4,5 _____
 14. LTR 7,4 _____
 15. LTR 6,4 _____
*16. LTR 4,6 _____
 17. LTR 5,5 _____
*18. LTR 4,7 _____

PROGRAMMING EXERCISES

Instructions: For each exercise, design the pseudocode and write the modular program to produce the output shown. Model your program after the sample programs presented in this chapter. Verify your output.

1. Overdue accounts: Write a program to provide management with information about their 90-day overdue customer accounts. Format the input as follows:

Chapter 6: Comparison and Conditional Branching

Columns	Field Names
01–03	Customer account number
04–18	Customer name
19–20	Number of days overdue
21–23	Balance overdue

Input data:

Account #	Customer Name	Days Overdue	Balance
101	David Ryan	90	$400
245	Marie Ross	30	754
273	Bonnie Fox	90	795
310	Vic Porter	90	550
408	Tim Adams	30	233
489	Amy Knox	30	700
526	Ron Wahl	30	625
635	Sue Farley	90	600
772	Bob Wilson	60	417
854	Mike Synan	90	900
920	Vern Ports	90	235
963	Pat Audi	60	342

Processing functions:

Determine which accounts are 90 days overdue and write them to the Overdue Accounts Report. Count the number of customers with a balance greater than $500. At the end of the report, print the count and the total number of customers with accounts that are 90 days overdue.

Program output (Overdue Accounts Report):

```
                R. D. CARRINGTON INCORPORATED
                    Overdue Accounts Report
                           mm/dd/yy


         ACCT #           CUSTOMER NAME           AMOUNT DUE

          101              David Ryan               400.00
           :                   :                       :
           :                   :                       :
          999              X--------X                999.99

              Number of overdue accounts:   999
              Number of accounts > $500.00 : 999
```

2. Insurance sales: Find the insurance agent who sold the most premiums for the year. The format for the input consists of the following:

Columns	Field Names
01–15	Insurance agent
16–18	Policy premium
25–27	Number of policies sold

Input data:

Agent	Premium per Policy	Policies Sold
Roy Marx	$750	100
Cathy Reed	423	231
Tex Lacey	217	175
Phillip Nye	486	109
Barbara Culp	343	254
Ryan Lane	336	125
Sandy Lee	266	111
Jason Burks	263	267
Devin Style	238	392

Processing functions:

Find the top agent of the year. Determine who sold the most premiums.

Premiums sold = premium per policy × policies sold.

Program output (Report):

Produce a report listing each agent and the premium sold by that agent. At the end of the report, print the name of the top sales agent and the premium sold.

```
              MUTUAL INSURANCE COMPANY
                       (year)

          AGENT              PREMIUM SOLD

         Roy Marx              75000.00
            :                      :
            :                      :
            :                      :
         X-------X              99999.99

       TOP AGENT:     X-------X
       PREMIUM SOLD:  99999.99
```

3. Modify the program in Exercise 2 to include the agent with the lowest sales for the year. Print the agent's name and premium sold as shown below:

```
                  MUTUAL INSURANCE COMPANY
                          (year)

              AGENT              PREMIUM SOLD

            Roy Marx                75000.00
               :                       :
               :                       :
               :                       :
            X--------X                99999.99

               TOP AGENT:    X--------X
            PREMIUM SOLD:    99999.99

               LOW AGENT:    X--------X
            PREMIUM SOLD:    99999.99
```

4. Grade report: Write a program to assign letter grades to test scores.

   Input data (Data is coded in the columns shown in parentheses.):

(10–13) Student-ID	(20–34) Student Name	(40–41) Test Scores
1000	Tom Hall	75
1500	Bill Noe	93
2000	Lou Wahl	80
3000	Susan West	52
4000	Tim Mills	77
5000	Dave Keys	87
6000	Bob Reid	60
7000	Mike Kehr	79
8000	Patrick Noll	98
9000	Barbara Carr	64

   Processing functions:

   Based on the test scores, assign the appropriate letter grade to each student. Use the table below to determine letter grades.

```
A:  90–100
B:  80–89
C:  70–79
D:  60–69
F:  00–59
```

Program output (Grade Report):

```
           Parker-Loren Community College
                   Grade Report

   Student      Student         Test        Letter
     ID          Name           Score       Grade
   -----------------------------------------------
     1000      Tom Hall          75           C
      :           :               :           :
      :           :               :           :
      :           :               :           :
     9000      Barb Carr         64           D
```

5. Modify the program in Exercise 4 to compute the grade distribution and print it at the end of the report.

```
           Parker-Loren Community College
                   Grade Report

   Student      Student         Test        Letter
     ID          Name           Score       Grade
   -----------------------------------------------
     1000      Tom Hall          75           C
      :           :               :           :
      :           :               :           :
      :           :               :           :
     9000      Barb Carr         64           D

         D i s t r i b u t i o n

         Letter         Frequency
         ------         ---------
           A                2
           B                :
           C                :
           D                :
           F                :
```

6. Modify the program in Exercise 5 to assign letter grades according to the table below and adjust the grade distribution to include the new grading scale.

   100–93: A   76–73: C
   92–90: A–   72–70: C–
   89–87: B+   69–67: D+
   86–83: B   66–63: D
   82–80: B–   62–60: D–
   79–77: C+   59–00: F

7. Accounts payable: Modify Exercise 8 in Chapter 5 to include an account status field with the following values: "P" = paid; "O" = outstanding. Position the field in column 55 of the input. Enter a P in column 55 for those records with a purchase order number beginning with an A, Y, P, D, or R. Otherwise enter an O. Accumulate two additional totals, one for the number of accounts paid (P) and one for the number of outstanding (O) accounts. Produce the output as shown in Exercise 8, but include the new totals at the end of the report.

8. Sales commission: Compute and print the weekly sales commission report for Perfecto Auto.

   Input data (The column positions are shown in parentheses.):

(01–20) Sales Employee	(25–29) Sales	(33–33) Years of Service
Jan Owens	$24122	3
Karen Heberling	3500	1
Amy Lambert	6000	2
Terry Karns	17900	4
Nat Wilcox	4350	4
Jason Stevens	8100	2
Pat Farley	3795	3
Joe Peterson	7446	5
Fred Langly	22000	2
Judy Marshall	7753	1
Bob Anthony	14570	2
Casey Roberts	4659	5

Processing functions:

Base pay = $200 \times$ years of service

Accumulate totals for sales, base pay, and commissions

Commission based on sales:

	Commission
0 < SALES ≤ 4,000	$ 0
4,000 < SALES ≤ 5,000	50
5,000 < SALES ≤ 7,500	75
7,500 < SALES ≤ 10,000	100
10,000 < SALES ≤ 20,000	200
20,000 < SALES	300

Program output (Weekly Sales Commission Report):

```
                  PERFECTO AUTO
           Weekly Sales Commission Report
                     mm/dd/yy

Sales Employee      Sales      Base Pay    Commission    Gross Pay

Jan Owens         24122.00      600.00       300.00        900.00
    :                :             :            :             :
    :                :             :            :             :
X-----------X     99999.99      999.99       999.99        999.99

         Totals: 999999.99     9999.99      9999.99
```

9. **Piece work:** Modify Exercise 7 in Chapter 5 to include three additional totals: (1) number of workers at quota, (2) number of workers exceeding quota, and (3) number of workers under quota. Print the same output as before and add the new information at the end of the report.

7 PAGE AND CONTROL BREAK PROCESSING

OVERVIEW

Learning Objectives
Performing Page Breaks
Sample Program CHAP7A
Performing Control Breaks
Sample Program CHAP7B
Key Review Terms
Review Exercises
Programming Exercises

LEARNING OBJECTIVES

After reading this chapter and completing the exercises, the reader should be able to:

- write programs to produce multi-page reports.
- code program loops using priming and looping read statements.
- use control fields and control break processing to accumulate and print report subtotals.

PERFORMING PAGE BREAKS

Computer-generated reports normally consist of multi-page output. For each page, we would like to maintain a one-inch margin at the top and bottom, and print 50–55 detail lines. When a page is full, the printer should stop, skip over the perforated line, and resume printing at the top of the next page.

In other words, a page break occurs when the number of lines to be printed equals or exceeds the limit established for one page. Accordingly, the printer advances to a new page, prints the appropriate title and column headings, and continues with the body of the report.

The process for determining page breaks depends mostly on the use of a line counter. Each time a line is printed, the line counter is incremented by one and compared to the maximum number of lines allowed per page. If we are also numbering the pages, then we need an additional variable: a page counter. The purpose of the page counter is to keep track of the number of pages printed; the purpose of the line counter is to keep track of the detail lines printed per page.

To further illustrate the concept of page breaks, let's look at the payroll report shown in Fig. 7.1. Assume we are printing forty detail lines per page. Once forty detail lines have been printed, the line counter is set to zero, one is added to the page counter, the printer advances to the next page, and the title lines, page number, and column headings are printed. The pseudocode version of the page break routine is shown in Fig. 7.2.

Given the limit of 40 lines per page, note the page and line counters shown in Fig. 7.2. For each page, the line counter advances from 1 to 40 as the detail lines are printed.

```
              PAYROLL REPORT                Page 1


    ID#   EMPLOYEE NAME         PAYRATE    HOURS WORKED
    ------------------------------------------------------
    101   Kara Anderson          12.00         40
     :        :                    :            :
     :        :                    :            :
     :        :                    :            :
     :        :                    :            :
    140   Hecter Pannacheck      10.00         39



              PAYROLL REPORT                Page 2


    ID#   EMPLOYEE NAME         PAYRATE    HOURS WORKED
    ------------------------------------------------------
    141   Clark Parsons           9.00         37
     :        :                    :            :
     :        :                    :            :
     :        :                    :            :
    165   Elinore Watson         14.00         40
```

FIGURE 7.1 Page Break Report

	Counters	
	Page	**Line**
:		
If line counter > 40		
Set line counter to 0	1	1–40
Add 1 to page counter	2	1–40
Advance to the next page	3	1–40
Print titles, page number, and column headings	:	:
:	:	
:	n	1-40

FIGURE 7.2 Page Break Logic

SAMPLE PROGRAM CHAP7A

This program illustrates page break processing and prints a personnel report for the Raintrax Manufacturing Company. Each detail line includes the division and department numbers, department supervisor, and employee count. The total number of nonsupervisory employees is accumulated and printed at the end of the report. Sample program CHAP7A is shown in Fig. 7.3; the program's output is shown in Fig. 7.4.

Input data:

A partial list of the input and the trailer record are shown below.

(1–2)	(3–5)	(6–25)	(26–27)
Division #	Department #	Department Supervisor	Employees
10	110	Tim Midden	10
10	120	Rob Clifford	06
10	130	Sarah Burnside	05
⋮	⋮	⋮	
00	000	End	00 (trailer record)

Processing functions:

    Print ten detail lines per page

    Accumulate the total number of nonsupervisory employees

Program output (Page Break Report):

```
          RAINTRAX MANUFACTURING COMPANY          Page 03
                 Personnel Report

DIVISION   DEPARTMENT                             EMPLOYEE
 NUMBER      NUMBER      DEPARTMENT SUPERVISOR     COUNT

    60         610       Robert Hall                 18
    60         620       Adam Uffner                 03
    60         630       Ron Null                    20
    70         710       Mike Redman                 19
    70         720       Jennifer Deihl              06


TOTAL EMPLOYEE COUNT:                              308
```

Pseudocode logic design:
>START
>Initialize registers
>Set line counter to 0
>Add 1 to page counter
>Advance to the next page
>Print titles, page number, and column headings
>LOOP until no more data
>>Read data
>>Accumulate total employees
>>If line counter > 10
>>>Set line counter to 0
>>>Add 1 to page counter
>>>Advance to the next page
>>>Print titles, page number, and column headings
>>Add 1 to line counter
>>Print detail line
>End LOOP
>Print total employees
>END

DISSECTION OF SAMPLE PROGRAM CHAP7A

Let's examine the processing of sample program CHAP7A beginning with the `HEADINGS` module. Note the functions that this module performs: It increments the page counter (register 8), advances the printer to the top of the next page, prints the report titles and column headings, and sets the line counter (register 9) to zero.

From here, we enter the heart of the program: the `DETAIL` module. Overall, it consists of a loop that controls the input and the processing of the data.

DETAIL PROCESSING LOOP:

```
49 DETAIL   GET   IPTFILE,IPTRECD
```

The above statement means: Read a record from the input file (`IPTFILE`) and store the record in the `IPTRECD` work area.

```
 1  *--------------- RAINTRAX PERSONNEL REPORT ---------------
 2  *     This program demonstrates page break processing.
 3  *
 4  *              PROGRAM-ID: CHAP7A
 5  *              PROGRAMMER: David M. Collopy
 6  *              RUN DATE:   mm/dd/yy
 7  ****************************************************************
 8  CHAP7A    CSECT                                        (system
 9            PRINT NOGEN                                 use and
10            BALR  2,0                                   general
11            USING *,2                              housekeeping)
12            OPEN  IPTFILE,PRINTER                    open files
13  *---------------------------------------------------------------
14  *                    MAINLINE CONTROL
15  *---------------------------------------------------------------
16  MAINLINE  BAL   10,SETUP                          program setup
17            BAL   4,HEADINGS                        print headings
18            BAL   10,DETAIL                    detail processing loop
19            BAL   10,TOTAL                         print total line
20            B     EXIT                                process exit
21  *---------------------------------------------------------------
22  *                    PROGRAM SET UP
23  *---------------------------------------------------------------
24  SETUP     SR    6,6                        set total employees to 0
25            SR    8,8                            set page count to 0
26            BR    10                             return to mainline
27  *---------------------------------------------------------------
28  *                    PRINT HEADINGS
29  *---------------------------------------------------------------
30  HEADINGS  SR    9,9                             set line count to 0
31            A     8,ONE                           add 1 to page count
32            CVD   8,DBLWORD                      convert page count...
33            UNPK  PAGE,DBLWORD                     ...to zone-decimal
34            MVZ   PAGE+1(1),PAGE                       replace sign
35            MVI   CCH1,C'1'                         skip to new page...
36            PUT   PRINTER,HDGLINE1             ...and print heading-1
37            MVI   CCH2,C' '                           single space...
```

FIGURE 7.3 Sample Program CHAP7A: Prints a personnel report for the Raintrax Manufacturing Company. The report displays the input data. The total number of nonsupervisory personnel is accumulated and printed at the end of the report.

```
38            PUT    PRINTER,HDGLINE2        ...and print heading-2
39            MVI    CCH3,C'-'                       triple space...
40            PUT    PRINTER,HDGLINE3        ...and print heading-3
41            MVI    CCH4,C' '                       single space...
42            PUT    PRINTER,HDGLINE4        ...and print heading-4
43            MVI    CCB,C' '                        single space...
44            PUT    PRINTER,BLKLINE              ...and blank line
45            BR     4                            return to mainline
46   *----------------------------------------------------------------
47   *              DETAIL PROCESSING LOOP
48   *----------------------------------------------------------------
49   DETAIL   GET    IPTFILE,IPTRECD                      read record
50            PACK   DBLWORD,IEMPLS          convert nbr employees...
51            CVB    5,DBLWORD                           ...to binary
52            CLC    EODFLAG,ISUPVR                      test for EOD
53            BE     LEAVE                     if EOD, leave module
54            BAL    3,PROCESS              accumulate total employees
55            C      9,MAXLINES              compare line count to 10
56            BL     PRTDTL              if page not full, print line
57            BAL    4,HEADINGS                       print headings
58   PRTDTL   BAL    3,OUTPUT                       print detail line
59            B      DETAIL                              repeat loop
60   LEAVE    BR     10                           return to mainline
61   *----------------------------------------------------------------
62   *              ACCUMULATE TOTAL EMPLOYEES
63   *----------------------------------------------------------------
64   PROCESS  AR     6,5                       add to total employees
65            BR     3                             return to detail
66   *----------------------------------------------------------------
67   *              PRINT DETAIL LINE
68   *----------------------------------------------------------------
69   OUTPUT   A      9,ONE                      add 1 to line count
70            MVI    CCD,C' '                   single space output
71            MVC    ODIV,IDIV                  move input to output
72            MVC    ODEPT,IDEPT                move input to output
73            MVC    OSUPVR,ISUPVR              move input to output
74            MVC    OEMPLS,IEMPLS              move input to output
75            PUT    PRINTER,DTLLINE               print detail line
76            BR     3                             return to detail
```

FIGURE 7.3 (cont.)

```
77  *-----------------------------------------------------------------
78  *                 PRINT TOTAL LINE
79  *-----------------------------------------------------------------
80  TOTAL     MVI    CCT,C'-'                     triple space output
81            CVD    6,DBLWORD                convert employee total...
82            UNPK   TOTEMPLS,DBLWORD              ...to zone-decimal
83            MVZ    TOTEMPLS+2(1),TOTEMPLS              replace sign
84            PUT    PRINTER,TOTLINE                 print total line
85            BR     10                           return to mainline
86  *
87  EXIT      CLOSE  IPTFILE,PRINTER                      close files
88            EOJ                                         end of job
89  ****************************************************************
90  *                 I/O FILE DEFINITIONS
91  *-----------------------------------------------------------------
92  IPTFILE   DTFCD  DEVADDR=SYSIPT,IOAREA1=IPTBUFF,DEVICE=2501,    X
                    WORKA=YES,EOFADDR=EXIT
93  PRINTER   DTFPR  DEVADDR=SYSLST,IOAREA1=PRTBUFF,DEVICE=1403,    X
                    CTLCHR=YES,WORKA=YES,BLKSIZE=80
94  *
95  IPTBUFF   DS     CL80                         input file buffer
96  PRTBUFF   DS     CL80                       printer file buffer
97  *-----------------------------------------------------------------
98  *                 RECORD/DATA DEFINITIONS
99  *-----------------------------------------------------------------
100 IPTRECD   DS     0CL80                  I N P U T   R E C O R D
101 IDIV      DS     CL2          (01 - 02)         division number
102 IDEPT     DS     CL3          (03 - 05)       department number
103 ISUPVR    DS     CL20         (06 - 25)   department supervisor
104 IEMPLS    DS     CL2          (26 - 27)     number of employees
105           DS     CL53         (28 - 80)                  unused
106 *
107 HDGLINE1  DS     0CL80                  H E A D I N G   L I N E - 1
108 CCH1      DS     CL1                              carriage control
109           DC     CL24' '                                    unused
110           DC     CL30'RAINTRAX MANUFACTURING COMPANY'
111           DC     CL7' '
112           DC     CL5'Page '
```

FIGURE 7.3 (cont.)

```
113 PAGE       DS    CL2
114            DC    CL11' '
115 *
116 HDGLINE2 DS    0CL80              H E A D I N G    L I N E - 2
117 CCH2      DS    CL1                          carriage control
118            DC    CL31' '
119            DC    CL16'Personnel Report'
120            DC    CL32' '
121 *
122 HDGLINE3 DS    0CL80              H E A D I N G    L I N E - 3
123 CCH3      DS    CL1                          carriage control
124            DC    CL9' '
125            DC    CL11'DIVISION'
126            DC    CL37'DEPARTMENT'
127            DC    CL22'EMPLOYEE'
128 *
129 HDGLINE4 DS    0CL80              H E A D I N G    L I N E - 4
130 CCH4      DS    CL1                          carriage control
131            DC    CL10' '
132            DC    CL12'NUMBER'
133            DC    CL11'NUMBER'
134            DC    CL25'DEPARTMENT SUPERVISOR'
135            DC    CL21'COUNT'
136 *
137 DTLLINE   DS    0CL80               D E T A I L    L I N E
138 CCD       DS    CL1       (01 - 01)           carriage control
139            DC    CL12' '   (02 - 13)                   unused
140 ODIV      DS    CL2       (14 - 15)          division number
141            DC    CL9' '    (16 - 24)                   unused
142 ODEPT     DS    CL3       (25 - 27)         department number
143            DC    CL7' '    (28 - 34)                   unused
144 OSUPVR    DS    CL20      (35 - 54)      department supervisor
145            DC    CL7' '    (55 - 61)                   unused
146 OEMPLS    DS    CL2       (62 - 63)       number of employees
147            DC    CL17' '   (64 - 80)                   unused
148 *
149 TOTLINE   DS    0CL80                 T O T A L    L I N E
150 CCT       DS    CL1                           carriage control
151            DC    CL9' '
152            DC    CL50'TOTAL EMPLOYEE COUNT:'
```

FIGURE 7.3 (cont.)

```
153 TOTEMPLS  DS    CL3
154           DC    CL17' '
155 *
156 BLKLINE   DS    0CL80                   B L A N K   L I N E
157 CCB       DS    CL1                        carriage control
158           DC    CL79' '
159 *
160 MAXLINES  DC    F'10'         maximum detail lines per page
161 EODFLAG   DC    CL3'End'               end of data flag
162 ONE       DC    F'1'                            constant
163 DBLWORD   DS    D                  temporary holding area
164           END   CHAP7A
```

FIGURE 7.3 (cont.)

```
                RAINTRAX MANUFACTURING COMPANY      Page 01
                        Personnel Report


       DIVISION    DEPARTMENT                           EMPLOYEE
       NUMBER      NUMBER       DEPARTMENT SUPERVISOR   COUNT

         10          110        Tim Midden                10
         10          120        Rob Clifford              06
         10          130        Sarah Burnside            05
         10          140        Kristen Frame             13
         10          150        Kelly Bianco              30
         20          210        Joe Arsenault             27
         20          220        Sonia Reymon              14
         20          230        Brian Walsh               04
         30          310        Josh Tunney               02
         30          320        Steve Obetz               12
```

FIGURE 7.4 Program Output for CHAP7A

```
                RAINTRAX MANUFACTURING COMPANY        Page 02
                        Personnel Report


    DIVISION     DEPARTMENT                              EMPLOYEE
     NUMBER        NUMBER      DEPARTMENT SUPERVISOR      COUNT

       30           330        Scott Henderson              18
       30           340        John Brewster               03
       40           410        Brad Deckman                10
       40           420        Jason Hailey                10
       40           430        Larry Tuze                  20
       40           440        Kurtis Nuzum                24
       40           450        Nichole Deer                10
       40           460        Amy Lacomb                  05
       50           510        Linda Perry                 07
       50           520        Franklin Smalley            12

                RAINTRAX MANUFACTURING COMPANY        Page 03
                        Personnel Report


    DIVISION     DEPARTMENT                              EMPLOYEE
     NUMBER        NUMBER      DEPARTMENT SUPERVISOR      COUNT

       60           610        Robert Hall                 18
       60           620        Adam Uffner                 03
       60           630        Ron Null                    20
       70           710        Mike Redman                 19
       70           720        Jennifer Deihl              06


    TOTAL EMPLOYEE COUNT:                                 308
```

FIGURE 7.4 (cont.)

```
50              PACK    DBLWORD,IEMPLS
51              CVB     5,DBLWORD
```

The above statements mean: Pack the number of employees (IEMPLS) and place the result in DBLWORD. Then convert the packed-decimal value to binary and store it in register 5.

```
52              CLC     EODFLAG,ISUPVR
```

The above statement means: Compare the supervisor's name to End, the contents of the EODFLAG, and set the condition code. Once again, we are using a trailer record to detect the end of the file. The last record has End coded for supervisor's name.

```
53              BE      LEAVE
```

If the contents of EODFLAG and ISUPVR are equal, then control branches to the statement labeled LEAVE. Otherwise, control falls through and executes the next instruction.

```
54              BAL     3,PROCESS
```

The above statement means: Store the address of the next statement in register 3 and branch to the PROCESS module.

```
55              C       9,MAXLINES
```

The above statement means: Compare the maximum number of lines allowed per page to the line count, stored in register 9, and set the condition code.

```
56              BL      PRTDTL
```

The above statement means: If the line count is less than MAXLINE, then branch to the statement labeled PRTDTL. Otherwise, fall through and branch to the HEADINGS module.

```
57              BAL     4,HEADINGS
```

The above statement means: Store the address of the next instruction in register 4 and branch to HEADINGS.

```
           58 PRTDTL    BAL    3,OUTPUT
```

The above statement means: Store the address of the next statement in register 3 and branch to the `OUTPUT` module to print the detail line.

```
           59           B      DETAIL
```

The above statement means: Branch to the top of the loop and repeat the detail processing.

```
           60 LEAVE     BR     10
```

The above statement means: Branch back to the `MAINLINE` beginning at the address specified by the register operand.

PERFORMING CONTROL BREAKS

If the input records are arranged in ascending order according to a control field (such as customer number), then we can process the file in a special way to produce group totals or subtotals. A subtotal is part of the overall total, which is accumulated and printed in relationship to a control group.

For example, when the control field of the current record equals that of the previous, then the input is added to the subtotal for the related records. On the other hand, when the control fields change, then the program executes a control break, the previous subtotal is printed, and the input is added to the subtotal for the new group.

Control break processing involves grouping related records and then processing them together as a group. One or more subtotals may be accumulated for any given group. Hence, the control field is used to detect a change in the group and to determine when to print and clear the subtotals before moving on to the next group.

As an example, suppose the previous and current customer numbers—the control fields—are equal to 103. Therefore, we add the current sales amount to the group subtotal for customer number 103 as shown in Fig. 7.5.

On the other hand, a control break occurs when the customer number changes from 103 to 104. When the control break is detected, the group subtotal for customer number 103 ($6,350.00) is printed. Then, the subtotal field is reset to zero in preparation for the next group (104).

After all the data has been processed, the subtotal for the last group (104) is printed, along with the report total ($8,250.00).

The pseudocode version of the control break routine is shown in Fig. 7.6.

```
                    Customer Accounts
         Customer Number        Sales Amount

              103                 $1,400.00
              103                 $1,200.00
              103                 $2,000.00
              103                 $1,750.00

         Sales subtotal:          $6,350.00

              104                 $1,000.00
              104                 $ 900.00

         Sales subtotal:          $1,900.00

         ** Report total:         $8,250.00
```

FIGURE 7.5 Control Break Processing

```
                :
    If previous customer ≠ current customer
       Add 3 to line counter
       Print customer subtotal
       Set customer subtotal to zero
       Set previous customer = current customer
                :
```

FIGURE 7.6 Control Break Logic

SAMPLE PROGRAM CHAP7B

This program illustrates the use of page and control breaks. by producing the personnel report shown for the Raintrax Manufacturing Company. Sample program CHAP7B is shown in Fig. 7.7; the program's output is shown in Fig. 7.8.

Note the input is the same as the input for sample program CHAP7A. However, sample program CHAP7B uses the division number as a control field to process the data. Note also that the input is arranged in ascending order by division. This is significant to the operation of the program. Control break processing requires that the control fields be arranged in either ascending or descending order. Otherwise, a break will occur each time the control fields change values.

Input data:

A partial list of the input follows.

(1–2)	(3–5)	(6–25)	(26–27)
		Department	
Division #	**Department #**	**Supervisor**	**Employees**
10	110	Tim Midden	10
10	120	Rob Clifford	06
10	130	Sarah Burnside	05
10	140	Kristen Frame	13
10	150	Kelly Bianco	30
20	210	Joe Arsenault	27
		⋮	
		⋮	
00	000	End	00

Processing functions:

Print twenty lines per page

Accumulate division subtotals for employees

Accumulate total employees

Program output (Control Break Report):

```
         RAINTRAX MANUFACTURING COMPANY       Page 01
                 Personnel Report


   DIVISION    DEPARTMENT                              EMPLOYEE
   NUMBER       NUMBER       DEPARTMENT SUPERVISOR      COUNT

     10          110         Tim Midden                  10
     10          120         Rob Clifford                06
     10          130         Sarah Burnside              05
     10          140         Kristen Frame               13
     10          150         Kelly Bianco                30

   DIVISION TOTAL:                                       64

     20          210         Joe Arsenault               27
                                  :
                                  :
```

Program pseudocode:
```
START
Read data
Set previous division = current division
Initialize registers
Set line counter to 0
Add 1 to page counter
Advance to the next page
Print titles, page number, and column headings
LOOP until no more data
   If previous division ≠ current division
      Add 3 to line counter
      Print division total
      Set division total to zero
      Set previous division = current division
   Accumulate division total
   Accumulate report total
   If line counter > 20
      Set line counter to 0
      Add 1 to page counter
      Advance to the next page
      Print titles, page number, and column headings
   Add 1 to line counter
   Print detail line
   Read data
End LOOP
Print report total
END
```

DISSECTION OF SAMPLE PROGRAM CHAP7B

Review the program carefully. Notice the similarities between this program and sample program CHAP7A. Note also the three major changes made to incorporate the subtotal processing:

1. A record was read from the MAINLINE. This special read, commonly referred to as the priming read, was placed at the top of the mainline to begin the processing. It retrieves the first record and "sets the stage" for subsequent processing by allowing us to set the previous division equal to the current division.

```
 1   *--------------- RAINTRAX PERSONNEL REPORT ----------------
 2   *     This program demonstrates page and control breaks.
 3   *
 4   *              PROGRAM-ID:  CHAP7B
 5   *              PROGRAMMER:  David M. Collopy
 6   *              RUN DATE:    mm/dd/yy
 7   ***************************************************************
 8   CHAP7B   CSECT                                         (system
 9            PRINT NOGEN                                   use and
10            BALR  2,0                                     general
11            USING *,2                                housekeeping)
12            OPEN  IPTFILE,PRINTER                      open files
13   *--------------------------------------------------------------
14   *                    MAINLINE CONTROL
15   *--------------------------------------------------------------
16   MAINLINE BAL   3,GETDATA                           priming read
17            BAL   10,SETUP                           program setup
18            BAL   4,HEADINGS                         print headings
19            BAL   10,DETAIL                   detail processing loop
20            BAL   3,SUBTOTAL                         print subtotal
21            BAL   10,TOTAL                         print total line
22            B     EXIT                                 process exit
23   *--------------------------------------------------------------
24   *                    PROGRAM SET UP
25   *--------------------------------------------------------------
26   SETUP    MVC   PREVDIV,IDIV                   set divisions equal
27            SR    6,6                        set employee total to 0
28            SR    7,7                        set division total to 0
29            SR    8,8                           set page count to 0
30            BR    10                            return to mainline
31   *--------------------------------------------------------------
32   *                    PRINT HEADINGS
33   *--------------------------------------------------------------
34   HEADINGS SR    9,9                            set line count to 0
35            A     8,ONE                         add 1 to page count
36            CVD   8,DBLWORD                     convert page count...
37            UNPK  PAGE,DBLWORD                     ...to zone-decimal
38            MVZ   PAGE+1(1),PAGE                       replace sign
```

FIGURE 7.7 Sample Program CHAP7B: Demonstrates subtotal processing for the Raintrax Manufacturing Company. Employee head count is reported by division. The total number of nonsupervisory personnel is printed at the end of the report.

```
39              MVI     CCH1,C'1'                       skip to new page...
40              PUT     PRINTER,HDGLINE1                ...and print heading-1
41              MVI     CCH2,C' '                            single space...
42              PUT     PRINTER,HDGLINE2                ...and print heading-2
43              MVI     CCH3,C'-'                            triple space...
44              PUT     PRINTER,HDGLINE3                ...and print heading-3
45              MVI     CCH4,C' '                            single space...
46              PUT     PRINTER,HDGLINE4                ...and print heading-4
47              MVI     CCB,C' '                             single space...
48              PUT     PRINTER,BLKLINE                 ...and print blank line
49              BR      4                                    return to mainline
50     *-----------------------------------------------------------------
51     *                DETAIL PROCESSING LOOP
52     *-----------------------------------------------------------------
53     DETAIL   CLC     EODFLAG,ISUPVR                            test for EOD
54              BE      LEAVE                            if EOD, leave module
55              CLC     PREVDIV,IDIV                         compare divisions
56              BE      SKIPIT                         if equal, skip SUBTOTAL
57              BAL     3,SUBTOTAL                              print subtotal
58     SKIPIT   BAL     3,PROCESS                           accumulate totals
59              C       9,MAXLINES                    compare line count to 20
60              BL      PRTDTL                    if page not full, print line
61              BAL     4,HEADINGS                              print headings
62     PRTDTL   BAL     3,OUTPUT                             print detail line
63              BAL     3,GETDATA                                 looping read
64              B       DETAIL                                     repeat loop
65     LEAVE    BR      10                                  return to mainline
66     *-----------------------------------------------------------------
67     *                GET DATA
68     *-----------------------------------------------------------------
69     GETDATA  GET     IPTFILE,IPTRECD                            read record
70              PACK    DBLWORD,IEMPLS              convert nbr employees...
71              CVB     5,DBLWORD                                 ...to binary
72              BR      3                                     return to detail
73     *-----------------------------------------------------------------
74     *                ACCUMULATE TOTALS
75     *-----------------------------------------------------------------
76     PROCESS  AR      7,5                       add employees to div total
77              AR      6,5                       add employees to rpt total
78              BR      3                                     return to detail
```

FIGURE 7.7 (cont.)

```
 79  *----------------------------------------------------------------
 80  *                 PRINT DETAIL LINE
 81  *----------------------------------------------------------------
 82  OUTPUT    A      9,ONE                      add 1 to line count
 83            MVI    CCD,C' '                   single space output
 84            MVC    ODIV,IDIV                  move input to output
 85            MVC    ODEPT,IDEPT                move input to output
 86            MVC    OSUPVR,ISUPVR              move input to output
 87            MVC    OEMPLS,IEMPLS              move input to output
 88            PUT    PRINTER,DTLLINE            print detail line
 89            BR     3                          return to detail
 90  *----------------------------------------------------------------
 91  *                 PRINT SUBTOTAL
 92  *----------------------------------------------------------------
 93  SUBTOTAL  A      9,THREE                    add 3 to line count
 94            MVI    CCST,C'0'                  double space output
 95            CVD    7,DBLWORD                  convert div total...
 96            UNPK   SUBTOT,DBLWORD             ...to zone-decimal
 97            MVZ    SUBTOT+1(1),SUBTOT         replace sign
 98            PUT    PRINTER,SUBTLINE           print subtotal line
 99            SR     7,7                        set div total to 0
100            MVC    PREVDIV,IDIV               set divisions equal
101            MVI    CCB,C' '                   single space...
102            PUT    PRINTER,BLKLINE            ...and print blank line
103            BR     3                          return to detail
104  *----------------------------------------------------------------
105  *                 PRINT TOTAL LINE
106  *----------------------------------------------------------------
107  TOTAL     MVI    CCT,C'-'                   triple space output
108            CVD    6,DBLWORD                  convert employee total...
109            UNPK   TOTEMPLS,DBLWORD           ...to zone-decimal
110            MVZ    TOTEMPLS+2(1),TOTEMPLS     replace sign
111            PUT    PRINTER,TOTLINE            print total line
112            BR     10                         return to mainline
113  *
114  EXIT      CLOSE  IPTFILE,PRINTER            close files
115            EOJ                               end of job
116  ****************************************************************
117  *                 I/O FILE DEFINITIONS
118  *----------------------------------------------------------------
119  IPTFILE   DTFCD  DEVADDR=SYSIPT,IOAREA1=IPTBUFF,DEVICE=2501,    X
                     WORKA=YES,EOFADDR=EXIT
```

FIGURE 7.7 (cont.)

```
120 PRINTER   DTFPR DEVADDR=SYSLST,IOAREA1=PRTBUFF,DEVICE=1403,  X
                   CTLCHR=YES,WORKA=YES,BLKSIZE=80
121 *
122 IPTBUFF   DS    CL80                         input file buffer
123 PRTBUFF   DS    CL80                       printer file buffer
124 *---------------------------------------------------------------
125 *                RECORD/DATA DEFINITIONS
126 *---------------------------------------------------------------
127 IPTRECD   DS    0CL80                   I N P U T   R E C O R D
128 IDIV      DS    CL2       (01 - 02)             division number
129 IDEPT     DS    CL3       (03 - 05)           department number
130 ISUPVR    DS    CL20      (06 - 25)       department supervisor
131 IEMPLS    DS    CL2       (26 - 27)         number of employees
132           DS    CL53      (28 - 80)                      unused
133 *
134 HDGLINE1  DS    0CL80               H E A D I N G   L I N E - 1
135 CCH1      DS    CL1                             carriage control
136           DC    CL24' '                                   unused
137           DC    CL30'RAINTRAX MANUFACTURING COMPANY'
138           DC    CL7' '
139           DC    CL5'Page '
140 PAGE      DS    CL2
141           DC    CL11' '
142 *
143 HDGLINE2  DS    0CL80               H E A D I N G   L I N E - 2
144 CCH2      DS    CL1                             carriage control
145           DC    CL31' '
146           DC    CL16'Personnel Report'
147           DC    CL32' '
148 *
149 HDGLINE3  DS    0CL80               H E A D I N G   L I N E - 3
150 CCH3      DS    CL1                             carriage control
151           DC    CL9' '
152           DC    CL11'DIVISION'
153           DC    CL37'DEPARTMENT'
154           DC    CL22'EMPLOYEE'
155 *
156 HDGLINE4  DS    0CL80               H E A D I N G   L I N E - 4
157 CCH4      DS    CL1                             carriage control
158           DC    CL10' '
159           DC    CL12'NUMBER'
160           DC    CL11'NUMBER'
```

FIGURE 7.7 (cont.)

```
161            DC     CL25'DEPARTMENT SUPERVISOR'
162            DC     CL21'COUNT'
163  *
164  DTLLINE   DS     0CL80                    D E T A I L   L I N E
165  CCD       DS     CL1          (01 - 01)         carriage control
166            DC     CL12' '      (02 - 13)                   unused
167  ODIV      DS     CL2          (14 - 15)          division number
168            DC     CL9' '       (16 - 24)                   unused
169  ODEPT     DS     CL3          (25 - 27)        department number
170            DC     CL7' '       (28 - 34)                   unused
171  OSUPVR    DS     CL20         (35 - 54)    department supervisor
172            DC     CL7' '       (55 - 61)                   unused
173  OEMPLS    DS     CL2          (62 - 63)      number of employees
174            DC     CL17' '      (64 - 80)                   unused
175  *
176  SUBTLINE  DS     0CL80                  S U B T O T A L   L I N E
177  CCST      DS     CL1                              carriage control
178            DC     CL9' '
179            DC     CL51'DIVISION TOTAL:'
180  SUBTOT    DS     CL2
181            DC     CL17' '
182  *
183  TOTLINE   DS     0CL80                        T O T A L   L I N E
184  CCT       DS     CL1                              carriage control
185            DC     CL9' '
186            DC     CL50'TOTAL EMPLOYEE COUNT:'
187  TOTEMPLS  DS     CL3
188            DC     CL17' '
189  *
190  BLKLINE   DS     0CL80                        B L A N K   L I N E
191  CCB       DS     CL1                              carriage control
192            DC     CL79' '
193  *
194  MAXLINES  DC     F'20'           maximum details lines per page
195  EODFLAG   DC     CL3'End'                      end of data flag
196  ONE       DC     F'1'                                 constant
197  THREE     DC     F'3'                                 constant
198  PREVDIV   DS     CL2                          previous division
199  DBLWORD   DS     D                      temporary holding area
200            END    CHAP7B
```

FIGURE 7.7 (cont.)

```
            RAINTRAX MANUFACTURING COMPANY         Page 01
                     Personnel Report


   DIVISION      DEPARTMENT                              EMPLOYEE
   NUMBER          NUMBER      DEPARTMENT SUPERVISOR      COUNT

     10             110        Tim Midden                  10
     10             120        Rob Clifford                06
     10             130        Sarah Burnside              05
     10             140        Kristen Frame               13
     10             150        Kelly Bianco                30

   DIVISION TOTAL:                                         64

     20             210        Joe Arsenault               27
     20             220        Sonia Reymon                14
     20             230        Brian Walsh                 04

   DIVISION TOTAL:                                         45

     30             310        Josh Tunney                 02
     30             320        Steve Obetz                 12
     30             330        Scott Henderson             18
     30             340        John Brewster               03

   DIVISION TOTAL:                                         35
```

FIGURE 7.8 Program Output for CHAP7B

```
                RAINTRAX MANUFACTURING COMPANY         Page 02
                       Personnel Report

 DIVISION      DEPARTMENT                              EMPLOYEE
  NUMBER        NUMBER       DEPARTMENT SUPERVISOR      COUNT

    40            410        Brad Deckman                 10
    40            420        Jason Hailey                 10
    40            430        Larry Tuze                   20
    40            440        Kurtis Nuzum                 24
    40            450        Nichole Deer                 10
    40            460        Amy Lacomb                   05

 DIVISION TOTAL:                                          79

    50            510        Linda Perry                  07
    50            520        Franklin Smalley             12

 DIVISION TOTAL:                                          19

    60            610        Robert Hall                  18
    60            620        Adam Uffner                  03
    60            630        Ron Null                     20

 DIVISION TOTAL:                                          41


                RAINTRAX MANUFACTURING COMPANY         Page 03
                       Personnel Report


 DIVISION      DEPARTMENT                              EMPLOYEE
  NUMBER        NUMBER       DEPARTMENT SUPERVISOR      COUNT

    70            710        Mike Redman                  19
    70            720        Jennifer Deihl               06

 DIVISION TOTAL:                                          25


 TOTAL EMPLOYEE COUNT:                                   308
```

FIGURE 7.8 (cont.)

2. Two statements were added to the SETUP module. Note that the MVC is used to move a copy of the input division to the previous division, a necessary step before the processing begins. For the first record, we have no previous division. By copying the control field to the previous division, we can avoid an untimely break on the first record.
3. Register 7 was added to the SETUP module. It is initialized to zero and used to hold the division subtotal. Sample program CHAP7B uses the division number as the control field to perform the subtotal processing. When division changes values, the program executes a control break and prints the subtotal for the previous division.

DETAIL PROCESSING LOOP:

```
53 DETAIL    CLC    EODFLAG,ISUPVR
54           BE     LEAVE
```

The above statements mean: Test for the end of the file indicator and branch to LEAVE when the supervisor's name equals End.

```
55           CLC    PREVDIV,IDIV
```

The above statement means: Compare previous division to the input division number and set the condition code based upon the outcome.

```
56           BE     SKIPIT
```

The above statement means: If the division codes are equal, skip the SUBTOTAL module and continue processing the current division.

```
57           BAL    3,SUBTOTAL
```

The above statement means: If the division codes are not equal, store the address of the next instruction in register 3 and branch to SUBTOTAL and perform the processing given there.

```
58           BAL    3,PROCESS
59           C      9,MAXLINES
60           BL     PRTDTL
61           BAL    4,HEADINGS
62 PRTDTL    BAL    3,OUTPUT
```

Since the above code is the same as the code for sample program CHAP7A, we will not review it here.

```
            63              BAL     3,GETDATA
```

The above statement means: Store the address of the next instruction in register 3 and branch to GETDATA. Since this statement is placed inside the loop, it is called the looping read statement. The priming read retrieves the first record and the looping read statement retrieves the rest of the file.

```
            64              B       DETAIL
```

The above statement means: Branch to the top of the loop and repeat the detail processing.

```
            65 LEAVE        BR      10
```

The above statement means: Branch back to the mainline beginning at the address specified by the register operand.

PRINT SUBTOTAL:

```
            93 SUBTOTAL A           9,THREE
```

The above statement means: Add 3 to the line count stored in register 9 (1 for a blank line before, 1 for the subtotal line, and 1 for a blank line after).

```
            94              MVI     CCST,C'0'
```

The above statement means: Move zero to carriage control of the subtotal line to double-space the output. The double space is used to separate the last detail line printed from the subtotal line.

```
            95              CVD     7,DBLWORD
            96              UNPK    SUBTOT,DBLWORD
            97              MVZ     SUBTOT+1(1),SUBTOT
            98              PUT     PRINTER,SUBTLINE
```

Statements 95–98 prepare the output for the printer by converting the subtotal from binary to zone-decimal. The sign is replaced and the subtotal line printed.

```
            99              SR      7,7
```

The above statement means: Subtract register 7 from register 7 to reset the subtotal to zero.

```
            100             MVC     PREVDIV,IDIV
```

The above statement means: Move the input division to previous division. This move is used to set up processing for the next division group.

```
            101             MVI     CCB,C' '
            102             PUT     PRINTER,BLKLINE
```

The above statements mean: Move a space to carriage control of the blank line to single-space the output. A single blank line is used to separate the subtotal from the first detail line of the next division group.

```
            103             BR      3
```

The above statement means: Branch back to the detail module beginning at the address specified by the register operand.

KEY REVIEW TERMS

Define the following terms:

looping read	page break	report total
page counter	subtotal	priming read
control break	control field	line counter

REVIEW EXERCISES

1. Translate the page break routine shown in Fig. 7.2 into Assembler statements.
*2. Translate the control break routine shown in Fig. 7.6 into Assembler statements.
3. Explain what happens when a page break is encountered by the program.
*4. After the priming read, why is it necessary to initialize the previous division to the value of the current division?
5. Data for the control break program was arranged in ascending order. Would the program work if the data were arranged in descending order? Explain your answer.

6. Is there a difference between a priming read and looping read? In what way do they enhance the programming structure developed thus far?

PROGRAMMING EXERCISES

Instructions: For each exercise, design the pseudocode and write the modular structured program to produce the given output. Model your program after samples presented in this chapter. Verify your output.

1. Video store: Write a program to produce an inventory report for the Parker Video Store. Use the following format for the input:

Columns	Field Names
01–06	Viewing category/type
07–09	Tape number
34–35	Quantity on hand
36–37	Cost
40–41	Selling price

   Input data:

Type	Tape Number	Quantity	Cost	Selling Price
ACTION	200	10	$35	$70
ACTION	100	20	30	60
ACTION	300	12	20	40
COMEDY	850	15	25	50
COMEDY	410	20	20	40
DRAMA	900	14	35	70
DRAMA	800	11	33	65
DRAMA	500	16	35	70
DRAMA	400	12	35	79
SCIFI	700	20	30	60
SCIFI	600	18	21	43

   Processing functions:

   Print seven detail lines per page

   Profit = quantity × (price − cost)

   Accumulate and print totals for quantity and profit

Program output (Inventory Report):

```
P A R K E R   V I D E O   S T O R E        Page 1
         Inventory Report
              mm/dd/yy


             TAPE        QTY ON      POTENTIAL
  TYPE       NUMBER      HAND        PROFIT
  -------------------------------------------

  ACTION      200          10          350.00
    :          :            :             :
    :          :            :             :
    :          :            :             :
    :          :            :             :
  DRAMA       999          99          999.99


        P A R K E R   V I D E O   S T O R E      Page 2
               Inventory Report
                    mm/dd/yy


                   TAPE        QTY ON      POTENTIAL
        TYPE       NUMBER      HAND        PROFIT
        -------------------------------------------

        DRAMA       999          99          999.99
          :          :            :             :
          :          :            :             :
        SCIFI       999          99          999.99


        REPORT TOTAL:            999         9999.99
```

2. Modify the program in Exercise 1 to include control break processing. Group and list the video tapes by type and print a subtotal for the potential profit for each group. Print a blank line before and after the subtotal. Be sure to include the blank lines in your line count. Print eighteen detail lines per page. Model the logic after sample program CHAP7B.

```
         P A R K E R   V I D E O   S T O R E        Page 1
                 Inventory Report
                     mm/dd/yy


                  TAPE      QTY ON     POTENTIAL
         TYPE    NUMBER      HAND       PROFIT
         ------------------------------------------

         ACTION    200        10        350.00
           :        :          :           :
           :        :          :           :
         ACTION    300        12        240.00

         TYPE TOTAL:                    9999.99

         COMEDY    850        15        375.00
           :        :          :           :
           :        :          :           :
           :        :          :           :

              . . . . . . . . . . .


           :        :          :           :
         X-----X   999        99        999.99

         TYPE TOTAL:                    9999.99


         REPORT TOTAL:                  9999.99
```

3. Staff performance: Code an Assembler program to compute and print a sales staff performance report for Shawger-LaGrange Incorporated.

   Input data:

(1–4)	(5–24)	(30–34) Sales This Year	(35–39) Sales Last Year
Department	**Employee**		
D100	Zack Spencer	$6129	$5136
D100	Andy Payne	7200	7462
D100	Tony Frame	10982	8766
D100	Shirley Nichols	6174	7593

(1–4)	(5–24)	(30–34)	(35–39)
		Sales	Sales
Department	Employee	This Year	Last Year
D150	Kevin Berkley	$8851	$8075
D150	Dennis Swenson	5457	5123
D200	Beth Davidson	6349	6938
D200	Ron Hanzel	9915	7750
D200	Mike Ridenour	9422	6992
D300	Karen Smith	9638	9841
D300	Brad Parker	5029	7193
D300	Jon Stotts	7483	6739
D300	David Brown	8976	9124
D300	Victor Moore	10314	10690
D370	Larry Pifer	9683	10431
D370	Joanne Bradford	6134	7558
D370	Bobby Vaas	7892	9100
D370	Josh Williams	6807	5737
D400	Brian Reisinger	9114	10233
D400	Hilda Frazer	5929	5768
D400	Vern Cronin	10458	10335

Processing functions:

Print nine detail lines per page.

Difference in sales = this year – last year

If the difference is positive, print "+"; otherwise, print "–" on the detail line with the record.

Accumulate and print the total sales for this year and last year.

Accumulate and print the number of employees with sales over and under last year's sales.

Program output (Performance Report):

```
            SHAWGER - LAGRANGE INCORPORATED         Page 1
                 Sales Staff Performance
                        mm/dd/yy


                                ACCUMULATIVE SALES         SALES
 DEPT    SALES EMPLOYEE      THIS YEAR    LAST YEAR      UP/DOWN
 -----------------------------------------------------------------
 D100    Zack Spencer          6129.00      5136.00         +
 D100    Andy Payne            7200.00      7462.00         -
   :        :                     :            :            :
   :        :                     :            :            :
   :        :                     :            :            :
   :        :                     :            :            :
 XXXX    X-------------X       9999.99      9999.99         X



            SHAWGER - LAGRANGE INCORPORATED         Page 2
                 Sales Staff Performance
                        mm/dd/yy


                                ACCUMULATIVE SALES         SALES
 DEPT    SALES EMPLOYEE      THIS YEAR    LAST YEAR      UP/DOWN
 -----------------------------------------------------------------
 XXXX    X-------------X       9999.99      9999.99         X
   :        :                     :            :            :
   :        :                     :            :            :
   :        :                     :            :            :
   :        :                     :            :            :
 XXXX    X-------------X       9999.99      9999.99         X

 Report totals:                99999.99     99999.99

 Employees with sales up:      99
 Employees with sales down:    99
```

4. Modify Exercise 3 to include control break processing. Group and list employees by department and print a subtotal for this year's and last year's sales for each group. Print 26 detail lines per page.

5. Bonus pay: Write a page break program to calculate holiday bonus pay for the newspaper carriers of the Mayfield Reporter.

   Input data:

(1–4) District	(5–7) Route #	(8–27) Paper Carrier	(28–29) Subscribers	(30–31) Complaints
1010	121	Debra Boyd	40	0
1010	122	Timothy Hahns	38	0
1010	123	Mike Morgan	52	1
2005	210	Doug Allen	47	0
2005	211	Angie Davis	59	2
3100	342	Ryan Courtney	34	1
3100	343	Pat Anderson	61	3
3100	344	Teresa North	45	1
3100	345	Brian Wickline	43	0
4510	417	Joey Turner	57	0
4510	418	Andrew Bundy	39	4
4510	419	Jenney Vargus	41	2
5209	563	Seth Walters	55	1
5209	564	Donna White	52	0
5209	565	Sonia Paterson	49	3
5209	566	Betty Adams	60	2
6357	601	Dave Cooper	47	1
6357	602	Katrina Ryan	63	1

   Processing functions:

   Print seven detail lines per page.

   Bonus = (subscribers × $2) – (complaints × $5)

   Accumulate a total for bonus pay.

Program output (Bonus Pay Report):

```
                  THE MAYFIELD REPORTER
                    Bonus Pay Report                    Page 1
                       mm/dd/yy


     DISTRICT                                              BONUS
       CODE      ROUTE#    PAPER CARRIER    SUBSCRIBERS     PAY

       1010       121      Debra Boyd           40        $80.00
         :         :           :                :            :
         :         :           :                :            :
         :         :           :                :            :
         :         :           :                :            :
       9999       999      X-----------X        99        $99.99


                  THE MAYFIELD REPORTER
                    Bonus Pay Report                    Page 2
                       mm/dd/yy


     DISTRICT                                              BONUS
       CODE      ROUTE#    PAPER CARRIER    SUBSCRIBERS     PAY

       9999       999      X-----------X        99        $99.99
         :         :           :                :            :
         :         :           :                :            :
         :         :           :                :            :
         :         :           :                :            :
       9999       999      X-----------X        99        $99.99

     TOTAL BONUSES PAID:                                 $999.99
```

6. Change the program in Exercise 5 to include control break processing. Group the paper carriers by district and print a subtotal for bonus pay for each group. Print eighteen detail lines per page.

8 PACKED-DECIMAL OPERATIONS

OVERVIEW

Learning Objectives
Packed-Decimal Data
Packed-Decimal Operations
Packed-Decimal DC Statement
Packed-Decimal DS Statement
Add Packed (AP) Instruction
Zero and Add Packed (ZAP) Instruction
Subtract Packed (SP) Instruction
Multiply Packed (MP) Instruction
Divide Packed (DP) Instruction
Compare Packed (CP) Instruction
Sample Program CHAP8
Key Review Terms
Review Exercises
Programming Exercises

LEARNING OBJECTIVES

After reading this chapter and completing the exercises, the reader should be able to:

- code statements to convert zone-decimal constants to packed-decimal.
- define packed-decimal constants and storage variables.
- design, write, and test structured programs using packed-decimal operations.
- discuss the advantages of using packed-decimal operations.

PACKED-DECIMAL DATA

Beginning in Chapter 2, we have studied how to write Assembler programs using binary operations. Now, we will learn how to write Assembler programs using a different set of commands—packed-decimal operations.

Remember, zone-decimal represents data in character form, and each character occupies one byte of storage. Likewise, numeric data is stored internally in zone-decimal format with one digit per byte. As an example, consider the decimal value 1234 and its zone-decimal equivalent:

```
ZONE-DECIMAL FORMAT: F1 F2 F3 F4

Note: byte F1 = 1111 0001        └── sign
```

Each byte (eight binary digits) is made up of a zone character (F) and a decimal digit. The zone character F in the right-most byte represents the sign of the number. The spaces between the bytes are not part of the zone-decimal format. They were added to separate the bytes, so that they would be easier to read.

Assembler has a set of commands that processes data in decimal form. Hence, it isn't always necessary to convert numeric values to binary, unless there is a need to increase processing speed.

We can save storage space by converting (packing) numeric zone-decimal data to decimal. The Pack statement performs this conversion for us. Consider, for example, the zone-decimal value `F1F2F3F4` and its packed-decimal equivalent:

```
PACKED-DECIMAL FORMAT: 01 23 4C
```

Packed-Decimal Operations

Sign Character	Valve
F, C	positive
B, D	negative

TABLE 8.1 Sign Characters

Decimal storage items pack two digits into each byte, except for the last byte. The sign occupies the right-most four bits of the last byte. The C represents the sign of the constant. (Refer to Table 8.1 for the sign characters.)

Note the leading zero in the first byte. It was placed there to pad the byte to two digits. Since each byte must hold two digits, Assembler pads any single-digit byte with a zero on the left.

Once numeric data have been converted to decimal, we may use any of the packed-decimal operations to process them. The conversion process follows these steps:

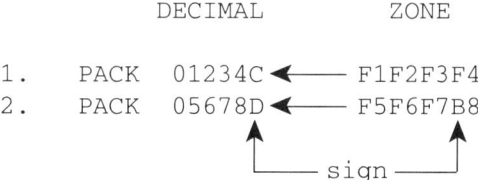

The zone bits are dropped during the conversion and the decimal digits are packed two per byte. Packing occurs from low order (right) to high order (left), and the sign is placed in the right-most four bits of the last byte. If the zone sign character is either a C or an F, then the number is positive and the decimal sign is set to C. For negative numbers (zone sign B or D), the decimal sign is set to D.

PACKED-DECIMAL OPERATIONS

We will now examine in detail the following new statements:

    DC   Define Packed Decimal Constant
    DS   Define Packed Decimal Storage
    AP   Add Packed
    ZAP   Zero and Add Packed

Chapter 8: Packed-Decimal Operations

SP Subtract Packed
MP Multiply Packed
DP Divide Packed
CP Compare Packed

Programming in packed-decimal has advantages. First, decimal numbers are easier to work with than binary or hexadecimal numbers. We're all familiar with decimal arithmetic and use it daily.

Second, variable names are used as operands instead of registers. This difference has three advantages: (1) It's easier to remember the name of a variable than it is to recall a register number. For example, variable names like `PAYRATE`, `ACCTNUM`, `INCOME`, and `EXPENSE` tell us something about their data, whereas register numbers, such as 3, 5, 7, and 10, do not relate in an obvious way to the data they contain. (2) We need never worry about running out of names for operands. For programs using binary operations, there are a limited number of registers available. And while registers may be reused by constantly storing and loading data, this technique is inconvenient and increases the complexity of the program. (3) Using decimal operations and data manipulation reduces memory space by "packing" two digits per byte. This advantage is not as significant today, when add-on memory is relatively cheap, as it was twenty years ago, when memory was limited and expensive. However, memory use is still a concern.

One disadvantage to programming in packed-decimal is a loss of speed. However, unless you are writing an application that requires speed while processing hundreds upon hundreds of mathematical operations, you should program in packed-decimal.

NOTE: The rules of algebra apply to the use of signs for packed-decimal as they do for binary. Field lengths for operands may vary. They do not have to be the same size. For AP, SP, MP, and DP statements, you should use the larger of the two fields as the first operand, since it receives the result of the operation.

PACKED-DECIMAL DEFINE CONSTANT (DC) STATEMENT

Format:

```
1--------10----16-----------columns
Label    DC    P'constant'              Label = constant
```

Purpose: To define and initialize packed-decimal constants. The P in column 16 indicates that the constant enclosed within single quotes is stored internally in packed-decimal format.

Enough bytes are allocated implicitly in memory to hold the constant. The LABEL field assigns a symbolic name to the storage area and is initialized to the value specified by the decimal constant.

Examples:

```
    Label    DC      P'constant'    PACKED-DECIMAL       LENGTH
    1--------10----16----------------------------------------
1.  PNUM1    DC      P'1234'        01 23 4C             3 bytes
2.  PNUM2    DC      P'655'         65 5C                2 bytes
3.  PNUM3    DC      P'01023'       01 02 3C             3 bytes
4.  NBRX     DC      P'18'          01 8C                2 bytes
5.  NEG      DC      P'-173'        17 3D                2 bytes
6.  SIZE     DC      PL4'6880'      00 06 88 0C          4 bytes
```

Note that each byte contains two digits. If the constant specified by the DC statement does not have enough digits to fill a byte, then Assembler pads the empty positions on the left with zeros. Examples 1, 4, and 6 illustrate zero padding.

Look at the negative constant defined in Example 5. In packed decimal, the minus sign is converted to the character D and is placed at the end of the number.

Now look at Example 6. The PL4 beginning in column 16 is coded explicitly to set the length of the constant to four bytes. However, the other examples have their lengths defined implicitly by the constant. In other words, the number of digits in the constant determines the actual number of bytes allocated to the variable.

PACKED-DECIMAL DEFINE STORAGE (DS) STATEMENT

Format:

```
1--------10----16---------columns
Label    DS      PLn                   Label = n-byte field
```

Purpose: To define packed-decimal variables. As you may recall, storage items are part of neither the input nor the output, but are required by the program in order to carry out the processing functions.

Chapter 8: Packed-Decimal Operations

The Label field refers to the label or name assigned to the program variable and DS stands for define storage. The `PLn` beginning in column 16 stands for Packed Length and allocates n bytes of storage to the decimal variable.

Examples:

```
                                       STORAGE
     Label    DS     PLn         SPACE ALLOCATED
     1--------10----16-----------------------
1.   PHOURS   DS     PL3             3 bytes
2.   PAYMNT   DS     PL4             4 bytes
3.   PRATE    DS     PL5             5 bytes
4.   LINECNT  DS     PL2             2 bytes
```

For the above examples, the `PLn` defines the variables as packed-decimal and allocates the specified number of bytes for each.

Look at the first example. Assembler allocates a 3-byte storage area to the variable `PHOURS`, but it does not initialize it. Whatever resides in memory at those three bytes becomes its value. This means that it is possible to have garbage stored in `PHOURS`. This is not significant, as long as we move the correct value to `PHOURS` prior to using the variable.

ADD PACKED (AP) INSTRUCTION

Format:

```
1--------10----16---------columns
         AP     S1,S2                         S1 = S1 + S2
                ←
```

Purpose: To add packed-decimal constants. Add Pack computes the sum for the decimal constants located at storage operand (`S2`) and storage operand (`S1`). The arrow indicates that the resulting sum is placed in `S1`, thus destroying the original value stored there. The contents of `S2` remain unchanged and may be used again as needed.

Example:

```
          AP      ANSWER,NUM                  ANSWER | NUM
                  :                                  |
                  :                BEFORE:   121C    |  8C
                  :                AFTER:    129C    |  8C
ANSWER    DC      P'121'
NUM       DC      P'8'
```

During execution, the sum 121 + 8 is computed and stored in the ANSWER operand. The before and after values for the NUM operand remain the same (8C). Note that ANSWER = 121C + 8C, or ANSWER = 129C:

```
          AP      ANSWER,NUM  ───▶  ANSWER  =  ANSWER  +  NUM
                                    ANSWER  =   121C   +   8C
                                    ANSWER  =   129C
```

ZERO AND ADD PACKED (ZAP) INSTRUCTION

Format:

```
1--------10----16---------columns
          ZAP     S1,S2                            S1 = 0 + S2
                  ←
```

Purpose: To initialize packed-decimal storage items. ZAP may be used to initialize a decimal operand to a specific value or to move a decimal constant from one operand to another, usually from a short operand (one with few bytes) to a longer one.

According to the general format, the value of the first storage operand (S1) is set to zero. Then ZAP computes the sum of the values stored at S2 and S1. In short, the decimal value stored at S2 is copied to S1.

Examples:

1. ZAP   COUNTER,ZERO

	COUNTER	ZERO
BEFORE:	100C	0C
AFTER:	000C	0C

NOTE: COUNTER = 000C + 0C or COUNTER = 000C:

```
ZAP   COUNTER,ZERO  ──▶  COUNTER = COUNTER + ZERO
                         COUNTER =   000C   +  0C
                         COUNTER =   000C
```

2. ZAP   OFFSET,NUM

	OFFSET	NUM
BEFORE:	17250C	020D
AFTER:	00020D	020D

NOTE: OFFSET = 00000C + 020D or OFFSET = 00020D:

```
ZAP   OFFSET,NUM  ──▶  OFFSET = OFFSET + NUM
                       OFFSET = 00000C + 020D
                       OFFSET = 00020D
```

3. ZAP   LONG,SHORT

	LONG	SHORT
BEFORE:	56134C	9C
AFTER:	00009C	9C

NOTE: LONG = 00000C + 9C or LONG = 00009C:

```
ZAP   LONG,SHORT  ──▶  LONG  =  LONG   + SHORT
                       LONG  =  00000C +   9C
                       LONG  =  00009C
```

Example 1 initializes COUNTER to zero, and Examples 2 and 3 set the first operand equal to the value of the second. In Example 2, note that the sign of the negative constant NUM has been preserved.

SUBTRACT PACKED (SP) INSTRUCTION

Format:

```
1--------10----16---------columns
        SP    S1,S2                        S1 = S1 - S2
              ←
```

Purpose: To subtract packed-decimal constants. The Subtract Packed instruction computes the difference between the decimal constants located at storage operands S1 and S2. Note the direction of the operation. According to the notation (S1 = S1 – S2), the difference replaces the original value of S1 and the contents of S2 remain unchanged.

Example:

```
SP     FIRST,SECOND              FIRST  | SECOND
                                 -------+-------
                        BEFORE:   500C  |  300C
                        AFTER:    200C  |  300C
```

During execution, the decimal value 300 is subtracted from 500. The difference, 200, is placed in the FIRST operand. Note that FIRST = 500C – 300C, or FIRST = 200C:

```
SP     FIRST,SECOND ──────▶  FIRST  =  FIRST  -  SECOND

                             FIRST  =  500C   -  300C
                             FIRST  =  200C
```

MULTIPLY PACKED (MP) INSTRUCTION

Format:

```
1--------10----16---------columns
        MP    S1,S2                        S1 = S1 × S2
              ←
```

Chapter 8: Packed-Decimal Operations

Purpose: To multiply packed-decimal constants. The Multiply Pack instruction computes the product of the decimal value stored at the first operand (S1) and the value located at the second operand (S2). The resulting product has no impact on the value of S2; however, it does replace the previous value stored at S1.

As a rule, the first operand (S1) should have as many bytes of leading zeros as there are bytes in the multiplier (S2); otherwise, the multiplicand will not be large enough to store the product.

There is one exception to this rule: If we know the maximum size (in bytes) for the multiplicand and the multiplier, we can determine the exact number of bytes required by the multiplicand to hold the largest possible product.

Example:

```
MP      NUM1,NUM2
```

	NUM1	NUM2
BEFORE:	0000025C	011C
AFTER:	0000275C	011C

When the above statement executes, the decimal product 25 × 11 is computed and placed in NUM1. The second operand, NUM2, remains unchanged as a result of the multiplication. Note that NUM1 = 0000025C × 011C, or NUM1 = 0000275C:

```
MP      NUM1,NUM2   ⟶   NUM1  =  NUM1      ×  NUM2
                        NUM1  =  0000025C  ×  011C
                        NUM1  =  0000275C
```

DIVIDE PACKED (DP) INSTRUCTION

Format:

```
1--------10----16---------columns
         DP    S1,S2                           S1 = S1 ÷ S2
               ←
```

Purpose: To divide packed-decimal constants. The value of the first storage operand (S1) is divided by the contents of the second operand (S2). Both the resulting quotient and remainder are placed in S1, thus destroying the

Divide Packed (DP) Instruction

previous value stored there. The remainder occupies the right-most part of `S1`, while the quotient occupies the left. Execution of the division statement has no impact on the value stored at the second operand.

Example:

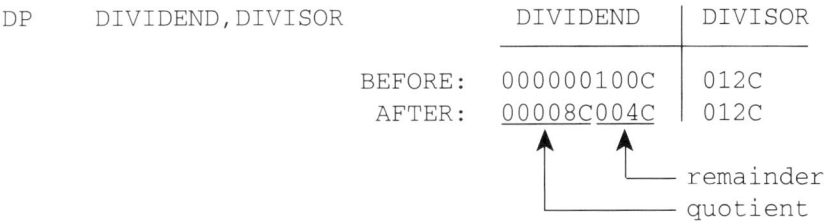

During the execution process, the decimal constant 100 is divided by 12. Both the resulting quotient (00008C) and the remainder (004C) are stored in `DIVIDEND`; each has its own sign. Note that `DIVIDEND` = 000000100C ÷ 012C, or `DIVIDEND` = 00008C (quotient) and 004C (remainder):

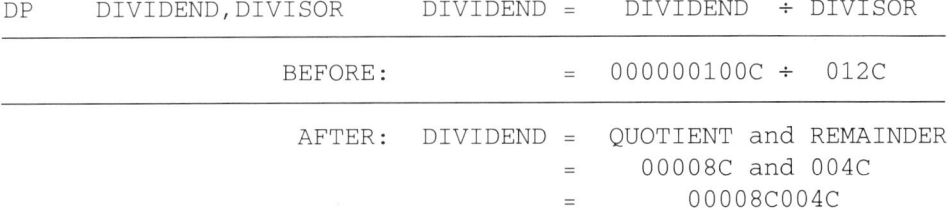

Care must be taken to assure that the first operand (`DIVIDEND`) is large enough to hold the quotient and the remainder. By definition, the remainder and `DIVISOR` occupy the same number of bytes. After the dividend is divided by the divisor, the remainder is placed in the right-most two bytes of `DIVIDEND`, and the quotient is stored in the remaining three bytes on the left (Fig. 8.1).

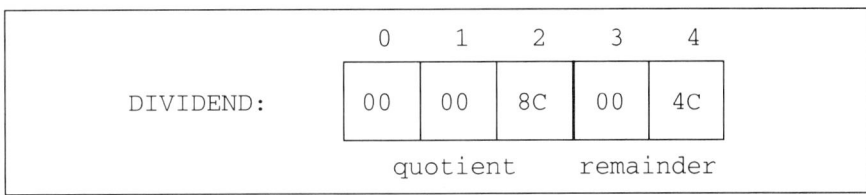

FIGURE 8.1 Dividend Operand after Executing DP

In Figure 8.1, we see that `DIVIDEND` occupies five bytes of memory. Remember, bytes are numbered starting with 0. We may reference either the quotient or the remainder by using the following relative addressing notation:

`DIVIDEND(3)`: Specifies that the quotient is located in the `DIVIDEND` operand, which is the first three bytes. The following Add statement illustrates how we may express the quotient as a relative part of the `DIVIDEND` operand.

```
AP     SUM,DIVIDEND(3)          add quotient to sum
```

`DIVIDEND+3(2)`: Specifies that the 2-byte remainder is located in the `DIVIDEND` operand, beginning with byte number 3. The following example illustrates how we may express the remainder in terms of its relative position within `DIVIDEND`.

```
ZAP    TOTAL,DIVIDEND+3(2)      initialize TOTAL to
                                value of the remainder.
```

COMPARE PACKED (CP) INSTRUCTION

Format:

```
1--------10----16---------columns              type A:B
        CP    S1,S2                 arithmetic compare
```

Purpose: To compare packed-decimal constants. This statement compares the contents of two packed-decimal operands and sets the condition code based on the outcome. The decimal constant located at the second storage operand (`S2`) is compared to the contents of the first (`S1`), which is the base operand.

Possible outcomes for the condition code are shown in Table 8.2:

Any one of the following branch statements may be used to test the condition code set by the Compare Packed instruction: BE, BNE, BL, BNL, BH and BNH. For more information on branch statements, refer to Chapter 6.

	Condition Codes	**CP** S1:S2
1.	1000	=
2.	0111	≠
3.	0010	>
4.	1101	≯
5.	0100	<
6.	1011	≮

TABLE 8.2 Arithmetic Condition Code Settings

Example:

```
      :
CP    MAXIMUM,INCOME
BE    EVEN
BH    TOOMUCH
AP    COUNT,ONE
      :
```

The decimal constants stored at operands MAXIMUM and INCOME are compared and the condition code set. If the constants are equal, then control branches to the statement in the program labeled EVEN. Otherwise, processing falls through to the Branch on High (BH) statement, where the condition code is tested for high. If MAXIMUM is greater than INCOME, then control skips to the statement labeled TOOMUCH. Otherwise, processing continues with the statement on the next line.

SAMPLE PROGRAM CHAP8

The specifications for sample program CHAP8 are the same as the specifications for sample program CHAP7B. As you may recall, sample program CHAP7B uses both page and control breaks to produce the personnel report for the Raintrax Manufacturing Company. Sample program CHAP8 is shown in Fig. 8.2; the program's output is shown in Fig. 8.3. A partial listing of the output follows:

```
            RAINTRAX MANUFACTURING COMPANY         Page 01
                     Personnel Report

DIVISION    DEPARTMENT                              EMPLOYEE
 NUMBER      NUMBER     DEPARTMENT SUPERVISOR        COUNT

   10          110      Tim Midden                     10
   10          120      Rob Clifford                   06
   10          130      Sarah Burnside                 05
   10          140      Kristen Frame                  13
   10          150      Kelly Bianco                   30

DIVISION TOTAL:                                        64

   20          210      Joe Arsenault                  27
                              :
                              :
```

You will notice that the output hasn't changed. However, the instructions that process the data have changed: Instead of binary instructions, the program uses primarily packed-decimal operations.

Although the pseudocode for sample program CHAP8 hasn't changed from the previous program's, we present it here as a review. Look over the logic before moving on to the program.

Pseudocode logic design:

    START
    Read data
    Set previous division = current division
    Initialize registers
    Set line counter to 0
    Add 1 to page counter
    Advance to the next page
    Print titles, page number, and column headings
    LOOP until no more data
      If previous division ≠ current division
        Add 3 to line counter
        Print division total
        Set division total to zero
        Set previous division = current division

> Accumulate division total
> Accumulate report total
> If line counter > 20
>   Set line counter to 0
>   Add 1 to page counter
>   Advance to the next page
>   Print titles, page number, and column headings
> Add 1 to line counter
> Print detail line
> Read data
> End LOOP
> Print report total
> END

DISSECTION OF SAMPLE PROGRAM CHAP8

Since most of the logic for this program was discussed in Chapter 7, we will highlight only the major functions performed by the program.

M A I N L I N E   C O N T R O L:

Six submodules are called by MAINLINE: GET DATA, PROGRAM SET UP, PRINT HEADINGS, DETAIL PROCESSING LOOP, PRINT SUBTOTAL, and PRINT TOTAL LINE. In brief, these modules perform the following tasks:

1. GET DATA: Retrieves the first record (priming read).
2. PROGRAM SET UP: Initializes the following decimal variables to zero: employee total, division total (the employee count subtotal), and page count.
3. PRINT HEADINGS: Increments page number, sets the line count to zero, and prints the report titles and headings at the top of the page.
4. DETAIL PROCESSING LOOP: Controls the detailed processing performed by the following modules: GET DATA, ACCUMULATE SUBTOTAL, PRINT HEADINGS, PRINT DETAIL LINE, and PRINT SUBTOTAL. Note that GET DATA and PRINT HEADINGS are called by MAINLINE as well as by DETAIL PROCESSING LOOP.

```
 1  *--------------- RAINTRAX PERSONNEL REPORT -----------------
 2  * This program demonstrates use of packed-decimal operations.
 3  *
 4  *               PROGRAM-ID: CHAP8
 5  *               PROGRAMMER: David M. Collopy
 6  *               RUN DATE:   mm/dd/yy
 7  **************************************************************
 8  CHAP8     CSECT                                        (system
 9            PRINT NOGEN                                  use and
10            BALR  2,0                                    general
11            USING *,2                               housekeeping)
12            OPEN  IPTFILE,PRINTER                     open files
13  *-------------------------------------------------------------
14  *                 MAINLINE CONTROL
15  *-------------------------------------------------------------
16  MAINLINE  BAL   3,GETDATA                           priming read
17            BAL   9,SETUP                            program setup
18            BAL   10,HEADINGS                        print headings
19            BAL   9,DETAIL                      detail processing loop
20            BAL   3,SUBTOTAL                         print subtotal
21            BAL   9,TOTAL                          print total line
22            B     EXIT                                 process exit
23  *-------------------------------------------------------------
24  *                 PROGRAM SET UP
25  *-------------------------------------------------------------
26  SETUP     MVC   PREVDIV,IDIV                   set divisions equal
27            ZAP   PTOTEMPL,ZERO               set employee total to 0
28            ZAP   PDIVTOT,ZERO                set division total to 0
29            ZAP   PPAGE,ZERO                     set page count to 0
30            BR    9                              return to mainline
31  *-------------------------------------------------------------
32  *                 PRINT HEADINGS
33  *-------------------------------------------------------------
34  HEADINGS  ZAP   LINECNT,ZERO                    set line count to 0
35            AP    PPAGE,ONE                      add 1 to page count
36            UNPK  PAGE,PPAGE                     convert page to ZD
37            MVI   CCH1,C'1'                       skip to new page...
38            PUT   PRINTER,HDGLINE1             ...and print heading-1
39            MVI   CCH2,C' '                           single space...
40            PUT   PRINTER,HDGLINE2             ...and print heading-2
```

FIGURE 8.2 Sample Program CHAP8: Packed-decimal version of the personnel report for the Raintrax Manufacturing Company.

```
41            MVI    CCH3,C'-'                       triple space...
42            PUT    PRINTER,HDGLINE3           ...and print heading-3
43            MVI    CCH4,C' '                       single space...
44            PUT    PRINTER,HDGLINE4           ...and print heading-4
45            MVI    CCB,C' '                        single space...
46            PUT    PRINTER,BLKLINE            ...and print blank line
47            BR     10                              return to mainline
48   *-----------------------------------------------------------------
49   *             DETAIL PROCESSING LOOP
50   *-----------------------------------------------------------------
51   DETAIL   CLC    EODFLAG,ISUPVR                       test for EOD
52            BE     LEAVE                      if EOD, leave module
53            CLC    PREVDIV,IDIV                    compare divisions
54            BE     SKIPIT                     if equal, skip SUBTOTAL
55            BAL    3,SUBTOTAL                         print subtotal
56   SKIPIT   BAL    3,PROCESS                      accumulate subtotal
57            CP     LINECNT,MAXLINES           compare line count to 20
58            BL     PRTDTL                     if page not full, print line
59            BAL    10,HEADINGS                        print headings
60   PRTDTL   BAL    3,OUTPUT                        print detail line
61            BAL    3,GETDATA                            looping read
62            B      DETAIL                               repeat loop
63   LEAVE    BR     9                               return to mainline
64   *-----------------------------------------------------------------
65   *             GET DATA
66   *-----------------------------------------------------------------
67   GETDATA  GET    IPTFILE,IPTRECD                        read record
68            PACK   PEMPLS,IEMPLS         convert nbr employees to PD
69            BR     3                                return to detail
70   *-----------------------------------------------------------------
71   *             ACCUMULATE TOTALS
72   *-----------------------------------------------------------------
73   PROCESS  AP     PDIVTOT,PEMPLS        add employees to div total
74            AP     PTOTEMPL,PEMPLS       add employees to rpt total
75            BR     3                                return to detail
76   *-----------------------------------------------------------------
77   *             PRINT DETAIL LINE
78   *-----------------------------------------------------------------
79   OUTPUT   AP     LINECNT,ONE                   add 1 to line count
80            MVI    CCD,C' '                      single space output
```

FIGURE 8.2 (cont.)

```
 81           MVC    ODIV,IDIV                   move input to output
 82           MVC    ODEPT,IDEPT                 move input to output
 83           MVC    OSUPVR,ISUPVR               move input to output
 84           MVC    OEMPLS,IEMPLS               move input to output
 85           PUT    PRINTER,DTLLINE                 print detail line
 86           BR     3                              return to detail
 87  *-----------------------------------------------------------------
 88  *                PRINT SUBTOTAL
 89  *-----------------------------------------------------------------
 90  SUBTOTAL AP     LINECNT,THREE               add 3 to line count
 91           MVI    CCST,C'0'                   double space output
 92           UNPK   SUBTOT,PDIVTOT         convert div total to ZD
 93           PUT    PRINTER,SUBTLINE             print subtotal line
 94           ZAP    PDIVTOT,ZERO                   set div total to 0
 95           MVC    PREVDIV,IDIV                set divisions equal
 96           MVI    CCB,C' '                         single spaces...
 97           PUT    PRINTER,BLKLINE           ...and print blank line
 98           BR     3                              return to detail
 99  *-----------------------------------------------------------------
100  *                PRINT TOTAL LINE
101  *-----------------------------------------------------------------
102  TOTAL    MVI    CCT,C'-'                    triple space output
103           UNPK   TOTEMPLS,PTOTEMPLS     convert empl total to ZD
104           PUT    PRINTER,TOTLINE                 print total line
105           BR     9                             return to mainline
106  *
107  EXIT     CLOSE  IPTFILE,PRINTER                       close files
108           EOJ                                          end of job
109  ****************************************************************
110  *                I/O FILE DEFINITIONS
111  *-----------------------------------------------------------------
112  IPTFILE  DTFCD  DEVADDR=SYSIPT,IOAREA1=IPTBUFF,DEVICE=2501,     X
                    WORKA=YES,EOFADDR=EXIT
113  PRINTER  DTFPR  DEVADDR=SYSLST,IOAREA1=PRTBUFF,DEVICE=1403,     X
                    CTLCHR=YES,WORKA=YES,BLKSIZE=80
114  *
115  IPTBUFF  DS     CL80                             input file buffer
116  PRTBUFF  DS     CL80                           printer file buffer
117  *-----------------------------------------------------------------
118  *                RECORD/DATA DEFINITIONS
119  *-----------------------------------------------------------------
```

FIGURE 8.2 (cont.)

```
120 IPTRECD   DS    0CL80                       I N P U T    R E C O R D
121 IDIV      DS    CL2         (01 - 02)              division number
122 IDEPT     DS    CL3         (03 - 05)            department number
123 ISUPVR    DS    CL20        (06 - 25)        department supervisor
124 IEMPLS    DS    CL2         (26 - 27)           number of employees
125           DS    CL53        (28 - 80)                        unused
126 *
127 HDGLINE1  DS    0CL80                     H E A D I N G    L I N E - 1
128 CCH1      DS    CL1                                    carriage control
129           DC    CL24' '                                          unused
130           DC    CL30'RAINTRAX MANUFACTURING COMPANY'
131           DC    CL7' '
132           DC    CL5'Page '
133 PAGE      DS    CL2
134           DC    CL11' '
135 *
136 HDGLINE2  DS    0CL80                     H E A D I N G    L I N E - 2
137 CCH2      DS    CL1                                    carriage control
138           DC    CL31' '
139           DC    CL16'Personnel Report'
140           DC    CL32' '
141 *
142 HDGLINE3  DS    0CL80                     H E A D I N G    L I N E - 3
143 CCH3      DS    CL1                                    carriage control
144           DC    CL9' '
145           DC    CL11'DIVISION'
146           DC    CL37'DEPARTMENT'
147           DC    CL22'EMPLOYEE'
148 *
149 HDGLINE4  DS    0CL80                     H E A D I N G    L I N E - 4
150 CCH4      DS    CL1                                    carriage control
151           DC    CL10' '
152           DC    CL12'NUMBER'
153           DC    CL11'NUMBER'
154           DC    CL25'DEPARTMENT SUPERVISOR'
155           DC    CL21'COUNT'
156 *
157 DTLLINE   DS    0CL80                           D E T A I L    L I N E
158 CCD       DS    CL1         (01 - 01)                 carriage control
159           DC    CL12' '     (02 - 13)                           unused
160 ODIV      DS    CL2         (14 - 15)                  division number
```

FIGURE 8.2 (cont.)

```
161            DC    CL9' '          (16 - 24)                         unused
162  ODEPT     DS    CL3             (25 - 27)              department number
163            DC    CL7' '          (28 - 34)                         unused
164  OSUPVR    DS    CL20            (35 - 54)          department supervisor
165            DC    CL7' '          (55 - 61)                         unused
166  OEMPLS    DS    CL2             (62 - 63)            number of employees
167            DC    CL17' '         (64 - 80)                         unused
168  *
169  SUBTLINE  DS    0CL80                         S U B T O T A L   L I N E
170  CCST      DS    CL1                                     carriage control
171            DC    CL9' '
172            DC    CL51'DIVISION TOTAL:'
173  SUBTOT    DS    CL2
174            DC    CL17' '
175  *
176  TOTLINE   DS    0CL80                                 T O T A L   L I N E
177  CCT       DS    CL1                                     carriage control
178            DC    CL9' '
179            DC    CL50'TOTAL EMPLOYEE COUNT:'
180  TOTEMPLS  DS    CL3
181            DC    CL17' '
182  *
183  BLKLINE   DS    0CL80                                 B L A N K   L I N E
184  CCB       DS    CL1                                     carriage control
185            DC    CL79' '
186  *
187  MAXLINES  DC    P'20'                     maximum detail lines per page
188  EODFLAG   DC    CL3'End'                            end of data flag
189  ZERO      DC    P'0'                                        constant
190  ONE       DC    P'1'                                        constant
191  THREE     DC    P'3'                                        constant
192  LINECNT   DS    PL2                                       line count
193  PPAGE     DS    PL2                                       page count
194  PREVDIV   DS    CL2                                  previous division
195  PEMPLS    DS    PL2                                         employees
196  PDIVTOT   DS    PL2                                    division total
197  PTOTEMPL  DS    PL3                        total number of employees
198            END   CHAP8
```

FIGURE 8.2 (cont.)

```
              RAINTRAX MANUFACTURING COMPANY         Page 01
                      Personnel Report


   DIVISION      DEPARTMENT                           EMPLOYEE
   NUMBER          NUMBER       DEPARTMENT SUPERVISOR   COUNT

     10             110         Tim Midden              10
     10             120         Rob Clifford            06
     10             130         Sarah Burnside          05
     10             140         Kristen Frame           13
     10             150         Kelly Bianco            30

   DIVISION TOTAL:                                      64

     20             210         Joe Arsenault           27
     20             220         Sonia Reymon            14
     20             230         Brian Walsh             04

   DIVISION TOTAL:                                      45

     30             310         Josh Tunney             02
     30             320         Steve Obetz             12
     30             330         Scott Henderson         18
     30             340         John Brewster           03

   DIVISION TOTAL:                                      35



              RAINTRAX MANUFACTURING COMPANY         Page 02
                      Personnel Report


   DIVISION      DEPARTMENT                           EMPLOYEE
   NUMBER          NUMBER       DEPARTMENT SUPERVISOR   COUNT

     40             410         Brad Deckman            10
     40             420         Jason Hailey            10
     40             430         Larry Tuze              20
```

FIGURE 8.3 Program Output for CHAP8

```
           40           440      Kurtis Nuzum            24
           40           450      Nichole Deer            10
           40           460      Amy Lacomb              05

    DIVISION TOTAL:                                      79

           50           510      Linda Perry             07
           50           520      Franklin Smalley        12


    DIVISION TOTAL:                                      19

           60           610      Robert Hall             18
           60           620      Adam Uffner             03
           60           630      Ron Null                20

    DIVISION TOTAL:                                      41



                    RAINTRAX MANUFACTURING COMPANY     Page 03
                              Personnel Report


        DIVISION     DEPARTMENT                        EMPLOYEE
        NUMBER        NUMBER       DEPARTMENT SUPERVISOR COUNT

           70           710      Mike Redman             19
           70           720      Jennifer Deihl          06

    DIVISION TOTAL:                                      25


    TOTAL EMPLOYEE COUNT:                               308
```

FIGURE 8.3 (cont.)

5. `PRINT SUBTOTAL`: Prints the division employee (total) subtotal line. This module too is called by `DETAIL PROCESSING LOOP` and `MAINLINE`.
6. `PRINT TOTAL LINE`: Prints the total number of employees at the end of the report. Control then returns to `MAINLINE`, where processing terminates.

D E T A I L   P R O C E S S I N G   L O O P:

Processing begins with the comparison on line 51, which checks for the end of file. The following Branch on Equal statement sends control back to `MAINLINE` when the trailer record is read. Otherwise, control falls through and executes the next sequential instruction.

On line 53, the program compares the current division number to the value of the previous division. If they are equal, control skips to `PROCESS` and adds the input employee count to the subtotal and the report total. If they are not equal, the program generates a control break, branches to `SUBTOTAL` to print the subtotal line, and then branches to `PROCESS` to increment the program totals. Upon returning, the computer encounters the Compare Pack on line 57.

During this comparison, the line counter is compared to `MAXLINES`. If the line counter equals twenty, processing continues to the `HEADINGS` module to print the titles lines and the column headings at the top of the next page. Otherwise, control falls through to the next instruction. In either case, processing skips to the `OUTPUT` module, increments the line counter, and prints the detail line.

The looping read on line 61 retrieves the next record. Afterwards, control branches to the top of the loop to repeat the detail processing.

P R I N T   S U B T O T A L:

Control branches when the division number changes value or the end of the file is reached. `SUBTOTAL` performs the following processing steps: It adds three to the line count, prints the subtotal for the previous division, resets the subtotal to zero for the next division, and moves the current division number to the previous division.

The Branch on Register statement on line 98 sends control back to the calling module: either `DETAIL PROCESSING LOOP` or `MAINLINE`.

KEY REVIEW TERMS

Define the following terms:

ZAP instruction
packed-decimal
  operations
SP instruction
AP instruction

C instruction
packed-decimal
  format
DP instruction

DC/P statement
relative addressing
DS/P statement
MP instruction

REVIEW EXERCISES

Show the contents of storage after the following constants have been assembled. Indicate the length (in bytes) of each storage item.

				Storage	Length
*1.	PNUM	DC	P'572916'		
2.	PKNBR	DC	P'135'		
*3.	YEAR	DC	PL3'63'		
4.	NEG1	DC	P'–49731'		
*5.	SIZE	DC	P'36'		
6.	DEC	DC	P'1000'		
*7.	NEG2	DC	PL4'–80'		
8.	POINT	DC	PL3'+49'		
*9.	HIGH	DC	PL6'123456'		
10.	HRS	DC	P'+9'		
*11.	MINUS	DC	PL4'–4'		
12.	VALU	DC	P'2001'		

Show the contents of storage and the major condition code setting after the following packed-decimal instructions have been executed. For each, assume the initial values given below.

```
ZERO  DC  P'0'       ONE   DC  P'1'        STOR: 045D
N10   DC  PL5'10'    NUM   DC  PL6'48'     PAC:  00014C
NBR   DC  P'5'       VALU  DC  P'12'       NET:  00020C
MINUS DC  P'-5'      NEG   DC  P'-10'      CNT:  0000029C
```

			Storage	Major CCode
*13.	ZAP	NBR,ZERO		
14.	SP	N10,ONE		

			Storage	Major CCode
*15.	AP	VALU,NUM	_____	_____
*16.	CP	CNT,STOR	_____	_____
17.	AP	NUM,NEG	_____	_____
*18.	MP	N10,NBR	_____	_____
19.	ZAP	NEG,ONE	_____	_____
*20.	DP	NUM,VALU	_____	_____
21.	SP	NEG,MINUS	_____	_____
22.	CP	NET,PAC	_____	_____
*23.	MP	N10,MINUS	_____	_____
24.	DP	N10,MINUS	_____	_____
*25.	ZAP	VALU,NBR	_____	_____
26.	MP	NUM,VALU	_____	_____
27.	CP	PAC,STOR	_____	_____
*28.	AP	NEG,MINUS	_____	_____
29.	SP	VALU,NEG	_____	_____
*30.	DP	NUM,NBR	_____	_____

PROGRAMMING EXERCISES

Instructions: For each exercise, design the pseudocode and write a structured program to produce the output specified. Model your program after sample program CHAP8. Verify your output.

1. Rewrite the program in Exercise 1 of Chapter 7 using packed-decimal operations.

2. Rewrite the program in Exercise 2 of Chapter 7 using packed-decimal operations.

3. Modify the page break program in Exercise 3 of Chapter 7 using packed-decimal statements.

4. Modify the control break program in Exercise 4 of Chapter 7 using packed-decimal statements.

5. Rewrite the page break program in Exercise 5 of Chapter 7 using packed-decimal operations.

6. Rewrite the control break program in Exercise 6 of Chapter 7 using packed-decimal operations.

9 SEQUENTIAL FILE UPDATING

OVERVIEW

Learning Objectives
Sequential File Maintenance
  Creating a File
  Updating a File
  Processing a File
Creating the Master File
  Sample Program CHAP9A
Reading and Printing the Master File
  Sample Program CHAP9B
Updating the Master File—Part I
  Sample Program CHAP9C
Updating the Master File—Part II
  Sample Program CHAP9D
Updating the Master File—Part III
  Sample Program CHAP9E
Key Review Terms
Review Exercises
Programming Exercises

LEARNING OBJECTIVES

After reading this chapter and completing the exercises, the reader should be able to:

- explain the process of updating and maintaining sequential files.
- write a program to create a sequential master file.
- read and print the contents of a sequential file.
- process a transaction file and update the master file.
- process a transaction file, check for input errors, and update the master file.

SEQUENTIAL FILE MAINTENANCE

Data processing applications provide information about many different aspects of a company. For example, most organizations require information about their customers, employees, products, and creditors. To provide this information, files are created and maintained to reflect the current business situation or financial conditions of the company.

In this book, we learned that data is organized into files to facilitate processing by the computer. There are two basic types of files: master files and transaction files. A master file contains permanent information about a particular application. A transaction file contains temporary information that updates the master file. For example, consider an inventory application: The master file contains information about each item stored in the warehouse; the transaction file contains information about items delivered to the warehouse and items sold to the customers this week.

CREATING A FILE

Let's continue with our example of an inventory application. Once management has decided that information is required about the inventory system, a master file is created. Data is collected about each item in the warehouse and stored on disk for future reference.

Since each record contains information about one item in the inventory, we will need some way of organizing the file so that any record can be accessed and processed by the computer. For our inventory file, we will use an item number as the control field or record key to uniquely identify each record. Hence, each record in the master file is stored sequentially in ascending (low to high) order according to the record key, or item number. A file organized in order by record key is called a *sequential file*.

UPDATING A FILE

As the physical inventory changes, so must the records in the inventory system. File updating refers to the process of updating the master file over time. Periodically, new records are added, old records are deleted, and updates are made to the current inventory. For example, when items are sold to customers, the on-hand quantity as recorded in the master file must be adjusted to reflect the sale. Similarly, when new products are offered to customers, new records must be added to the master file.

Even though the master file is a permanent repository of information, it is volatile and must be maintained. Customer orders, as well as other inventory-related activities, are batched to form a transaction file that represents changes to the master file. Once the transactions have been organized by item number, they are applied to the old master file to produce a new, updated master file. If errors are detected during the update process, they are written to the inventory error log (Fig. 9.1).

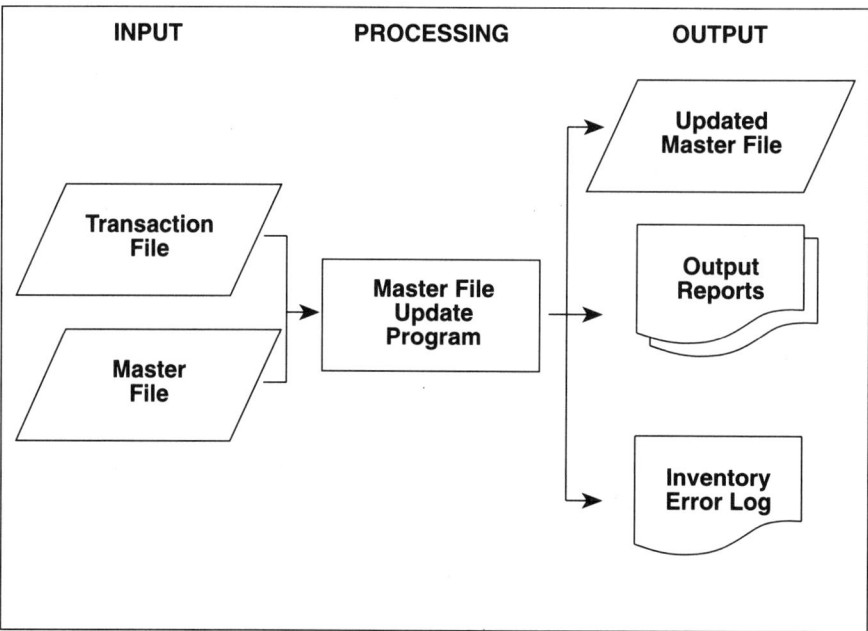

FIGURE 9.1 Sequential File Update

PROCESSING A FILE

Updates to the master file are usually scheduled on a regular basis. In Fig. 9.1, each time the master file is updated, various reports and documents are automatically created. For example, the update program could also provide the following information concerning the status of the inventory system:

- physical inventory counts for each item
- items to reorder, quantity to reorder, cost and vendor information
- total sales per item for a specific period of time
- transactions processed for the current week
- back-ordered items
- slow- and fast-moving items

This information can be used by management to monitor the inventory and to make decisions concerning the profit earned from sales for the current week. For instance, consider the slow- and fast-moving items shown in the preceding list. Slow-moving items could be deleted from the product line, and management could increase the on-hand quantity of fast-moving items.

CREATING THE MASTER FILE: SAMPLE PROGRAM CHAP9A

The inventory master file is created from the input data (Fig. 9.2). Since the keys for the input are in ascending order, each record is written to the disk sequentially. The specifications, pseudocode, and program listing follow.

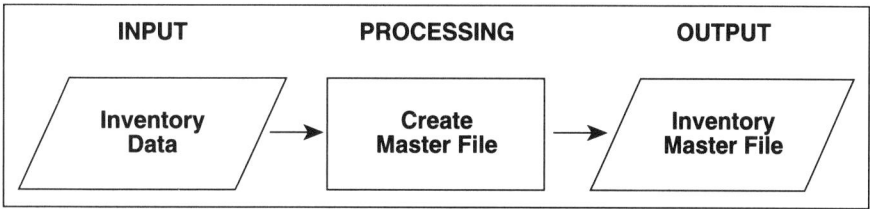

FIGURE 9.2 CHAP9A: Creating the Master File

Sample program CHAP9A is shown in Fig. 9.3; the program's output is shown in Fig. 9.4.

Input data:
>Inventory data: item number, item description, quantity on hand, and other information (not currently used).

Processing functions:
>Read an input record
>Move the input data to the master record
>Write the master record to the master file

Program output (Disk file):
>Inventory Master File. The output is shown in Fig. 9.4.

Pseudocode logic design:
>START
>Open files
>LOOP until no more data
>   Read a record
>   Move input to output
>   Write output to master file
>End LOOP
>Close files
>END

DISSECTION OF SAMPLE PROGRAM CHAP9A

Let's look at the processing performed by the build-disk-file module.

```
BUILD    DISK    FILE:

  22 BLDFILE    GET    IPTFILE,IPTRECD
  23            MVC    MSTKEY,IPTITEM
  24            MVC    MSTDESC,IPTDESC
  25            MVC    MSTQTY,IPTQTY
  26            MVC    MSTDATA,IPTDATA
  27            PUT    MAST,MSTRECD
  28            B      BLDFILE
  29 EOF        BR     10
```

Creating the Master File: Sample Program CHAP9A

```
 1  *------------------- CREATE MASTER FILE -------------------
 2  *   This program reads data and creates a sequential disk
 3  *   master file.
 4  *
 5  *              PROGRAM-ID: CHAP9A
 6  *              PROGRAMMER: David M. Collopy
 7  *              RUN DATE:   mm/dd/yy
 8  ************************************************************
 9  CHAP9A    CSECT                                     (system
10            PRINT NOGEN                              use and
11            BALR  2,0                                general
12            USING *,2                           housekeeping)
13            OPEN  IPTFILE,MAST                     open files
14  *----------------------------------------------------------
15  *              MAINLINE CONTROL
16  *----------------------------------------------------------
17  MAINLINE  BAL   10,BLDFILE                  build master file
18            B     EXIT                             process exit
19  *----------------------------------------------------------
20  *              BUILD DISK FILE
21  *----------------------------------------------------------
22  BLDFILE   GET   IPTFILE,IPTRECD                   read record
23            MVC   MSTKEY,IPTITEM            move input to output
24            MVC   MSTDESC,IPTDESC           move input to output
25            MVC   MSTQTY,IPTQTY             move input to output
26            MVC   MSTDATA,IPTDATA           move input to output
27            PUT   MAST,MSTRECD              write master record
28            B     BLDFILE                          repeat loop
29  EOF       BR    10                         return to mainline
30  *
31  EXIT      CLOSE IPTFILE,MAST                      close files
32            EOJ                                     end of job
33  ************************************************************
34  *              I/O FILE DEFINITIONS
35  *----------------------------------------------------------
36  IPTFILE   DTFCD DEVADDR=SYSIPT,IOAREA1=IPTBUFF,DEVICE=2540,  X
                   WORKA=YES,BLKSIZE=80,EOFADDR=EOF
```

FIGURE 9.3 Sample Program CHAP9A: Creates a sequential disk master file from the inventory data.

```
37 MAST       DTFSD DEVADDR=SYS005,IOAREA1=MSTBUFF,DEVICE=3330,   X
                    WORKA=YES,RECFORM=FIXUNB,BLKSIZE=80,          X
                    VERIFY=YES,TYPEFLE=OUTPUT
38 *
39 IPTBUFF   DS    CL80                           input file buffer
40 MSTBUFF   DS    CL80                          master file buffer
41 *----------------------------------------------------------------
42 *                RECORD/DATA DEFINITIONS
43 *----------------------------------------------------------------
44 IPTRECD   DS    0CL80                  I N P U T    R E C O R D
45 IPTITEM   DS    CL4       (01 - 04)                  item number
46 IPTDESC   DS    CL26      (05 - 30)             item description
47 IPTQTY    DS    CL3       (31 - 33)            quantity on hand
48 IPTDATA   DS    CL12      (34 - 45)                   other data
49           DS    CL35      (46 - 80)                       unused
50 *
51 MSTRECD   DS    0CL80                 M A S T E R   R E C O R D
52 MSTKEY    DS    CL4       (01 - 04)                   record key
53 MSTDESC   DS    CL26      (05 - 30)             item description
54 MSTQTY    DS    CL3       (31 - 33)             quantity on hand
55 MSTDATA   DS    CL12      (34 - 45)                   other data
56           DS    CL35      (46 - 80)                       unused
57 *
58           END   CHAP9A
```

FIGURE 9.3 (cont.)

```
1000 Description for item# 1000 100 *other data*
2000 Description for item# 2000 050 *other data*
3000 Description for item# 3000 025 *other data*
4000 Description for item# 4000 012 *other data*
5000 Description for item# 5000 024 *other data*
6000 Description for item# 6000 048 *other data*
7000 Description for item# 7000 030 *other data*
8000 Description for item# 8000 060 *other data*
9000 Description for item# 9000 090 *other data*
```

NOTE: Output to the disk is not actually visible to the programmer. Spaces between the fields are inserted to improve readability; they are not part of the file.

FIGURE 9.4 File Output for CHAP9A

Beginning with the statement on line 22, a record is read from the input file and is placed in the input work area. The four MVCs on lines 23–26 copy the input data to the master record and the Put statement writes the record to the master file.

The branch to `BLDFILE` sends control to the top of the loop to repeat the processing. The Branch Register on line 29 is tied-in with the DTF for the input file and will execute when the input file is out of data.

I / O F I L E D E F I N I T I O N S:

The following DTF defines a sequential disk (SD) file for the master file produced by the program.

```
MAST     DTFSD DEVADDR=SYS005,IOAREA1=MSTBUFF,DEVICE=3330,    X
               WORKA=YES,RECFORM=FIXUNB,BLKSIZE=80,           X
               VERIFY=YES,TYPEFLE=OUTPUT
```

Since the DTF uses several new parameters, we will define them as follows:

- VERIFY — Instructs the system to verify each record written to the disk, when VERIFY = YES.
- DEVICE — Specifies the system unit number for the 3330 disk storage device.
- RECFORM — Specifies the format of the input/output records. FIXUNB indicates that the records are fixed-length and unblocked.
- TYPEFLE — Specifies whether the file is used for input, output, or both (INOUT).

READING AND PRINTING THE MASTER FILE: SAMPLE PROGRAM CHAP9B

The master file created in the previous section was stored on disk. Since the records were written directly to the disk, we have no way of knowing what was actually placed there. We didn't see the output. Therefore, it would be wise to look at the file and verify the contents. We can do this by simply reading the file and printing a copy of the records.

As shown in Fig. 9.5, the inventory report is printed from the master file. Each record is read from the disk master file and is written to the inventory report.

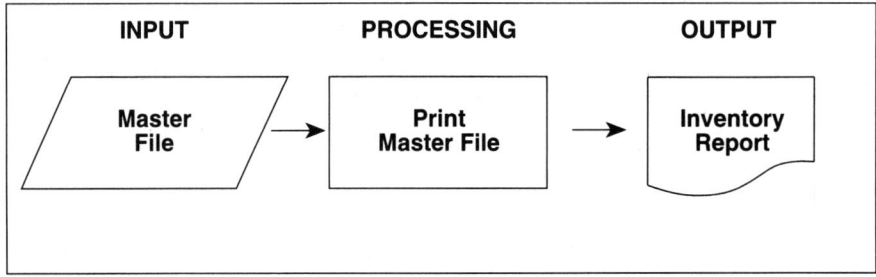

FIGURE 9.5 CHAP9B: Printing the Master File

Sample program CHAP9B is shown in Fig. 9.6; the program's output is shown in Fig. 9.7.

Input data:
    Inventory master file (see Fig. 9.4)

Processing functions:
    Read a master record.
    Move the contents of the master record to the output.
    Write the output to the inventory report.

Program output (Printer Report: Inventory Item Report)
    The output is shown in Fig. 9.7.

Pseudocode logic design:
    START
    Open files
    LOOP until no more data
        Read a record
        Move record to output
        Write output to printer
    End LOOP
    Close files
    END

```
1   *----------------- PRINT INVENTORY REPORT ------------------
2   *       This program demonstrates how to read and print a
3   *       sequential disk file.
4   *
5   *              PROGRAM-ID:  CHAP9B
6   *              PROGRAMMER:  David M. Collopy
7   *              RUN DATE:    mm/dd/yy
8   ***************************************************************
9   CHAP9B    CSECT                                        (system
10            PRINT  NOGEN                                 use and
11            BALR   2,0                                   general
12            USING  *,2                              housekeeping)
13            OPEN   MAST,PRINTER                       open files
14  *--------------------------------------------------------------
15  *                  MAINLINE CONTROL
16  *--------------------------------------------------------------
17  MAINLINE  BAL    10,HEADINGS                      print headings
18            BAL    10,REPORT                          print report
19            B      EXIT                              process exit
20  *--------------------------------------------------------------
21  *                  PRINT HEADINGS
22  *--------------------------------------------------------------
23  HEADINGS  MVI    CCH1,C'1'                     skip to new page...
24            PUT    PRINTER,HDGLINE1            ...and print heading-1
25            MVI    CCH2,C' '                         single space...
26            PUT    PRINTER,HDGLINE2            ...and print heading-2
27            MVI    CCH3,C' '                         single space...
28            PUT    PRINTER,HDGLINE3            ...and print heading-3
29            MVI    CCH4,C'-'                         triple space...
30            PUT    PRINTER,HDGLINE4            ...and print heading-4
31            MVI    CCH5,C' '                         single space...
32            PUT    PRINTER,HDGLINE5            ...and print heading-5
33            MVI    CCB,C' '                          single space...
34            PUT    PRINTER,BLKLINE             ...and print blank line
35            BR     10                             return to mainline
```

FIGURE 9.6 Sample Program CHAP9B: Prints an inventory report from a sequential disk master file.

276 Chapter 9: Sequential File Updating

```
36  *----------------------------------------------------------------
37  *                  PRINT REPORT
38  *----------------------------------------------------------------
39  REPORT    GET      MAST,MSTRECD                      read record
40            MVC      DTLKEY,MSTKEY          move input to output
41            MVC      DTLDESC,MSTDESC        move input to output
42            MVC      DTLQTY,MSTQTY          move input to output
43            MVC      DTLDATA,MSTDATA        move input to output
44            MVI      CCD,C' '                     single space...
45            PUT      PRINTER,DTLLINE    ...and write master record
46            B        REPORT                           repeat loop
47  EOF       BR       10                         return to mainline
48  *
49  EXIT      CLOSE    MAST,PRINTER                     close files
50            EOJ                                       end of job
51  ****************************************************************
52  *                  I/O FILE DEFINITIONS
53  *----------------------------------------------------------------
54  MAST      DTFSD    DEVADDR=SYS005,IOAREA1=MSTBUFF,DEVICE=3330,  X
                       WORKA=YES,RECFORM=FIXUNB,BLKSIZE=80,         X
                       TYPEFLE=INPUT,EOFADDR=EOF
55  PRINTER   DTFPR    DEVADDR=SYSLST,IOAREA1=PRTBUFF,DEVICE=1403,  X
                       CTLCHR=YES,WORKA=YES,BLKSIZE=80
56  *
57  MSTBUFF   DS       CL80                       master file buffer
58  PRTBUFF   DS       CL80                      printer file buffer
59  *----------------------------------------------------------------
60  *                  RECORD/DATA DEFINITIONS
61  *----------------------------------------------------------------
62  MSTRECD   DS       0CL80                 M A S T E R   R E C O R D
63  MSTKEY    DS       CL4        (01 - 04)                record key
64  MSTDESC   DS       CL26       (05 - 30)          item description
65  MSTQTY    DS       CL3        (31 - 33)         quantity on hand
66  MSTDATA   DS       CL12       (34 - 45)                other data
67            DS       CL35       (46 - 80)                    unused
68  *
69  HDGLINE1  DS       0CL80                 H E A D I N G   L I N E - 1
70  CCH1      DS       CL1                          carriage control
71            DC       CL25' '
```

FIGURE 9.6 (cont.)

```
 72              DC       CL26'WINSTON-SLATER CORPORATION'
 73              DC       CL28' '
 74  *
 75  HDGLINE2 DS          0CL80                    H E A D I N G   L I N E - 2
 76  CCH2     DS          CL1                                 carriage control
 77              DC       CL30' '
 78              DC       CL16'INVENTORY SYSTEM'
 79              DC       CL33' '
 80  *
 81  HDGLINE3 DS          0CL80                    H E A D I N G   L I N E - 3
 82  CCH3     DS          CL1                                 carriage control
 83              DC       CL34' '
 84              DC       CL8'mm/dd/yy'
 85              DC       CL37' '
 86  *
 87  HDGLINE4 DS          0CL80                    H E A D I N G   L I N E - 4
 88  CCH4     DS          CL1                                 carriage control
 89              DC       CL11' '
 90              DC       CL4'ITEM'
 91              DC       CL32' '
 92              DC       CL8'QUANTITY'
 93              DC       CL5' '
 94              DC       CL5'OTHER'
 95              DC       CL14' '
 96  *
 97  HDGLINE5 DS          0CL80                    H E A D I N G   L I N E - 5
 98  CCH5     DS          CL1                                 carriage control
 99              DC       CL10' '
100              DC       CL6'NUMBER'
101              DC       CL8' '
102              DC       CL16'ITEM DESCRIPTION'
103              DC       CL7' '
104              DC       CL7'ON HAND'
105              DC       CL3' '
106              DC       CL11'INFORMATION'
107              DC       CL11' '
108  *
109  DTLLINE  DS          0CL80                         D E T A I L   L I N E
110  CCD      DS          CL1        (01 - 01)          carriage control
```

FIGURE 9.6 (cont.)

```
111             DC      CL11' '         (02 - 12)                   unused
112  DTLKEY     DS      CL4             (13 - 16)              item number
113             DC      CL4' '          (17 - 20)                   unused
114  DTLDESC    DS      CL26            (21 - 46)         item description
115             DC      CL4' '          (47 - 50)                   unused
116  DTLQTY     DS      CL3             (51 - 53)         quantity on hand
117             DC      CL4' '          (54 - 57)                   unused
118  DTLDATA    DS      CL12            (58 - 69)               other data
119             DC      CL11' '         (70 - 80)                   unused
120 *
121  BLKLINE    DS      0CL80                             B L A N K    L I N E
122  CCB        DS      CL1                                   carriage control
123             DC      CL79' '
124 *
125             END     CHAP9B
```

FIGURE 9.6 (cont.)

```
                    WINSTON-SLATER CORPORATION
                         INVENTORY SYSTEM
                             mm/dd/yy


    ITEM                                        QUANTITY      OTHER
   NUMBER         ITEM DESCRIPTION              ON HAND    INFORMATION

    1000       Description for item# 1000         100      *other data*
    2000       Description for item# 2000         050      *other data*
    3000       Description for item# 3000         025      *other data*
    4000       Description for item# 4000         012      *other data*
    5000       Description for item# 5000         024      *other data*
    6000       Description for item# 6000         048      *other data*
    7000       Description for item# 7000         030      *other data*
    8000       Description for item# 8000         060      *other data*
    9000       Description for item# 9000         090      *other data*
```

FIGURE 9.7 Printer Output for CHAP9B

DISSECTION OF SAMPLE PROGRAM CHAP9B

Note the file type specified in the DTF that defines the master file. `TYPEFLE` equals `INPUT`. This means the master file has been declared as an input file. In other words, records will be read from the file rather than written to it.

M A I N L I N E   C O N T R O L :

Two modules are called from the mainline routine, `PRINT HEADINGS` and `PRINT REPORT`. Upon a return from the `PRINT REPORT` module, control branches to `EXIT`, closes the program files, and terminates the processing.

P R I N T   H E A D I N G S :

After the printer advances to the top of a new page, the title and headings are printed in the center of the report.

P R I N T   R E P O R T

This module contains a loop that reads a record, moves the input to the detail line, and prints the detail line to the body of the inventory report. The loop repeats until the input is out of data. At the end of the file, control branches to the statement labeled `EOF` and subsequently returns to the mainline to execute the exit procedure.

UPDATING THE MASTER FILE—PART I

Sample program CHAP9C does not actually update the master file. Since the update logic is involved and complex, our goal in sample program CHAP9C is to construct and test the top-level control logic. We will ignore the intricate details of how to perform the complete update.

The update performed by sample program CHAP9C is as follows: to compare the transaction and master keys and—based on the results of the comparison—print one of three messages, as shown in Table 9.1. In other words, we are printing messages that correspond to updates, rather than actually doing the updates.

As shown in Table 9.1, we print `UPDATE MASTER` when the keys are equal. Usually an update is performed by applying data stored in the transaction record to the master record. The update logic should also allow multiple transaction records to update any given master record.

TABLE 9.1 Update Messages

Compare Keys	Print Message
1. TRNKEY = MSTKEY	UPDATE MASTER (TRNKEY)
2. TRNKEY < MSTKEY	ADD NEW MASTER (TRNKEY)
3. TRNKEY > MSTKEY	WRITE MASTER (MSTKEY)

We print ADD NEW MASTER when the master key is greater than the transaction. Data for the new master record is stored in the transaction. Hence, a new record is added to the master by writing the transaction to the master file.

We print WRITE MASTER when the transaction is greater than the master key. This message implies that the old, or updated, master is written to the new master file.

In all three cases, we are assuming that the records of both files have been arranged in ascending order by item number.

SAMPLE PROGRAM CHAP9C

For sample program CHAP9C, a print file is created by applying the transactions to the master file (Fig. 9.8). Essentially, the keys are compared to determine the type of processing to perform. Sample program CHAP9C is shown in Fig. 9.9; the program's input and output are shown in Fig. 9.10.

Input data:
  Transaction file.
  Master file.

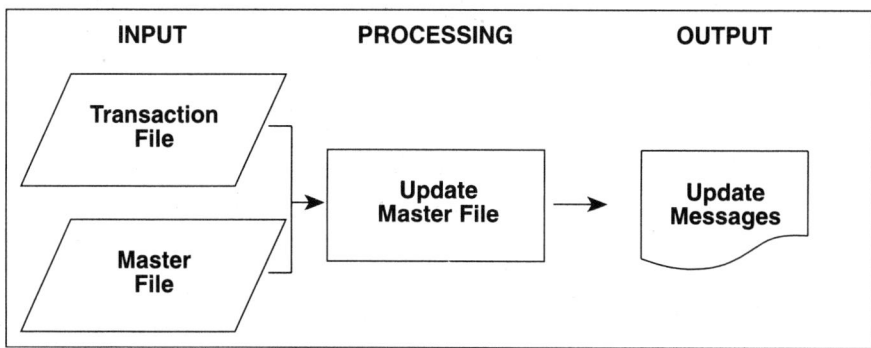

FIGURE 9.8 CHAP9C: Basic Update Logic

Processing functions:
Compare the transaction and master keys to determine the processing, and print the corresponding message (Table 9.1).

Program output (Printer Report: Update Messages):
The output is shown in Fig. 9.10.

Pseudocode logic design:
Two new conventions introduced in the following design require explanation. First, any statement enclosed within parentheses specifies a call or branch to the named module. Second, a block of pseudocode beginning with ENTER and ending with RETURN represents a module.

START
Open files
(Read transaction record)
(Read master record)
LOOP until no more data (both files empty)
   If TRNKEY = MSTKEY
     Print: UPDATE MASTER
     (Read transaction record)
   else
     If TRNKEY < MSTKEY
       Print: ADD NEW MASTER
       (Read transaction record)
     else
       Print: WRITE MASTER
       (Read master record)
End LOOP
Close files
END

ENTER (Read transaction record)
If more data remains
   Get transaction record
else
   Move EOF indicator to TRNKEY
RETURN

ENTER (Read master record)
If more data remains
   Get master record
else
   Move EOF indicator to MSTKEY
RETURN

```
 1  *----------------- BASIC UPDATE LOGIC --------------------
 2  *  This program illustrates the basic update logic. It reads
 3  *  the transaction and master files and prints the update.
 4  *
 5  *            PROGRAM-ID: CHAP9C
 6  *            PROGRAMMER: David M. Collopy
 7  *            RUN DATE:   mm/dd/yy
 8  ****************************************************************
 9  CHAP9C    CSECT                              (system
10            PRINT NOGEN                        use and
11            BALR  2,0                          general
12            USING *,2                          housekeeping)
13            OPEN  TRANS,MAST,PRINTER           open files
14  *---------------------------------------------------------------
15  *                 MAINLINE CONTROL
16  *---------------------------------------------------------------
17  MAINLINE  BAL   10,GETTRAN                   get trans record
18            BAL   10,GETMAST                   get mast record
19            BAL   9,UPDPROC                    update processing
20            B     EXIT                         process exit
21  *---------------------------------------------------------------
22  *                 UPDATE PROCESSING
23  *---------------------------------------------------------------
24  UPDPROC   CLC   MSTKEY,EOFKEY                test for EOM
25            BE    CKTRAN                       if EOM, test for EOT
26            B     CONTINUE                     else continue
27  CKTRAN    CLC   TRNKEY,EOFKEY                test for EOT
28            BE    QUIT                         if EOM & EOT, quit
29  CONTINUE  CLC   TRNKEY,MSTKEY                compare keys
30            BE    UPDMST                       if T = M, update mst
31            BL    ADDMST                       if T < M, add new mst
32  WRTMST    MVC   DTLMESG,WRTMESG              move mesg: write mst
33            MVC   DTLKEY,MSTKEY                move mst key
34            MVI   CCD,C' '                     single space...
35            PUT   PRINTER,DTLLINE              ...and print mst
36            BAL   10,GETMAST                   get mast record
37            B     REPEAT                       skip to repeat
```

FIGURE 9.9 Sample Program CHAP9C: Reads a transaction and master file, compares keys, and prints the result of the update.

Updating the Master File—Part I

```
38 UPDMST    MVC    DTLMESG,UPDMESG          move mesg: update mst
39           MVC    DTLKEY,TRNKEY                    move trn key
40           MVI    CCD,C' '                        single space...
41           PUT    PRINTER,DTLLINE         ...and print updated mst
42           BAL    10,GETTRAN                   get trans record
43           B      REPEAT                         skip to repeat
44 ADDMST    MVC    DTLMESG,ADDMESG         move mesg: add new mst
45           MVC    DTLKEY,TRNKEY                    move trn key
46           MVI    CCD,C' '                        single space...
47           PUT    PRINTER,DTLLINE           ...and print new mst
48           BAL    10,GETTRAN                   get trans record
49 REPEAT    B      UPDPROC                          repeat loop
50 QUIT      BR     9                                       return
51 *-----------------------------------------------------------
52 *                GET TRANSACTION RECORD
53 *-----------------------------------------------------------
54 GETTRAN   CLC    TRNKEY,EOFKEY                       test for EOT
55           BNE    READTRAN                if more data, read trans
56 EOT       MVC    TRNKEY,EOFKEY           else set key to '9999'
57           B      NOTRAN                               skip read
58 READTRAN  GET    TRANS,TRNRECD                       read trans
59 NOTRAN    BR     10                                      return
60 *-----------------------------------------------------------
61 *                GET MASTER RECORD
62 *-----------------------------------------------------------
63 GETMAST   CLC    MSTKEY,EOFKEY                       test for EOM
64           BNE    READMAST                 if more data, read mast
65 EOM       MVC    MSTKEY,EOFKEY           else set key to '9999'
66           B      NOMAST                               skip read
67 READMAST  GET    MAST,MSTRECD                         read mast
68 NOMAST    BR     10                                      return
69 *
70 EXIT      CLOSE  TRANS,MAST,PRINTER                 close files
71           EOJ                                        end of job
72 ***********************************************************
73 *                I/O FILE DEFINITIONS
74 *-----------------------------------------------------------
75 TRANS     DTFCD  DEVADDR=SYSIPT,IOAREA1=TRNBUFF,DEVICE=2540,   X
                   WORKA=YES,BLKSIZE=80,EOFADDR=EOT
```

FIGURE 9.9 (cont.)

```
 76 MAST       DTFSD DEVADDR=SYS005,IOAREA1=MSTBUFF,DEVICE=3330,    X
                     WORKA=YES,RECFORM=FIXUNB,BLKSIZE=80,            X
                     TYPEFLE=INPUT,EOFADDR=EOM
 77 PRINTER    DTFPR DEVADDR=SYSLST,IOAREA1=PRTBUFF,DEVICE=1403,    X
                     CTLCHR=YES,WORKA=YES,BLKSIZE=80
 78 *
 79 TRNBUFF    DS    CL80                       transaction file buffer
 80 MSTBUFF    DS    CL80                        old master file buffer
 81 PRTBUFF    DS    CL80                           printer file buffer
 82 *----------------------------------------------------------------
 83 *                RECORD/DATA DEFINITIONS
 84 *----------------------------------------------------------------
 85 TRNRECD    DS    0CL80           T R A N S A C T I O N   R E C O R D
 86 TRNKEY     DS    CL4      (01 - 04)                               key
 87 TRNDESC    DS    CL26     (05 - 30)                  item description
 88 TRNQTY     DS    CL3      (31 - 33)                          quantity
 89 TRNDATA    DS    CL12     (34 - 45)                        other data
 90            DS    CL35     (46 - 80)                            unused
 91 *
 92 MSTRECD    DS    0CL80                  M A S T E R   R E C O R D
 93 MSTKEY     DS    CL4      (01 - 04)                               key
 94 MSTDESC    DS    CL26     (05 - 30)                  item description
 95 MSTQTY     DS    CL3      (31 - 33)                          quantity
 96 MSTDATA    DS    CL12     (34 - 45)                        other data
 97            DS    CL35     (46 - 80)                            unused
 98 *
 99 DTLLINE    DS    0CL80                       D E T A I L   L I N E
100 CCD        DS    CL1      (01 - 01)                  carriage control
101 DTLMESG    DS    CL23     (02 - 24)                    update message
102 DTLKEY     DS    CL4      (25 - 28)                        record key
103            DC    CL52' '  (29 - 80)                            unused
104 *
105 EOFKEY     DC    CL4'9999'                    end of file indicator
106 UPDMESG    DC    CL23'UPDATE MASTER: TRNKEY= '
107 ADDMESG    DC    CL23'ADD NEW MASTER: TRNKEY='
108 WRTMESG    DC    CL23'WRITE MASTER: MSTKEY=  '
109            END   CHAP9C
```

FIGURE 9.9 (cont.)

```
Input: Transaction File         Input: Master File

4000 Description for...         1000 Description for...
5000 Description for...         2000 Description for...
5000 Description for...         3000 Description for...
7000 Description for...         4000 Description for...
8000 Description for...         5000 Description for...
8500 Description for...         6000 Description for...
                                7000 Description for...
                                8000 Description for...
                                9000 Description for...


              Output: Printer

        WRITE MASTER:  MSTKEY=   1000
        WRITE MASTER:  MSTKEY=   2000
        WRITE MASTER:  MSTKEY=   3000
        UPDATE MASTER: TRNKEY=   4000
        WRITE MASTER:  MSTKEY=   4000
        UPDATE MASTER: TRNKEY=   5000
        UPDATE MASTER: TRNKEY=   5000
        WRITE MASTER:  MSTKEY=   5000
        WRITE MASTER:  MSTKEY=   6000
        UPDATE MASTER: TRNKEY=   7000
        WRITE MASTER:  MSTKEY=   7000
        UPDATE MASTER: TRNKEY=   8000
        WRITE MASTER:  MSTKEY=   8000
        ADD NEW MASTER: TRNKEY=8500
        WRITE MASTER:  MSTKEY=   9000
```

FIGURE 9.10 Input and Output for CHAP9C

DISSECTION OF SAMPLE PROGRAM CHAP9C

M A I N L I N E   C O N T R O L:

The mainline begins by reading the first transaction and the first master record. (Both read statements are priming reads.) Then the program branches to the update routine (UPDPROC). After both files have been processed, control branches to EXIT, closes the files, and terminates the run.

Chapter 9: Sequential File Updating

GET TRANSACTION RECORD:

There may be times when the program will branch to GETTRAN even though the file is empty. Because of this, a check has been added to avoid reading past the last record.

When the program detects the end of the file, the EOFKEY (9999) is moved to the transaction key.

```
54 GETTRAN   CLC   TRNKEY,EOFKEY
```

The above statement means: Compare the key of the last transaction read to the end-of-file indicator (9999) and set the condition code accordingly.

```
55           BNE   READTRAN
```

The above statement means: If the end of the transaction file has not been reached, skip lines 56 and 57 and branch to READTRAN.

```
56 EOT       MVC   TRNKEY,EOFKEY
```

The above statement means: When the end of file has been detected, move the end-of-file key (9999) to the transaction key.

```
57           B     NOTRAN
```

The above statement means: Branch to NOTRAN and skip the looping read statement. Lines 56 and 57 work together to mark the end of the transaction file and to avoid reading past it.

```
58 READTRAN GET    TRANS,TRNRECD
```

The above statement means: Retrieve a record from the transaction file and store the contents of the record in the TRNRECD work area.

```
59 NOTRAN    BR    10
```

The above statement means: Branch back to the statement corresponding to the address stored in register 10.

GET MASTER RECORD:

Since the processing performed by GETMAST is similar to that shown for GETTRAN, we will not repeat it here.

UPDATE PROCESSING:

When two files are read and processed together, you must determine which file runs out of data first. For example, either the transaction file or the master file could run out of data first, or both could end together. (This occurrence is unlikely, but possible.) Statements 24–28 provide for any of these three situations.

```
24 UPDPROC   CLC    MSTKEY,EOFKEY
```

The above statement means: Compare the key of the last master record to the end-of-file indicator and set the condition code.

```
25            BE     CKTRAN
```

The above statement means: If the master file is empty, then branch to CKTRAN to see if the transaction file is also empty.

```
26            B      CONTINUE
```

The above statement means: If the master file is not empty, skip to line 29 and continue the update processing.

```
27 CKTRAN    CLC    TRNKEY,EOFKEY
```

The above statement means: Compare the key of the last transaction record to the end-of-file indicator and set the condition code.

```
28            BE     QUIT
```

The above statement means: If both files are empty, then the processing is complete and control skips to QUIT.

```
29 CONTINUE  CLC    TRNKEY,MSTKEY
30            BE     UPDMST
```

The above statements mean: Compare the keys and set the condition code. If the keys are equal, then branch to UPDMST to update the master record.

```
31            BL     ADDMST
```

The above statement means: If the transaction key is less than the master, then branch to ADDMST to add a new master record.

```
32  WRTMST     MVC    DTLMESG,WRTMESG
33             MVC    DTLKEY,MSTKEY
34             MVI    CCD,C' '
35             PUT    PRINTER,DTLLINE
```

Control reaches this point in the program when a match was not found for the previous branch statements. Hence, by default, the condition code is high: TRNKEY > MSTKEY. Therefore, the above statements direct the program to move the message WRITE MASTER and the master key to the detail line, set the carriage control to single space, and print the line.

```
36             BAL    10,GETMAST
37             B      REPEAT
```

The above statements mean: Branch to GETMAST, read the next master record, and skip to REPEAT.

```
38  UPDMST     MVC    DTLMESG,UPDMESG
39             MVC    DTLKEY,TRNKEY
40             MVI    CCD,C' '
41             PUT    PRINTER,DTLLINE
```

The above statements mean: Move the message UPDATE MASTER and the transaction key to the detail line, set the carriage control to single space, and print the output.

```
42             BAL    10,GETTRAN
43             B      REPEAT
```

The above statements mean: Get the next transaction and branch to REPEAT.

```
44  ADDMST     MVC    DTLMESG,ADDMESG
45             MVC    DTLKEY,TRNKEY
46             MVI    CCD,C' '
47             PUT    PRINTER,DTLLINE
48             BAL    10,GETTRAN
```

The above statements mean: Move ADD NEW MASTER and the transaction key to the detail line, single space the output, print the line, and read the next transaction.

```
49 REPEAT    B     UPDPROC
```

The above statement means: Branch to the top of the loop and repeat the processing.

```
50 QUIT      BR    9
```

The above statement means: Return to the statement corresponding to the address stored in register 9.

UPDATING THE MASTER FILE—PART II

Now that we have designed and programmed our top-level control logic, we are ready to update the master file. Once again, to avoid becoming entangled in unnecessary details, we will focus on the actual update logic and ignore the possibility of errors.

Let's pause briefly to discuss what to do if the update program ends abnormally (ABEND). An abend occurs when certain logic errors prevent the program from running to completion. Usually this means that part of the transactions was applied (correctly or incorrectly) to the master file. Once the errors are found and corrected, you must run the program again; don't assume that part of the update is correct and you can continue where the program ended during the last run. It is much safer to correct the errors and rerun the update program from the start.

Figure 9.11 shows the input and output for sample program CHAP9D.

In sample program CHAP9D, we will consider six types of updates that use a special code, called the transaction code, to tell the program what to do or how

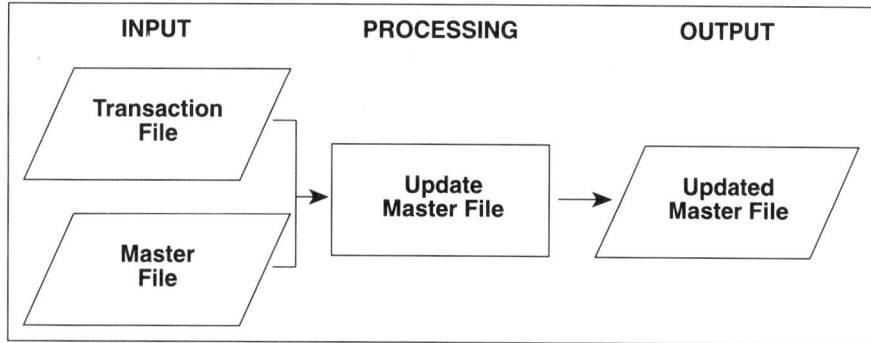

FIGURE 9.11 CHAP9D: Update Processing

to apply the transactions to the master file. These codes are defined as follows:

1	*add quantity received*	Items received from suppliers or returned by customers are added to the master file. The transaction quantity is added to the master quantity on hand.
2	*subtract quantity sold*	Items sold or scrapped (damaged) are removed from the master file. The transaction quantity is subtracted from the quantity stored in the master record.
3	*change master quantity*	When the physical inventory count does not agree with the quantity shown in the master file, it is adjusted to reflect the actual count. Hence, the transaction quantity replaces the value stored in the master record.
4	*change item description*	When the item description is incorrect it must be changed. The item description coded in the transaction record replaces the description stored in the master record.
5	*add new master record*	When new items are added to the product line, they are added to the master file. New records are coded as transactions and are inserted into the master file in their proper order.
6	*delete old master record*	Occasionally, obsolete or slow-moving items are removed from the inventory to make room for other products. Hence, the old master records are removed by not copying them to the new master file.

SAMPLE PROGRAM CHAP9D

Sample program CHAP9D processes the transactions one at a time and applies them, according to the update logic, to the old master file. It then produces the updated master file. Sample program CHAP9D is shown in Fig. 9.12; the program's input and output are shown in Fig. 9.13.

Input data:
    Transaction file
    Old master file

Processing functions:

Compare the transaction and master keys. If they are equal, use the transaction code to determine whether to perform a deletion or an update. If the transaction key is less than the master key, then add the new record to the master file. If the transaction key is greater than the master key, write the old master to the file.

Program output (Disk File: Updated Master File):

The output is shown in Fig. 9.13.

Pseudocode logic design:

START
Open I/O files
(Read transaction record)
(Read master record)
LOOP until no more data (both files empty)
   If TRNKEY = MSTKEY
      If transaction code = delete record
         (Read master record)
         (Read transaction record)
      else
         (Update master record)
   else
      If TRNKEY < MSTKEY
         Write transaction record to new master file
         (Read transaction record)
      else
         Write old master record to new master file
         (Read master record)
End LOOP
Close files
END

ENTER (Update master record)
If transaction code = add items
   Add transaction qty to master qty
If transaction code = subtract items
   Subtract transaction qty from master qty
If transaction code = change qty
   Move transaction qty to master qty
else
   Move transaction description to master description.
   (Read transaction record).
RETURN

```
 1  *--------------- SEQUENTIAL FILE UPDATE ------------------
 2  *   This program updates the master file; errors are not
 3  *   considered.
 4  *
 5  *              PROGRAM-ID: CHAP9D
 6  *              PROGRAMMER: David M. Collopy
 7  *              RUN DATE:   mm/dd/yy
 8  ***************************************************************
 9  CHAP9D    CSECT                                      (system
10            PRINT NOGEN                               use and
11            BALR  2,0                                  general
12            USING *,2                              housekeeping)
13            OPEN  TRANS,MAST,NEWMAST               open files
14  *-----------------------------------------------------------
15  *              MAINLINE CONTROL
16  *-----------------------------------------------------------
17  MAINLINE  BAL   10,GETTRAN                     get trans record
18            BAL   10,GETMAST                     get mast record
19            BAL   9,UPDPROC                      update processing
20            B     EXIT                              process exit
21  *-----------------------------------------------------------
22  *              UPDATE PROCESSING
23  *-----------------------------------------------------------
24  UPDPROC   CLC   MSTKEY,EOFKEY                    test for EOM
25            BE    CKTRAN                       if EOM, test for EOT
26            B     CONTINUE                        else continue
27  CKTRAN    CLC   TRNKEY,EOFKEY                    test for EOT
28            BE    QUIT                         if EOM & EOT, quit
29  CONTINUE  CLC   TRNKEY,MSTKEY                    compare keys
30            BE    UPDATE                       if T = M, update
31            BL    ADDREC                       if T < M, add record
32            BAL   5,WRTMST                     write master record
33            B     REPEAT                           skip to repeat
34  UPDATE    BAL   5,UPDMST                     update master record
35            B     REPEAT                           skip to repeat
36  ADDREC    BAL   5,ADDMST                     add new master record
37  REPEAT    B     UPDPROC                          repeat loop
38  QUIT      BR    9                                     return
```

FIGURE 9.12 Sample Program CHAP9D: Reads a transaction file and updates the master file.

```
39  *-----------------------------------------------------------------
40  *              UPDATE MASTER RECORD
41  *-----------------------------------------------------------------
42  UPDMST   CLI   TRNCODE,C'6'                    test trn code
43           BE    DLETMAST                 if equal, delete mst
44           B     UPDMASTR                      else update mst
45  DLETMAST BAL   10,GETMAST                    get mast record
46           B     NEXTRN                     skip to next tran
47  UPDMASTR CLI   TRNCODE,C'1'                    test trn code
48           BE    ADDQTY                      if equal, add qty
49           CLI   TRNCODE,C'2'                    test trn code
50           BE    SUBTQTY                if equal, subtract qty
51           CLI   TRNCODE,C'3'                    test trn code
52           BE    CHGQTY                   if equal, change qty
53  CHGDESC  MVC   MSTDESC,TRNDESC             change description
54           B     NEXTRN                     skip to next tran
55  ADDQTY   PACK  MQTY,MSTQTY                      convert to PD
56           PACK  TQTY,TRNQTY                      convert to PD
57           AP    MQTY,TQTY                     add trn quantity
58           UNPK  MSTQTY,MQTY                      convert to ZD
59           B     NEXTRN                     skip to next tran
60  SUBTQTY  PACK  MQTY,MSTQTY                      convert to PD
61           PACK  TQTY,TRNQTY                      convert to PD
62           SP    MQTY,TQTY                subtract trn quantity
63           UNPK  MSTQTY,MQTY                      convert to ZD
64           B     NEXTRN                     skip to next tran
65  CHGQTY   MVC   MSTQTY,TRNQTY                  change quantity
66  NEXTRN   BAL   10,GETTRAN                    get tran record
67           BR    5                                      return
68  *-----------------------------------------------------------------
69  *              ADD NEW MASTER RECORD
70  *-----------------------------------------------------------------
71  ADDMST   MVC   NMSTKEY,TRNKEY            move input to output
72           MVC   NMSTDESC,TRNDESC          move input to output
73           MVC   NMSTQTY,TRNQTY            move input to output
74           MVC   NMSTDATA,TRNDATA          move input to output
75           PUT   NEWMAST,NMSTRECD         write trn to new mst
76           BAL   10,GETTRAN                    get tran record
77           BR    5                                      return
```

FIGURE 9.12 (cont.)

```
 78  *----------------------------------------------------------------
 79  *              WRITE MASTER RECORD
 80  *----------------------------------------------------------------
 81  WRTMST   MVC    NMSTKEY,MSTKEY        move input to output
 82           MVC    NMSTDESC,MSTDESC      move input to output
 83           MVC    NMSTQTY,MSTQTY        move input to output
 84           MVC    NMSTDATA,MSTDATA      move input to output
 85           PUT    NEWMAST,NMSTRECD      write old mst to new mst
 86           BAL    10,GETMAST            get mast record
 87           BR     5                     return
 88  *----------------------------------------------------------------
 89  *              GET TRANSACTION RECORD
 90  *----------------------------------------------------------------
 91  GETTRAN  CLC    TRNKEY,EOFKEY         test for EOT
 92           BE     NOTRAN                if EOT, skip read
 93           B      READTRAN              else read trans
 94  EOT      MVC    TRNKEY,EOFKEY         set key to '9999'
 95           B      NOTRAN                skip read
 96  READTRAN GET    TRANS,TRNRECD         read trans
 97  NOTRAN   BR     10                    return
 98  *----------------------------------------------------------------
 99  *              GET MASTER RECORD
100  *----------------------------------------------------------------
101  GETMAST  CLC    MSTKEY,EOFKEY         test for EOM
102           BE     NOMAST                if EOM, skip read
103           B      READMAST              else read trans
104  EOM      MVC    MSTKEY,EOFKEY         set key to '9999'
105           B      NOMAST                skip read
106  READMAST GET    MAST,MSTRECD          read mast
107  NOMAST   BR     10                    return
108  *
109  EXIT     CLOSE  TRANS,MAST,NEWMAST    close files
110           EOJ                          end of job
111  ****************************************************************
112  *              I/O FILE DEFINITIONS
113  *----------------------------------------------------------------
114  TRANS    DTFCD  DEVADDR=SYSIPT,IOAREA1=TRNBUFF,DEVICE=2540,     X
                    WORKA=YES,BLKSIZE=80,EOFADDR=EOT
115  MAST     DTFSD  DEVADDR=SYS005,IOAREA1=MSTBUFF,DEVICE=3330,     X
```

FIGURE 9.12 (cont.)

```
                       WORKA=YES,RECFORM=FIXUNB,BLKSIZE=80,           X
                       TYPEFLE=INPUT,EOFADDR=EOM
116 NEWMAST    DTFSD   DEVADDR=SYS005,IOAREA1=NMSTBUF,DEVICE=3330,    X
                       WORKA=YES,RECFORM=FIXUNB,BLKSIZE=80,           X
                       TYPEFLE=OUTPUT
117 *
118 TRNBUFF    DS      CL80                    transaction file buffer
119 MSTBUFF    DS      CL80                    old master file buffer
120 NMSTBUF    DS      CL80                    new master file buffer
121 *------------------------------------------------------------------
122 *                  RECORD/DATA DEFINITIONS
123 *------------------------------------------------------------------
124 TRNRECD    DS      0CL80        T R A N S A C T I O N   R E C O R D
125 TRNKEY     DS      CL4          (01 - 04)                       key
126 TRNDESC    DS      CL26         (05 - 30)          item description
127 TRNQTY     DS      CL3          (31 - 33)                  quantity
128 TRNDATA    DS      CL12         (34 - 45)                other data
129            DS      CL4          (46 - 49)                    unused
130 TRNCODE    DS      CL1          (50 - 50)          transaction code
131            DS      CL30         (51 - 80)                    unused
132 *
133 MSTRECD    DS      0CL80            M A S T E R   R E C O R D
134 MSTKEY     DS      CL4          (01 - 04)                       key
135 MSTDESC    DS      CL26         (05 - 30)          item description
136 MSTQTY     DS      CL3          (31 - 33)                  quantity
137 MSTDATA    DS      CL12         (34 - 45)                other data
138            DS      CL35         (46 - 80)                    unused
139 *
140 NMSTRECD   DS      0CL80        N E W   M A S T E R   R E C O R D
141 NMSTKEY    DS      CL4          (01 - 04)                       key
142 NMSTDESC   DS      CL26         (05 - 30)          item description
143 NMSTQTY    DS      CL3          (31 - 33)                  quantity
144 NMSTDATA   DS      CL12         (34 - 45)                other data
145            DS      CL35         (46 - 80)                    unused
146 *
147 EOFKEY     DC      CL4'9999'               end of file indicator
148 MQTY       DS      PL2                     master qty (packed)
149 TQTY       DS      PL2                     transaction qty (packed)
150            END     CHAP9D
```

FIGURE 9.12 (cont.)

```
                    Input: Transaction File

3000                                                                    6
4000                              024                                   1
5000                              005                                   2
5000                              023                                   3
6500 Add new master record 6500 015 *other data*                        5
7000 Change description -- 7000                                         4
8000                              055                                   3
9500 Add new master record 9500 018 *other data*                        5


                      Input: Master File

    1000 Description for item# 1000 100 *other data*
    2000 Description for item# 2000 050 *other data*
    3000 Description for item# 3000 025 *other data*
    4000 Description for item# 4000 012 *other data*
    5000 Description for item# 5000 024 *other data*
    6000 Description for item# 6000 048 *other data*
    7000 Description for item# 7000 030 *other data*
    8000 Description for item# 8000 060 *other data*
    9000 Description for item# 9000 090 *other data*

                  Output: Updated Master File

    1000 Description for item# 1000 100 *other data*
    2000 Description for item# 2000 050 *other data*
    4000 Description for item# 4000 036 *other data*
    5000 Description for item# 5000 023 *other data*
    6000 Description for item# 6000 048 *other data*
    6500 Add new master record 6500 015 *other data*
    7000 Change description  -- 7000 030 *other data*
    8000 Description for item# 8000 055 *other data*
    9000 Description for item# 9000 090 *other data*
    9500 Add new master record 9500 018 *other data*
```

FIGURE 9.13 Input and Output for CHAP9D

NOTE: It is important to realize that we cannot physically see the update performed by the program. Therefore, it is a good idea to run a report program, similar to the one shown in Figure 9.5, to print the master file and verify that the update is correct.

DISSECTION OF SAMPLE PROGRAM CHAP9D

After the first transaction and master records have been read, the program proceeds to perform the update processing. In fact, all the modules work together to apply the transactions to the master file.

UPDATE PROCESSING:

```
24 UPDPROC   CLC   MSTKEY,EOFKEY
25           BE    CKTRAN
26           B     CONTINUE
27 CKTRAN    CLC   TRNKEY,EOFKEY
28           BE    QUIT
```

This part of the update logic remains the same as it was in sample program CHAP9C. The transaction and master keys are checked to see if there are any more records to read. If there are, the program continues with the update. Otherwise, control exits the module and returns to the Mainline.

```
29 CONTINUE  CLC   TRNKEY,MSTKEY
30           BE    UPDATE
31           BL    ADDREC
32           BAL   5,WRTMST
33           B     REPEAT
```

The above statements mean: Compare the keys; if they are equal, skip to UPDATE. If the transaction key is less than the master, then skip to ADDREC. Otherwise, the program falls through to the next statement, branches to the WRTMST module, and, upon returning, skips to REPEAT.

```
34 UPDATE    BAL   5,UPDMST
35           B     REPEAT
```

The above statements mean: Branch to the UPDMST module, update the master record, and skip to REPEAT.

```
36 ADDREC    BAL   5,ADDMST
37 REPEAT    B     UPDPROC
```

The above statements mean: Branch to the ADDMST module, add the new master record, and skip to the top of the loop to repeat the processing.

```
38 QUIT      BR    9
```

The above statement means: Return to the mainline at the statement corresponding to the address stored in register 9.

U P D A T E   M A S T E R   R E C O R D :

```
42 UPDMST    CLI   TRNCODE,C'6'
43           BE    DLETMAST
44           B     UPDMASTR
```

The above statements mean: Compare the transaction code to 6 (delete master). If they are equal, skip to DLETMAST. Otherwise, skip to UPDMASTR.

```
45 DLETMAST  BAL   10,GETMAST
46           B     NEXTRN
```

The above statements mean: Delete the old master record. By reading the next master and the next transaction, the previous master record is skipped and not written to the new master file.

```
47 UPDMASTR  CLI   TRNCODE,C'1'
48           BE    ADDQTY
```

The above statements mean: Compare the transaction code to 1 (add quantity). If they are equal, branch to ADDQTY.

```
49           CLI   TRNCODE,C'2'
50           BE    SUBTQTY
```

The above statements mean: Compare the transaction code to 2 (subtract quantity). If they are equal, branch to SUBTQTY.

Updating the Master File—Part II

```
51              CLI     TRNCODE,C'3'
52              BE      CHGQTY
```

The above statements mean: Compare the transaction code to 3 (change quantity). If they are equal, branch to CHGQTY.

```
53   CHGDESC   MVC     MSTDESC,TRNDESC
54              B       NEXTRN
```

If the transaction code does not equal 3, change the item description. Move the description coded in the transaction to the old master record and branch to read the next transaction.

```
55   ADDQTY    PACK    MQTY,MSTQTY
56              PACK    TQTY,TRNQTY
57              AP      MQTY,TQTY
58              UNPK    MSTQTY,MQTY
59              B       NEXTRN
```

The above statements mean: Add the transaction quantity to the master quantity on hand. Store the sum in the old master record and branch to read the next transaction.

```
60   SUBTQTY   PACK    MQTY,MSTQTY
61              PACK    TQTY,TRNQTY
62              SP      MQTY,TQTY
63              UNPK    MSTQTY,MQTY
64              B       NEXTRN
```

The above statements mean: Subtract the transaction quantity from the master quantity on hand. Store the result in the old master record and branch to read the next transaction.

```
65   CHGQTY    MVC     MSTQTY,TRNQTY
66   NEXTRN    BAL     10,GETTRAN
67   RETURN    BR      5
```

The above statements mean: Change the quantity on hand. Move the transaction quantity to the old master record, read the next transaction, and return to the UPDPROC module.

ADD NEW MASTER RECORD:

```
71  ADDMST   MVC   NMSTKEY,TRNKEY
72           MVC   NMSTDESC,TRNDESC
73           MVC   NMSTQTY,TRNQTY
74           MVC   NMSTDATA,TRNDATA
75           PUT   NEWMAST,NMSTRECD
76           BAL   10,GETTRAN
77           BR    5
```

The above statements mean: Add a new record to the master file. Move the data stored in the transaction to the new master record, and write it to the new master file. Read the next transaction and return to the UPDPROC module.

WRITE MASTER RECORD:

```
81  WRTMST   MVC   NMSTKEY,MSTKEY
82           MVC   NMSTDESC,MSTDESC
83           MVC   NMSTQTY,MSTQTY
84           MVC   NMSTDATA,MSTDATA
85           PUT   NEWMAST,NMSTRECD
86           BAL   10,GETMAST
87           BR    5
```

The above statements mean: Write the old master record to the new master file. Remember: The old master record may contain updates applied by a previous transaction. In either case, the old master record is written to the new master file. The branch register returns control to the UPDPROC module.

UPDATING THE MASTER FILE—PART III

With sample program CHAP9D, we have a working copy of the update program. Errors were not considered in the last program, but we are now ready to look for them. In sample program CHAP9E, we will check for the following errors: (1) adding master records that already exist, (2) processing transactions that do not match a master record, and (3) processing transaction codes that are invalid.

Figure 9.14 shows the input and output for sample program CHAP9E.

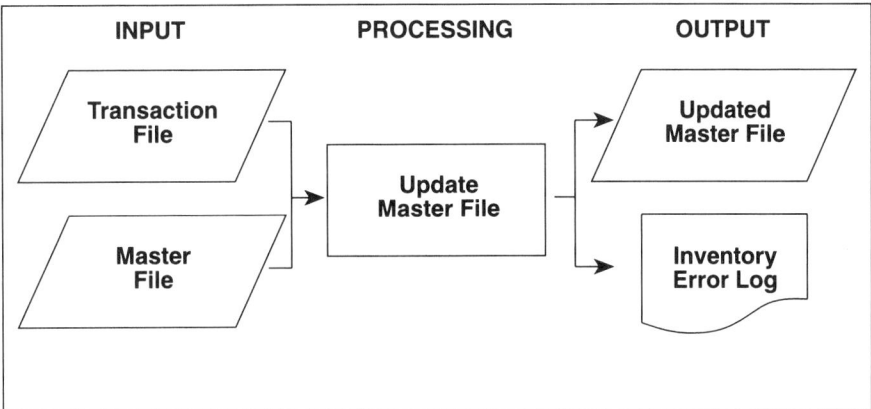

FIGURE 9.14 CHAP9E: Updating with Error Checking

SAMPLE PROGRAM CHAP9E

As shown in Figure 9.14, the Updated Master File and the Inventory Error Log are produced by applying the transactions to the old master file. Errors are considered and checks have been added to the update logic. Sample program CHAP9E is shown in Fig. 9.15; the program's input and output are shown in Fig. 9.16.

Input data:
    Transaction file
    Old master file

Processing functions:
    Compare the keys. If they are equal, use the transaction code to determine the processing: (1) delete the master record, (2) update the master record, or (3) print the error message MASTER EXISTS. But if the transaction key is less than the master, then use the transaction code to determine whether to add a new master record or print the error message UNMATCHED TRANSACTION. Otherwise, write the old master record to the new master file.

Program output (Disk File: Updated Master File; Printer Report: Inventory Error Log):
    The program output is shown in Fig. 9.16.

Pseudocode logic design:
START
Open I/O files
(Read transaction record)
(Read master record)
LOOP until no more data (both files empty)
   If TRNKEY = MSTKEY
      If transaction code = delete record
         (Read master record)
         (Read transaction record)
      else
         If transaction code = add record
            Print error message MASTER EXISTS
            (Read transaction record)
         else
            (Update master record)
   else
      If TRNKEY < MSTKEY
         If transaction code = add record
            Write transaction record to new master file
            (Read transaction record)
         else
            Print error message UNMATCHED
                TRANSACTION
            (Read transaction record)
      else
         Write old master record to new master file
         (Read master record)
End LOOP
Close files
END

ENTER (Update master record)
If transaction code = add items
   Add transaction qty to master qty.
If transaction code = subtract items
   Subtract transaction qty from master qty.
If transaction code = change qty
   Move transaction qty to master qty.
If transaction code = change description
   Move transaction description to master description.

else
>Print error message BAD TRANSACTION CODE.
>(Read transaction record).

RETURN

```
 1  *---------------- SEQUENTIAL FILE UPDATE -----------------
 2  *  This program reads a transaction file, updates the
 3  *  master file, and checks for errors.
 4  *
 5  *           PROGRAM-ID: CHAP9E
 6  *           PROGRAMMER: David M. Collopy
 7  *           RUN DATE:   mm/dd/yy
 8  ****************************************************************
 9  CHAP9E    CSECT                                        (system
10            PRINT NOGEN                                  use and
11            BALR  2,0                                    general
12            USING *,2                                housekeeping)
13            OPEN  TRANS,MAST,NEWMAST,PRINTER         open files
14  *---------------------------------------------------------------
15  *              MAINLINE CONTROL
16  *---------------------------------------------------------------
17  MAINLINE  BAL   10,HEADING                         print heading
18            BAL   10,GETTRAN                       get trans record
19            BAL   10,GETMAST                       get mast record
20            BAL   9,UPDPROC                       update processing
21            B     EXIT                                 process exit
22  *---------------------------------------------------------------
23  *              PRINT HEADING
24  *---------------------------------------------------------------
25  HEADING   MVI   CCH,C'1'                         skip to new page...
26            PUT   PRINTER,HDGLINE                  ...and print heading
27            MVI   CCB,C' '                         single space...
28            PUT   PRINTER,BLKLINE                  ...and print blank line
29            BR    10                               return to mainline
```

FIGURE 9.15 Sample Program CHAP9E: Reads a transaction file, updates the master file, and checks for errors.

```
30 *-------------------------------------------------------------------
31 *               UPDATE PROCESSING
32 *-------------------------------------------------------------------
33 UPDPROC   CLC   MSTKEY,EOFKEY                      test for EOM
34           BE    CKTRAN                  if EOM, test for EOT
35           B     CONTINUE                       else continue
36 CKTRAN    CLC   TRNKEY,EOFKEY                      test for EOT
37           BE    QUIT                    if EOM & EOT, quit
38 CONTINUE  CLC   TRNKEY,MSTKEY                     compare keys
39           BE    UPDATE                      if T = M, update
40           BL    ADDREC                  if T < M, add record
41           BAL   5,WRTMST                 write master record
42           B     REPEAT                         skip to repeat
43 UPDATE    BAL   5,UPDMST                update master record
44           B     REPEAT                         skip to repeat
45 ADDREC    BAL   5,ADDMST                add new master record
46 REPEAT    B     UPDPROC                            repeat loop
47 QUIT      BR    9                                       return
48 *-------------------------------------------------------------------
49 *               UPDATE MASTER RECORD
50 *-------------------------------------------------------------------
51 UPDMST    CLI   TRNCODE,C'6'                      test trn code
52           BE    DLETMAST                 if equal, delete mst
53           CLI   TRNCODE,C'5'                      test trn code
54           BE    BADADD                     if equal, bad add
55           B     UPDMASTR                      else update mst
56 DLETMAST  BAL   10,GETMAST                     get mast record
57           B     NEXTRN                    skip to next tran
58 UPDMASTR  CLI   TRNCODE,C'1'                      test trn code
59           BE    ADDQTY                     if equal, add qty
60           CLI   TRNCODE,C'2'                      test trn code
61           BE    SUBTQTY                 if equal, subtract qty
62           CLI   TRNCODE,C'3'                      test trn code
63           BE    CHGQTY                     if equal, change qty
64           CLI   TRNCODE,C'4'                      test trn code
65           BE    CHGDESC                 if equal, change desc
66 BADTCODE  MVC   ERRMESG,ERMSG3        trn code out of range (1-6)
67           MVC   ERRKEY,TRNKEY                move key to report
68           MVC   ERRDESC,TRNDESC             move desc to report
```

FIGURE 9.15 (cont.)

```
 69            MVC    ERRQTY,TRNQTY               move qty to report
 70            MVC    ERRDATA,TRNDATA            move data to report
 71            MVI    CCE,C' '                       single space...
 72            PUT    PRINTER,ERRRECD       ...and write error record
 73            B      NEXTRN                      skip to next tran
 74 CHGDESC    MVC    MSTDESC,TRNDESC             change description
 75            B      NEXTRN                      skip to next tran
 76 ADDQTY     PACK   MQTY,MSTQTY                    convert to PD
 77            PACK   TQTY,TRNQTY                    convert to PD
 78            AP     MQTY,TQTY                     add trn quantity
 79            UNPK   MSTQTY,MQTY                    convert to ZD
 80            B      NEXTRN                      skip to next tran
 81 SUBTQTY    PACK   MQTY,MSTQTY                    convert to PD
 82            PACK   TQTY,TRNQTY                    convert to PD
 83            SP     MQTY,TQTY                subtract trn quantity
 84            UNPK   MSTQTY,MQTY                    convert to ZD
 85            B      NEXTRN                      skip to next tran
 86 BADADD     MVC    ERRMESG,ERMSG1           master already exists
 87            MVC    ERRKEY,TRNKEY              move key to report
 88            MVC    ERRDESC,TRNDESC           move desc to report
 89            MVC    ERRQTY,TRNQTY              move qty to report
 90            MVC    ERRDATA,TRNDATA           move data to report
 91            MVI    CCE,C' '                       single space...
 92            PUT    PRINTER,ERRRECD       ...and write error record
 93            B      NEXTRN                       skip to next trn
 94 CHGQTY     MVC    MSTQTY,TRNQTY                change quantity
 95 NEXTRN     BAL    10,GETTRAN                   get tran record
 96            BR     5                                      return
 97 *----------------------------------------------------------------
 98 *                 ADD NEW MASTER RECORD
 99 *----------------------------------------------------------------
100 ADDMST     CLI    TRNCODE,C'5'                     test trn code
101            BNE    BADTRN                  if not equal, bad trn
102            MVC    NMSTKEY,TRNKEY          move input to output
103            MVC    NMSTDESC,TRNDESC        move input to output
104            MVC    NMSTQTY,TRNQTY          move input to output
105            MVC    NMSTDATA,TRNDATA        move input to output
106            PUT    NEWMAST,NMSTRECD        write trn to new mst
107            B      READTRAN                  skip to read tran
```

FIGURE 9.15 (cont.)

```
108 BADTRN     MVC    ERRMESG,ERMSG2              unmatched trn
109            MVC    ERRKEY,TRNKEY            move key to report
110            MVC    ERRDESC,TRNDESC         move desc to report
111            MVC    ERRQTY,TRNQTY            move qty to report
112            MVC    ERRDATA,TRNDATA         move data to report
113            MVI    CCE,C' '                     single space...
114            PUT    PRINTER,ERRRECD     ...and write error record
115 READTRN    BAL    10,GETTRAN                   get next trn
116            BR     5                                  return
117 *------------------------------------------------------------
118 *                 WRITE MASTER RECORD
119 *------------------------------------------------------------
120 WRTMST     MVC    NMSTKEY,MSTKEY          move input to output
121            MVC    NMSTDESC,MSTDESC        move input to output
122            MVC    NMSTQTY,MSTQTY          move input to output
123            MVC    NMSTDATA,MSTDATA        move input to output
124            PUT    NEWMAST,NMSTRECD    write old mst to new mst
125            BAL    10,GETMAST                  get mast record
126            BR     5                                  return
127 *------------------------------------------------------------
128 *                 GET TRANSACTION RECORD
129 *------------------------------------------------------------
130 GETTRAN    CLC    TRNKEY,EOFKEY                  test for EOT
131            BE     NOTRAN                      if EOT, skip read
132            B      READTRAN                     else read trans
133 EOT        MVC    TRNKEY,EOFKEY            set key to '9999'
134            B      NOTRAN                              skip read
135 READTRAN   GET    TRANS,TRNRECD                    read trans
136 NOTRAN     BR     10                                  return
137 *------------------------------------------------------------
138 *                 GET MASTER RECORD
139 *------------------------------------------------------------
140 GETMAST    CLC    MSTKEY,EOFKEY                  test for EOM
141            BE     NOMAST                      if EOM, skip read
142            B      READMAST                     else read trans
143 EOM        MVC    MSTKEY,EOFKEY            set key to '9999'
144            B      NOMAST                              skip read
145 READMAST   GET    MAST,MSTRECD                      read mast
146 NOMAST     BR     10                                  return
```

FIGURE 9.15 (cont.)

```
147 *
148 EXIT      CLOSE TRANS,MAST,NEWMAST,PRINTER         close files
149           EOJ                                      end of job
150 **************************************************************
151 *                  I/O FILE DEFINITIONS
152 *--------------------------------------------------------------
153 TRANS     DTFCD DEVADDR=SYSIPT,IOAREA1=TRNBUFF,DEVICE=2540,   X
                  WORKA=YES,BLKSIZE=80,EOFADDR=EOT
154 MAST      DTFSD DEVADDR=SYS005,IOAREA1=MSTBUFF,DEVICE=3330,   X
                  WORKA=YES,RECFORM=FIXUNB,BLKSIZE=80,            X
                  TYPEFLE=INPUT,EOFADDR=EOM
155 NEWMAST   DTFSD DEVADDR=SYS005,IOAREA1=NMSTBUF,DEVICE=3330,   X
                  WORKA=YES,RECFORM=FIXUNB,BLKSIZE=80,            X
                  TYPEFLE=OUTPUT
156 PRINTER   DTFPR DEVADDR=SYSLST,IOAREA1=PRTBUFF,DEVICE=1403,   X
                  CTLCHR=YES,WORKA=YES,BLKSIZE=80
157 *
158 TRNBUFF   DS    CL80                     transaction file buffer
159 MSTBUFF   DS    CL80                     old master file buffer
160 NMSTBUF   DS    CL80                     new master file buffer
161 PRTBUFF   DS    CL80                     printer file buffer
162 *--------------------------------------------------------------
163 *                  RECORD/DATA DEFINITIONS
164 *--------------------------------------------------------------
165 TRNRECD   DS    0CL80      T R A N S A C T I O N   R E C O R D
166 TRNKEY    DS    CL4        (01 - 04)                        key
167 TRNDESC   DS    CL26       (05 - 30)           item description
168 TRNQTY    DS    CL3        (31 - 33)                   quantity
169 TRNDATA   DS    CL12       (34 - 45)                 other data
170           DS    CL4        (46 - 49)                     unused
171 TRNCODE   DS    CL1        (50 - 50)           transaction code
172           DS    CL30       (51 - 80)                     unused
173 *
174 MSTRECD   DS    0CL80              M A S T E R   R E C O R D
175 MSTKEY    DS    CL4        (01 - 04)                        key
176 MSTDESC   DS    CL26       (05 - 30)           item description
177 MSTQTY    DS    CL3        (31 - 33)                   quantity
178 MSTDATA   DS    CL12       (34 - 45)                 other data
179           DS    CL35       (46 - 80)                     unused
```

FIGURE 9.15 (cont.)

```
180 *
181 HDGLINE   DS    0CL80               H E A D I N G   L I N E
182 CCH       DS    CL1                      carriage control
183           DC    CL20' '
184           DC    CL19'INVENTORY ERROR LOG'
185           DC    CL40' '
186 *
187 BLKLINE   DS    0CL80               B L A N K   L I N E
188 CCB       DS    CL1                      carriage control
189           DC    CL79' '
190 *
191 NMSTRECD  DS    0CL80          N E W   M A S T E R   R E C O R D
192 NMSTKEY   DS    CL4       (01 - 04)                          key
193 NMSTDESC  DS    CL26      (05 - 30)             item description
194 NMSTQTY   DS    CL3       (31 - 33)                     quantity
195 NMSTDATA  DS    CL12      (34 - 45)                   other data
196           DS    CL35      (46 - 80)                       unused
197 *
198 ERRRECD   DS    0CL80                 E R R O R   R E C O R D
199 CCE       DS    CL1                      carriage control
200 ERRKEY    DS    CL4       (01 - 04)                          key
201 ERRDESC   DS    CL26      (05 - 30)             item description
202 ERRQTY    DS    CL3       (31 - 33)                     quantity
203 ERRDATA   DS    CL12      (34 - 45)                   other data
204           DC    CL2' '    (46 - 47)                       unused
205 ERRMESG   DS    CL15      (48 - 62)                error message
206           DC    CL17' '   (63 - 80)                       unused
207 *
208 EOFKEY    DC    CL4'9999'            end of file indicator
209 MQTY      DS    PL2                  master qty (packed)
210 TQTY      DS    PL2             transaction qty (packed)
211 ERMSG1    DC    CL15'MASTER EXISTS'       error message-1
212 ERMSG2    DC    CL15'UNMATCHED TRANS'     error message-2
213 ERMSG3    DC    CL15'BAD TRANS CODE'      error message-3
214           END   CHAP9E
```

FIGURE 9.15 (cont.)

```
                    Input: Transaction File

3000                                                          6
4000                              024                         1
4500                                                          6
5000                              005                         2
5000                              012                         7
5000 Add new master record 5000 144 *other data*              5
6500 Add new master record 6500 015 *other data*              5
7000 Change description -- 7000                               4
8000                              055                         3
9500 Add new master record 9500 018 *other data*              5
9700                              035                         3

                     Input: Master File

  1000 Description for item# 1000 100 *other data*
  2000 Description for item# 2000 050 *other data*
  3000 Description for item# 3000 025 *other data*
  4000 Description for item# 4000 012 *other data*
  5000 Description for item# 5000 024 *other data*
  6000 Description for item# 6000 048 *other data*
  7000 Description for item# 7000 030 *other data*
  8000 Description for item# 8000 060 *other data*
  9000 Description for item# 9000 090 *other data*

                  Output: Updated Master File

  1000 Description for item# 1000 100 *other data*
  2000 Description for item# 2000 050 *other data*
  4000 Description for item# 4000 036 *other data*
  5000 Description for item# 5000 019 *other data*
  6000 Description for item# 6000 048 *other data*
  6500 Add new master record 6500 015 *other data*
  7000 Change description -- 7000 030 *other data*
  8000 Description for item# 8000 055 *other data*
  9000 Description for item# 9000 090 *other data*
  9500 Add new master record 9500 018 *other data*
```

FIGURE 9.16 File Input and Output for CHAP9E

```
                     INVENTORY  ERROR  LOG
4500                                                    UNMATCHED TRANS
5000                                  012               BAD TRANS CODE
5000  Add new master record 5000  144 *other data*      MASTER EXISTS
9700                                  035               UNMATCHED TRANS
```

FIGURE 9.16 (cont.)

DISSECTION OF SAMPLE PROGRAM CHAP9E

With the exception of the error checks and the Inventory Error Log, the logic in sample program CHAP9E is similar to the logic in sample program CHAP9D. The update routine remains basically the same.

Two error checks were added to the UPDMST module: BADADD (bad add/master exists—we may not add a record to the master file because the record is already in the master file) and BADTCODE (bad transaction code—we may not process transaction codes that fall outside the range of acceptable values). A third error check was added to the ADDMST module: BADTRN (bad transaction/unmatched transaction—we may not process transactions, other than new record additions, that do not match an existing master record).

When the program detects an error, the transaction record and the appropriate error message are written to the Inventory Error Log. The code used for processing errors follows:

```
UPDATE     MASTER     RECORD:
                :
     66  BADTCODE  MVC    ERRMESG,ERMSG3
     67            MVC    ERRKEY,TRNKEY
     68            MVC    ERRDESC,TRNDESC
     69            MVC    ERRQTY,TRNQTY
     70            MVC    ERRDATA,TRNDATA
     71            MVI    CCE,C' '
     72            PUT    PRINTER,ERRRECD
     73            B      NEXTRN
                :
```

When the transaction and master keys are equal, control branches to UPDMST and checks the transaction code to determine the type of update to perform. If the transaction code falls outside the range of 1–6, then it is illegal, and we have an error.

The message BAD TRANS CODE is moved to the error record, along with the data stored in the transaction, and the error record is written to the Inventory Error Log. Control then branches to NEXTRN and reads the next transaction.

```
            :
86 BADADD   MVC    ERRMESG,ERMSG1
87          MVC    ERRKEY,TRNKEY
88          MVC    ERRDESC,TRNDESC
89          MVC    ERRQTY,TRNQTY
90          MVC    ERRDATA,TRNDATA
91          MVI    CCE,C' '
92          PUT    PRINTER,ERRRECD
93          B      NEXTRN
            :
```

Control branches to BADADD when the transaction and master keys are equal, and the transaction code specifies a record addition (5). Since it is impossible to add a record that already exists, the transaction is obviously in error.

The message MASTER EXISTS is moved to the error record, along with the data stored in the transaction, and the error record is written to the Inventory Error Log. The program then branches and reads the next transaction.

ADD NEW MASTER RECORD:

```
            :
108 BADTRN  MVC    ERRMESG,ERMSG2
109         MVC    ERRKEY,TRNKEY
110         MVC    ERRDESC,TRNDESC
111         MVC    ERRQTY,TRNQTY
112         MVC    ERRDATA,TRNDATA
113         MVI    CCE,C' '
114         PUT    PRINTER,ERRRECD
115 READTRN BAL    10,GETTRAN
            :
```

When the transaction key is less than the master key and the transaction code specifies processing other than a new record addition, then we have an unmatched transaction.

The message UNMATCHED TRANS is moved to the error record, along with the data stored in the transaction, the error record is written to the Inventory Error Log, and the next transaction is read.

KEY REVIEW TERMS

Define the following terms:

Inventory Error Log	error check	file creation
file update	ABEND	control field
RECFORM	master file	transaction code
transaction file	TYPEFLE	file maintenance
DTFSD	sequential file	VERIFY
file processing	record key	

REVIEW EXERCISES

1. Earlier in this chapter, we listed six types of information that describe the status of the inventory: physical inventory counts for each item, items to reorder, total sales per item for a specific period, transactions processed for the current week, back-ordered items, and slow- and fast-moving items. Can you identify at least three other types of useful information that help describe the status of the inventory?
*2. When the master file is updated, why is it necessary for the transactions to include all the fields contained in the master record?
3. List the transaction codes used by the program to update the master file. Explain the purpose of each. Which transaction codes actually update the old master records?
4. When testing and debugging an update program, is it necessary to reconstruct the master file prior to executing the program? Explain your answer.
5. What relationship exists, if any, between the keys used to create the master file and the keys used by the transaction file?
6. What is the purpose of the Create Master program? Explain how it works.
*7. Why do we print a hard copy of the master file after it has been created and after each update run?

8. Explain the methods you use to locate and correct program errors. In what ways could you improve your debugging skills?

9. Identify three input errors that the update program should catch.

*10. Using the update and error-checking logic given for sample program CHAP9E, would the program catch a transaction coded to delete a record that is not on the master file? Explain your answer.

11. What is the purpose of the error log? Is it necessary to print the error log during an update run, or should errors be handled differently?

12. Explain in detail how the update logic works for sample program CHAP9E.

PROGRAMMING EXERCISES

Instructions: For each exercise, design the pseudocode and write the modular structured program to produce the output given. Model your program after the sample programs. Verify your output.

1. Sample program CHAP9B updates the master file and checks for errors. It does not, however, check for sequence errors in the input. Include an error check in the read modules to assure the record keys are in ascending order. Modify the transaction and master files to include sequence errors. When a sequence error is detected, print the appropriate error message (MST OUT OF SEQ or TRN OUT OF SEQ), along with the record found in error, and continue processing.

2. Production work: Write a program to create the production master file (on disk) for the Rollbent Manufacturing Company. After creating the file, write a second program to read and list the master records to the printer to verify that the file was built correctly.

    The master records consist of the following fields:

Columns	Record Fields
01–03	Employee number
04–23	Employee name
24–27	Product number
28–30	Production quota
31–33	Pieces made

Input data (Master File):

Employee #	Employee Name	Product #	Quota	Pieces
169	Tim Duffy	A174	100	100
173	Bob Wells	E001	057	062
213	Sarah Rodock	H037	125	119
383	Sonia Bowers	X341	089	070
409	Brian Ayers	E849	043	043
445	Scott Beale	R939	072	089
615	Trisha Morris	C292	039	039
663	Kirt Jones	F456	055	067
718	Seth Cossin	T215	112	099
727	Carrie Ross	Y771	045	043
811	Pat Willits	B119	075	075
823	Trevor Miller	D017	060	060

Processing functions:

Create the master file and, for verification purposes, read and list a copy of the file to the printer.

Program output:

Production master file. Print a title line across the top of the page, skip a line, and list the unedited records to the report.

3. Update the master file created in Exercise 2. Use the following transactions to update the production master file. Assume there are no errors.

Column	Transaction Code (TC)
40–40	Used to tell the computer how to process or apply the transaction to the master file. C1—change employee name C2—change product number C3—change quota C4—change pieces made AR—add new master record DR—delete old master record

Upon completing the update, write a second program to read and print the production report shown under "Program Output."

NOTE: The record fields for the transactions are identical to those of the master file, with the exception of the transaction code.

Input data (Master File):
　See Exercise 2.
Input data (Transaction File):

Employee #	Employee Name	Product #	Quota	Pieces	TC
108	Jodie Pifer	D963	065	065	AR
173			060		C3
213		H373			C2
409					DR
615	Trisha McMorris				C1
659	Ron Parker	V019	040	045	AR
718				110	C4
727				047	C4
823					DR
855	Jenny Scanlon	W604	035	031	AR

Processing functions:
　Update the master file. Afterwards, read the master file and print the daily production report.

Program output (Production Report):

```
              ROLLBENT MANUFACTURING COMPANY
                  Daily Production Report
                        mm/dd/yy


   EMPL#         EMPLOYEE NAME         PRODUCT#    QUOTA    OUTPUT

    169       Tim Duffy                  A174       100       100
     :            :                       :          :         :
     :            :                       :          :         :
     :            :                       :          :         :
    999       X----------------X         XXXX       999       999
```

4. Change Exercise 3 to include error checks for illegal transaction codes, unmatched transactions, and illegal record additions. Insert the following transactions into the transaction file used in Exercise 3. Be sure to insert them in record-key (employee-number) order.

Transactions:

Employee #	Employee Name	Product #	Quota	Pieces	TC
169					AC
214		D184			C2
445	Scott Beale	R939	072	089	AR
663			109		C6
727	Carrie Ross	Y771	045	043	AR

5. Modify Exercise 4 to include input sequence checking. Test your program by making up 4–5 additional transaction and master records. Place them in the input files used in Exercise 4. Be sure they are inserted in out-of-sequence order.

6. Enrollment survey: Write a program to create the school enrollment master file. Then write a second program to read and list the master records to the printer to verify that the output is correct. The master records consist of the following fields:

Columns	Record Fields
01–02	School Identification Code
03–22	Name of school
23–23	Education-type code
	E—Elementary school
	M—Middle school
	J—Junior high school
	H—High school
24–27	Student Population
28–30	Staff Size

Input data (Master File):

School ID	School Name	Education-Type Code	Student Population	Staff Size
10	Karla Buckley	E	0425	018
15	Northbrook	E	0400	016
21	Hanna Eppley	M	1600	064
23	Adam E. Myers	J	0800	033
25	Woodman Heights	H	3500	117
36	Ellis Watts	E	0300	012
39	Wahrfield	E	0350	014
45	McKinley	M	1335	053
51	Eastbrook	M	0650	027
63	Weststone	H	2400	080

Processing functions:

> Create the master file and, for verification, read and list a copy of the file to the printer.

Program output:

> School enrollment master file. Print a title line at the top of the page, skip a line, and list the unedited master records to the report.

7. Using the following transaction file, update the school enrollment master file created in Exercise 6. Assume there are no errors in the input.

Column	Transaction Code (TC)
45–45	Tells the computer how to process or apply the transaction to the master file. 1—Add new master record 2—Delete old master record 3—Change name of school 4—Change education type code 5—Change student population 6—Change staff size

Upon completing the update, write a second program to read and print the school enrollment survey shown under "Program Output."

NOTE: Except for the transaction code, the data fields of the transactions are identical to those of the master file.

> *Input data (Master File):*
>
> See Exercise 6.
>
> *Input data (Transaction File):*

School ID	School Name	Education-Type Code	Student Population	Staff Size	TC
10				017	6
15					2
15	Westwood	E	0430	018	1
25			3528		5
36	Ellis B. Watson				3
42	Cooper Run	E	0412	016	1
51		J			4

Processing functions:
Update the master file. Afterwards, read the master file and print the school enrollment survey.

Program output (Enrollment Survey):

```
         PLAINFIELD CITY SCHOOL SYSTEM
              School Enrollment Survey
                     mm/dd/yy


SCHOOL     NAME OF SCHOOL        EDUCATION     STUDENT       SIZE OF
  ID                             TYPE CODE    POPULATION      STAFF

  10       Karla Buckley             E           0425          018
   :            :                    :             :            :
   :            :                    :             :            :
   :            :                    :             :            :
  99       X----------------X        X           9999          999
```

8. Change Exercise 7 to include error checks for illegal transaction codes, unmatched transactions, and illegal record additions. Insert the following transactions into the transaction file used in Exercise 7. Be sure to insert them in record-key (school-ID) order.

    Transactions:

School ID	School Name	Education-Type Code	Student Population	Staff Size	TC
10	Charles Grant	E	0425	018	1
21		H			7
30			3600		5
45	John Q. Adams	M	1400	054	1
67	Boyd Mauger				3

9. Modify Exercise 8 to check for input sequence errors. Test your program by making up 4–5 additional transaction and master records. Place them in the input files used in Exercise 8. Be sure they are inserted in out-of-sequence order.

A | ENTERING AND RUNNING YOUR FIRST PROGRAM

PC 370 Assembler will run with DOS. Use the following procedures as a guideline to enter your source program and to run the Assembler compiler.

LOGGING ON

If your computer system has two floppy-disk drives, follow the steps under "Two-Drive System." If your computer has a hard drive and floppy drive(s), follow the steps under "Hard-Drive System."

TWO-DRIVE SYSTEM

1. Turn on the computer, the monitor, and the printer. Insert your DOS disk in drive A.
2. Enter the current date, if requested, and press RETURN (<R>). Enter the current time, if requested, and press <R>. Put your formatted work disk in drive B.
3. We will use a text editor to enter, edit, save, and load Assembler programs and datasets. Your instructor or supervisor will let you know which text editor to use. Remove your DOS disk from drive A, and insert the text editor program disk you will be using.
4. Skip the following section, "Hard Drive System," and continue with "Keying-in Your Program."

HARD-DRIVE SYSTEM

1. Turn on the computer, the monitor, and the printer.
2. Enter the current date, if requested, and press RETURN (<R>). Enter the current time, if requested, and press <R>. Insert your formatted work disk in drive B.
3. We will use a text editor to enter, edit, save, and load Assembler programs and datasets. Your instructor or supervisor will let you know which text editor to use.

Appendix A: Entering and Running Your First Program

KEYING-IN YOUR PROGRAM

1. Using the editor, key-in the following test program. Enter it exactly as shown, noting the column positions. Do not key-in the column position line; it is not part of the program. Enter your name as the programmer and the current date.

```
1--------1-----1------------------------ column positions
         0     6


// JOB FIRST1 your name
// OPTION LINK
// EXEC ASSEMBLY
*------------- FIND THE SUM OF THREE INTEGERS --------------
*
*         PROGRAM-ID: FIRST1.ASM
*         PROGRAMMER: enter your name
*         RUN DATE:   enter the date
**************************************************************
FIRST1    CSECT
          PRINT NOGEN
          BALR  2,0
          USING *,2
          L     7,NUM1
          A     7,NUM2
          A     7,NUM3
          ST    7,SUM
          PDUMP NUM1,SUM+4
          EOJ
NUM1      DC    F'10'
NUM2      DC    F'15'
NUM3      DC    F'20'
SUM       DS    F
          END   FIRST1
/*
// EXEC LNKEDT
// EXEC
/*
/&
```

2. Proofread your program. Double-check spelling and spacing carefully. Be sure your program matches the preceding code. If you need to make corrections, ask your instructor or supervisor for help with the editor.
3. When your program is correctly keyed-in, you are ready to save it; refer to the section "Saving Your Program."

NOTE: Statements beginning with a slash (/) represent Job Control Language (JCL) statements. They are used to communicate and issue commands to the operating system. Key them in as shown. They are required and are included with the program. Refer to Appendix B for a brief introduction to JCL.

SAVING YOUR PROGRAM

1. Save your program on drive B. Use FIRST1.ASM as your file name. Be sure to save the program as an ASCII or text document. PC 370 Assembler reads only programs and datasets that have been saved in ASCII format.
2. For backup purposes, save your program twice: If you accidentally lose the program, you will have a backup copy with which to work. Use the file name FIRST1.BAK to save your backup copy. The extension BAK stands for backup.

EXECUTING ASSEMBLER AND RUNNING YOUR PROGRAM

1. Make sure you are online to the printer before running the program.
2. Exit the text editor program, and return to DOS.
3. If your system has two floppy-disk drives, remove the text editor program disk from drive A and insert the PC 370 Assembler System disk in drive A.
4. Type: ASM
   Press: <R>
   This command loads Assembler.
5. Assembler will prompt you to enter the name of the program. Key-in the name of the program without the .ASM extension.
   Type: FIRST1
   Press: <R>

Appendix A: Entering and Running Your First Program

6. If your program has no errors, it will execute successfully. After a successful run, skip to the section "Logging Off." Otherwise, an error message may appear on the screen.
7. For errors, list a copy of the screen to the printer. Press simultaneously SHIFT and PRINT SCREEN. With some keyboards, you need press only PRINT SCREEN.
8. If you are using a system with two floppy-disk drives, remove the PC 370 Assembler System disk from drive A and insert the text editor program disk.
9. Restart the text editor program.
10. Load your Assembler program into the editor.
11. Fix the errors made and resave the program. Use FIRST1.ASM as your file name. Remember to save a backup copy as well. Always save your program after making changes to it.
12. Now you're ready to run the program again. Return to Step 1 of this section.

LOGGING OFF

1. Remove any disks from the computer system.
2. If your computer contains a hard drive, check with your instructor or supervisor for any special instructions before turning off the computer.
3. Turn off the computer, the monitor, and the printer before leaving the lab.

B | INTRODUCTION TO DOS JOB CONTROL LANGUAGE

The purpose of the operating system is to maintain order, manage resources, and execute programs. It acts as an interface between the program and the computer. The operating system allows the user to enter and execute programs without the cumbersome burden of manually overseeing the interaction between the hardware and the software. Overall, it performs a variety of functions, including (but not limited to) managing the computer's internal resources, controlling the input and output operations, translating source programs into machine code, scheduling and running programs, and organizing and manipulating files.

Programmers communicate with the operating system in Job Control Language (JCL). JCL is used to issue commands to the operating system, such as telling it when to execute a program, process data, and read/write files. We need JCL to tell the operating system what to do.

We shall be using the microcomputer as if it were a mainframe. Because of this configuration, the PC 370 Assembler system equates a micro-disk drive to a direct-access storage device (DASD). Hence, a disk file for the micro is treated as if it were a DASD file for the mainframe. For the sake of simplicity, we will modify a few programming procedures, but overall we will follow the mainframe conventions used for creating and processing DASD files.

In this text, we will illustrate the use of the Disk Operating System (DOS) as it applies to the PC 370 Assembler Compiler that accompanies this text. Ask your instructor or supervisor for the JCL required to run Assembler on your computer system.

SAMPLE JCL-1: SOURCE PROGRAM WITH NO DATA

The following job control statements are required to execute a program that does not read data.

```
// JOB FIRST1 DMCOLLOPY
// OPTION LINK
```

```
// EXEC ASSEMBLY
(source program statements)
/*
// EXEC LNKEDT
// EXEC
/*
/&
```

DISSECTION OF SAMPLE JCL-1

```
// JOB FIRST1 DMCOLLOPY
```

Job statement: This statement alerts the operating system that a new job or program is ready to execute. The slashes in columns 1 and 2 indicate that the statement represents a JCL command, as opposed to a program statement. DOS JCL commands usually begin with slashes. Column 3 must be blank and the keyword JOB (called the operation code) must appear in columns 4–6. The keyword JOB signals the start of a new job. The operands that follow identify the job name and the programmer. Both must be separated by a blank space.

Job name identifies the name of the program and may contain a maximum of eight alphanumeric characters. In our sample program, the job name is FIRST1. Job name may also refer to a system of programs that is processed as a single job. However, we will not use it to mean this, since each of our jobs will consist of one program.

As stated, blank spaces are used as delimiters to separate the operands. For the last operand, we enter our name as the programmer.

```
// OPTION LINK
```

Option statement: This statement tells the operating system to include the link option during execution of the job. The keyword OPTION indicates the presence of the named job options. In this case, the only option coded is LINK. It tells the operating system to load the object module (produced during the assembly step) into the program storage area and to perform the required link-edit operations. Although other options are available, PC 370 Assembler requires and accepts only the link option.

```
// EXEC ASSEMBLY
(source program statements)
```

Execution statement: This statement calls the Assembler compiler and instructs it to start translating the source program into machine code and to create the object module. The complete source program is placed instream and follows the `// EXEC ASSEMBLY` statement.

```
/*
```

Delimiter statement: The `/*` represents a delimiter statement. In this case, the `/*` is used to mark the end of the source code program.

```
// EXEC LNKEDT
```

Execute statement: This statement calls the linkage editor program and tells it to perform the necessary link-edit operations to the object module and to create an executable load module.

```
// EXEC
```

Execute statement: This statement executes the load module. In other words, it runs the program and performs the processing specified.

```
/*
/&
```

Delimiter statements: Both statements represent delimiters. The `/*` marks the end of the previous execution step. The `/&` specifies the end of the program or job. It tells the operating system that the current job is finished.

SAMPLE JCL-2: SOURCE PROGRAM WITH INSTREAM DATA

The following job control statements are required to execute a program that reads and processes an instream data file.

```
// JOB SECOND1 DMCOLLOPY
// OPTION LINK
// EXEC ASSEMBLY
(source program statements)
/*
// EXEC LNKEDT
// EXEC
(program data)
/*
/&
```

DISSECTION OF SAMPLE JCL-2

```
// JOB SECOND1 DMCOLLOPY
// OPTION LINK
// EXEC ASSEMBLY
(source program statements)
/*
```

Since this part of the job is the same as Sample JCL-1, we will begin our discussion with the following `// EXEC LNKEDT` statement.

```
// EXEC LNKEDT
// EXEC
(program data)
/*
/&
```

Most of the code shown here has also been covered in our discussion of Sample JCL-1. Notice how the input data has been included with the program by inserting it between the `// EXEC` and the `/*` statements. Overall, this part of the JCL instructs the operating system to perform the link-edit and to execute the program, which accesses and processes the data coded instream.

During execution, the program reads and processes the data. Accordingly, the access method looks for an instream data record each time a read statement is executed by the program. The `/*` delimiter is used here to mark the end of the instream data. As before, the `/&` is used to alert the operating system that the job is finished.

SAMPLE JCL-3: SOURCE PROGRAM WITH TWO DATA FILES

The following job control statements are required to execute a program that reads and processes two input files: one coded instream and one stored on disk.

```
// JOB THIRD1 DMCOLLOPY
// OPTION LINK
// EXEC ASSEMBLY
(source program statements)
```

```
/*
// EXEC LNKEDT
// ASSGN SYS005,3330,VOL=213045,SHR          (Input:
// DLBL MAST,'B:MAST.DAT'                        disk file)
// EXEC
(program data)
/*
/&
```

DISSECTION OF SAMPLE JCL-3

Most of Sample JCL-3 is similar to Sample JCL-2. However, two new JCL statements—ASSGN and DLBL—require explanation.

```
// ASSGN SYS005,3330,VOL=213045,SHR
```

Assign statement: This statement assigns the logical unit SYS005, defined by the DTF statement in the Assembler program, to the 3330 disk drive. This statement tells the computer operator to load the disk pack with volume label 213045 on the 3330 disk drive.

Note the last operand: SHR. It refers to the disposition of the file. SHR (share) indicates that the disk volume may be shared with other programs while we are using it to read and process MAST. Sharing improves program productivity and utilization of system resources. Since more than one program may access the disk pack, wait time is reduced.

```
// DLBL MAST,'B:MAST.DAT'
```

Disk label statement: When the appropriate volume has been mounted on the disk drive specified by ASSGN, then DLBL is used to associate the filename MAST, defined by the DTF in the program, with the physical data stored on the disk.

The disk filename enclosed within single quotes tells the operating system where the data can be found. Hence, each time the program reads a record from MAST, a record is retrieved from MAST.DAT and placed in the input (IOAREA1) buffer.

NOTE: The filenames of the program file and the physical file may be different. For example, INMAST may be retrieved from MAST.DAT.

The file-ID B:MAST.DAT, varies somewhat from DASD file-naming conventions. For convenience, we will use the file-naming standard shown.

B: indicates that the file is stored on the disk in drive B, and `MAST.DAT` specifies the name of the file. Disk filenames may contain a maximum of eight characters and include an extension of three characters following a period. DTF filenames, on the other hand, may consist of up to seven characters.

NOTE: In summary, `ASSGN` tells the operator which volume to mount on the disk drive, and `DLBL` tells the system-access method where to find the data. Together they provide the program with access to the data stored on the disk.

SAMPLE JCL-4: SOURCE PROGRAM WITH ONE INPUT AND ONE OUTPUT FILE

The following job control statements are required to execute a program that reads an instream data file and creates an output disk file.

```
// JOB FOURTH1 DMCOLLOPY
// OPTION LINK
// EXEC ASSEMBLY
(source program statements)
/*
// EXEC LNKEDT
// ASSGN SYS005,3330,VOL=213045,SHR        (Output:
// DLBL MAST,'B:MAST.DAT'                     disk
// EXTENT SYS005,213045,,,4,2                   file)
// EXEC
(program data)
/*
/&
```

DISSECTION OF SAMPLE JCL-4

`// EXTENT SYS005,213045,,,4,2`

Extent statement: Extent statements are required for output files and are used to tell the access method where to store the output on the disk.

In Sample JCL-4, the access method is told to place the output on volume 213045, which has been mounted on logical unit SYS005. Furthermore, the output is to be written to the disk beginning at the fourth track and has been given the name `MAST.DAT` by the `DLBL` statement. The last operand specifies the number of tracks (2) reserved for the file.

The operands for the EXTENT are positional. We may skip an operand when it isn't required, but must maintain its relative position by inserting a comma in its place. In Sample JCL-4, two operands were omitted: Extent Type and Sequence Number. Since we don't need them, we indicate their absence and relative position by coding the commas as shown.

ADDITIONAL JCL SAMPLES

The following samples show the job control statements used to execute the programs in Chapter 9.

1. Sample JCL: CHAP9A (Creating the Master File)

```
// JOB CHAP9A DMCOLLOPY
// OPTION LINK
// EXEC ASSEMBLY
(source program statements)
/*
// EXEC LNKEDT
// ASSGN SYS005,3330,VOL=213045,SHR        (Output:
// DLBL MAST,'B:MAST.DAT'                   disk
// EXTENT SYS005,213045,,,4,2                  file)
// EXEC
(program data)
/*
/&
```

2. Sample JCL: CHAP9B (Printing the Master File)

```
// JOB CHAP9B DMCOLLOPY
// OPTION LINK
// EXEC ASSEMBLY
(source program statements)
/*
// EXEC LNKEDT
// ASSGN SYS005,3330,VOL=213045,SHR        (Input:
// DLBL MAST,'B:MAST.DAT'                    Master File)
// EXEC
/*
/&
```

3. Sample JCL: CHAP9C (Updating the Master File)

```
// JOB CHAP9C DMCOLLOPY
// OPTION LINK
// EXEC ASSEMBLY
(source program statements)
/*
// EXEC LNKEDT
// ASSGN SYS005,3330,VOL=213045,SHR      (Input:
// DLBL MAST,'B:MAST.DAT'                        disk file)
// EXEC
(program data)
/*
/&
```

4. Sample JCL: CHAP9D (Updating the Master File)

```
// JOB CHAP9D DMCOLLOPY
// OPTION LINK
// EXEC ASSEMBLY
(source program statements)
/*
// EXEC LNKEDT
// ASSGN SYS005,3330,VOL=213045,SHR    (Input:
// DLBL MAST,'B:MAST.DAT'                      Master File)
// ASSGN SYS005,3330,VOL=213045,SHR    (Output:
// DLBL NEWMAST,'B:NEWMAST.DAT'                New Master
// EXTENT SYS005,213045,,,6,2                   File)
// EXEC
(instream data)                         (Input: Transaction
/*                                              File)
/&
```

5. Sample JCL: CHAP9E (Updating the Master File)

```
// JOB CHAP9E DMCOLLOPY
// OPTION LINK
// EXEC ASSEMBLY
(source program statements)
/*
// EXEC LNKEDT
```

```
// ASSGN SYS005,3330,VOL=213045,SHR    (Input:
// DLBL MAST,'B:MAST.DAT'                  Master File)
// ASSGN SYS005,3330,VOL=213045,SHR    (Output:
// DLBL NEWMAST,'B:NEWMAST.DAT'            New Master
// EXTENT SYS005,213045,,,6,2              File)
// EXEC
(instream data)                        (Input: Transaction
/*                                            File)
/&
```

C | SUMMARY REFERENCE: ASSEMBLER INSTRUCTIONS

The following instructions represent the Assembler statements introduced in this book.

```
      INSTRUCTION                LABEL   OPCODE   OPERAND FORMAT
      -------------------------1--------10----16---------------------
  *   Add                                A        R,S
  *   Add Packed                         AP       S1,S2
  *   Add Register                       AR       R1,R2
      Branch                             B        L
      Branch and Link                    BAL      R,L
      Branch on Count                    BCT      R,L
      Branch on Equal                    BE       L
      Branch on High                     BH       L
      Branch on Low                      BL       L
      Branch on Minus                    BM       L
      Branch on Not Minus                BNE      L
      Branch on Not High                 BNH      L
      Branch on Not Low                  BNL      L
      Branch on Not Minus                BNM      L
      Branch on Not Positive             BNP      L
      Branch on Not Zero                 BNZ      L
      Branch on Positive                 BP       L
      Branch Register                    BR       R
      Branch on Zero                     BZ       L
      Close                              CLOSE    (file names)
  *   Compare                            C        R,S
  *   Compare Logical Character          CLC      S1,S2
  *   Compare Logical Immediate          CLI      S,'I'
  *   Compare Packed                     CP       S1,S2
  *   Compare Register                   CR       R1,R2
      Control Section            L       CSECT
      Convert to Binary                  CVB      R,S
      Convert to Decimal                 CVD      R,S
```

Summary Reference: Assembler Instructions

```
    INSTRUCTION              LABEL   OPCODE  OPERAND FORMAT
----------------------------1--------10----16----------------------
    Divide                           D       R,S
    Define Constant          L       DC      C'string'
    Define Constant          L       DC      F'constant'
    Define Constant          L       DC      H'constant'
    Define Constant          L       DC      P'constant'
    Define Constant          L       DC      X'constant'
    Divide Packed                    DP      S1,S2
    Divide Register                  DR      R1,R2
    Define Storage           L       DS      CLn
    Define Storage           L       DS      D
    Define Storage           L       DS      F
    Define Storage           L       DS      H
    Define Storage           L       DS      PLn
    Define Storage           L       DS      XLn
    Define the File          L       DTF     (multiple operands)
*   Edit                             ED      S1,S2
    End                              END     L
    End of Job                       EOJ
    Equate                   L       EQU     *
    Get                              GET     F,S      (F = file name)
    Load                             L       R,S
    Load Register                    LR      R1,R2
*   Load and Test Register           LTR     R1,R2
    Multiply                         M       R,S
    Multiply Packed                  MP      S1,S2
    Multiply Register                MR      R1,R2
    Move Character                   MVC     S1,S2
    Move Immediate                   MVI     S,C'I'
    Move Zone                        MVZ     S1,S2
    Open                             OPEN    (file names)
    Pack                             PACK    S1,S2
    Partial Dump                     PDUMP   S1,S2
    Put                              PUT     F,S      (F = file name)
*   Subtract                         S       R,S
*   Subtract Packed                  SP      S1,S2
*   Subtract Register                SR      R1,R2
    Store                            ST      R,S
    Unpack                           UNPK    S1,S2
*   Zero and Add Packed              ZAP     S1,S2
```

* Denotes an instruction that sets the condition code.

Appendix C: Summary Reference: Assembler Instructions

LEGEND

- L = Label (shown for instructions which either require a label or use a label)
- R = Register
- S = Storage area
- C = Character
- P = Packed
- H = Halfword
- F = Fullword
- D = Doubleword
- X = Hexadecimal
- I = Immediate

D | SUMMARY REFERENCE: EBCDIC CODES

An abbreviated list of EBCDIC codes follows. For a complete list of EBCDIC codes, refer to the IBM System/370 Reference Summary published by the IBM Corporation.

	HEXADECIMAL	CHARACTER	ZONE BITS	DIGIT BITS
Special	40	blank	0100	0000
symbols	4B	.	0100	1011
	4C	<	0100	1100
	4D	(	0100	1101
	4E	+	0100	1110
	50	&	0101	0000
	5A	!	0101	1010
	5B	$	0101	1011
	5C	*	0101	1100
	5D	)	0101	1101
	5E	;	0101	1110
	60	-	0110	0000
	61	/	0110	0001
	6B	,	0110	1011
	6C	%	0110	1100
	6E	>	0110	1110
	6F	?	0110	1111
	7A	:	0111	1010
	7B	#	0111	1011
	7C	@	0111	1100
	7D	'	0111	1101
	7E	=	0111	1110
	7F	"	0111	1111

Appendix D: Summary Reference: EBCDIC Codes

	HEXADECIMAL	CHARACTER	ZONE BITS	DIGIT BITS
Letters	C1	A	1100	0001
	C2	B	1100	0010
	C3	C	1100	0011
	C4	D	1100	0100
	C5	E	1100	0101
	C6	F	1100	0110
	C7	G	1100	0111
	C8	H	1100	1000
	C9	I	1100	1001
	D1	J	1101	0001
	D2	K	1101	0010
	D3	L	1101	0011
	D4	M	1101	0100
	D5	N	1101	0101
	D6	O	1101	0110
	D7	P	1101	0111
	D8	Q	1101	1000
	D9	R	1101	1001
	E2	S	1110	0010
	E3	T	1110	0011
	E4	U	1110	0100
	E5	V	1110	0101
	E6	W	1110	0110
	E7	X	1110	0111
	E8	Y	1110	1000
	E9	Z	1110	1001
Digits	F0	0	1111	0000
	F1	1	1111	0001
	F2	2	1111	0010
	F3	3	1111	0011
	F4	4	1111	0100
	F5	5	1111	0101
	F6	6	1111	0110
	F7	7	1111	0111
	F8	8	1111	1000
	F9	9	1111	1001

E | POWERS OF TWO AND SIXTEEN TABLES

POWERS OF TWO

p	2^p
0	1
1	2
2	4
3	8
4	16
5	32
6	64
7	128
8	256
9	512
10	1,024
11	2,048
12	4,096
13	8,192
14	16,384
15	32,768

POWERS OF SIXTEEN

p	16^p
0	1
1	16
2	256
3	4,096
4	65,536
5	1,048,576
6	16,777,216
7	268,435,456
8	4,294,967,296
9	68,719,476,736
10	1,099,511,627,776
11	17,592,186,044,416
12	281,474,976,710,656
13	4,503,599,627,370,496
14	72,057,594,037,927,936
15	1,152,921,504,606,848,976

F | HEXADECIMAL AND DECIMAL CONVERSION TABLE

	POSITIONS					
	6	5	4	3	2	1
HEX DIGIT						
0	0	0	0	0	0	0
1	1,048,576	65,536	4,096	256	16	1
2	2,097,152	131,072	8,192	512	32	2
3	3,145,728	196,608	12,288	768	48	3
4	4,194,304	262,144	16,384	1,024	64	4
5	5,242,880	327,680	20,480	1,280	80	5
6	6,291,456	393,216	24,576	1,536	96	6
7	7,340,032	458,752	28,672	1,792	112	7
8	8,388,608	524,288	32,768	2,048	128	8
9	9,437,184	589,824	36,864	2,304	144	9
A	10,485,760	655,360	40,960	2,560	160	10
B	11,534,336	720,896	45,056	2,816	176	11
C	12,582,912	786,432	49,152	3,072	192	12
D	13,631,488	851,968	53,248	3,328	208	13
E	14,680,064	917,504	57,344	3,584	224	14
F	15,728,640	983,040	61,440	3,849	240	15

CONVERTING FROM DECIMAL TO HEXADECIMAL

Example: Convert 45992 to hexadecimal.

Subtract the largest possible table value from the decimal number and note the remainder. Record the corresponding hex digit in the given position. Repeat the process with the remainders until complete.

Hence, the hexadecimal result of 45992 is: B3A8.

$$\begin{array}{r} 45992 \\ -45056 \longrightarrow B\_\_\_ \\ \hline 936 \\ -768 \longrightarrow B\,3\_\_ \\ \hline 168 \\ -160 \longrightarrow B\,3\,A\_ \\ \hline 8 \longrightarrow B\,3\,A\,8 \end{array}$$

CONVERTING FROM HEXADECIMAL TO DECIMAL

Example: Convert 47DC to decimal.

positions 4 3 2 1
hex: 4 7 D C

Locate the value at the intersection of:
    position 1 and hex digit C: 12
    position 2 and hex digit D: 208
    position 3 and hex digit 7:   1,792
    position 4 and hex digit 4:   16,384

Hence, the decimal result of hexadecimal 47DC is: 18,396

G | ANSWERS TO ASTERISKED EXERCISES

CHAPTER 1

1. true   2. false   3. true
5. false   7. false   10. false
11. true   13. true   15. true
17. true   19. true   21. false
23. false   25. true

CHAPTER 2

1. 409 decimal

```
      ┌─── 9×1    =   9     4×10² + 0×0¹ + 9×0⁰ = 409
      ├─── 0×10   =   0
      └─── 4×100  = 400
                    ───
                    409
```

3. 1 1 0 1 1 0 1 binary

$$1\times 2^6 + 1\times 2^5 + 0\times 2^4 + 1\times 2^3 + 1\times 2^2 + 0\times 2^1 + 1\times 2^0 = 109$$

5. 1 2 3 hexadecimal
    - 3 × 1 = 3
    - 2 × 16 = 32
    - 1 × 256 = 256

    291 decimal

    $1 \times 16^2 + 2 \times 16^1 + 3 \times 16^0 = 291$

7. $111\ 1011_2$ $7B_{16}$
9. 1447_{10} $0101\ 1010\ 0111_{16}$
11. 125_{10} $7D_{16}$
13. $0011\ 1110\ 1000_2$ $3E8_{16}$
15. 43981_{10} $1010\ 1011\ 1100\ 1101_2$
16. $1\ 1100_2$ 111_{16} $1\ 1010_2$ $5F0E4_{16}$
18. $1\ 1100_2$ $590E_{16}$ $00\ 0011_2$ $111E6_{16}$
20. $110\ 1101_2$ $6CEB_{16}$ $10\ 1001_2$ $1FFFE_{16}$
21. $1111\ 1111\ 1000\ 0011_2$
23. $1111\ 1111\ 1111\ 0110_2$
25. $1111\ 0101\ 0100\ 1011_2$
26. 214_{10}
28. -157_{10}
30. -207_{10}
31. $1111\ 0001\ 1010\ 0100\ 1001\ 1110\ 1100\ 1011_2$
33. $F6D17B8C_{16}$
35. C1E2E2C5D4C2D3C5D9
37. C3E3C3C840F2F3F8
39. F1F9F840C3D9

CHAPTER 3

1. $0000\ 0064_{16}$
3. 0019_{16}

Answers to Asterisked Exercises

4. $0000\ 06E5_{16}$
5. $FFFF\ FFD2_{16}$
6. $FF3A_{16}$
7. C8C5D3D3D6
9. C8C94040
11. WHAT   DC   H'-233'
13. WHO   DC   F'-194'
14. TRYIT   DC   F'-3830'
15. NOTE2   DC   C'DATA-IN'
17. ANS   DC   F'44637'
19. NUM   DC   H'-1'
21. $0000\ 000E_{16}$ $0000\ 0032_{16}$
22. $0000\ 000C_{16}$ $0000\ 000C_{16}$
23. $0000\ 0078_{16}$ $0000\ 0052_{16}$
24. $0000\ 004E_{16}$ $0000\ 003B_{16}$
25. $0000\ 003E_{16}$ $0000\ 002D_{16}$
26. $FFFF\ FFC4_{16}$ $0000\ 0055_{16}$
27. $FFFF\ FFF3_{16}$ $FFFF\ FFD3_{16}$
28. $0000\ 21C0_{16}$ $FFFF\ EE48_{16}$
29. $0000\ 0360_{16}$ $FFFF\ FC58_{16}$
30. $0000\ 0002_{16}$ $0000\ 0007_{16}$
    $0000\ 0000_{16}$ $0000\ 0024_{16}$
31. $0000\ 0000_{16}$ $0000\ 000C_{16}$
    $0000\ 0007_{16}$ $FFFF\ FFFB_{16}$

CHAPTER 4

1. INPUT   EQU   * --------- Read record ------------
   PROCESS EQU   * --------- Process data ----------
   PNTLINE EQU   * --------- Print detail line ------
   TOTAL   EQU   * --------- Compute total ---------

Appendix G: Answers to Asterisked Exercises

```
2.  CRDHRS    EQU   5
    TEXTEXP   EQU   7
    CHGFEE    EQU   8
    TUITION   EQU   9

3.  INVEN     DS    0CL80    I N V E N T O R Y   R E C O R D
    CCI       DS    CL1                   carriage control
              DS    CL5' '                          unused
    ITEMNBR   DS    CL4                        item number
              DS    CL1' '                          unused
    DESCRIPT  DS    CL23                  item description
              DS    CL' '                           unused
    QUANT     DS    CL3                  quantity on hand
              DS    CL1' '                          unused
    PRICE     DS    CL3                     selling price
              DS    CL38' '                         unused

4.
PRINTER   DTFPR DEVADDR=SYSLST,IOAREA1=BUFFOUT,DEVICE=1403, X
              CTLCHR=YES,WORKA=YES,BLKSIZE=80

5.  CVD       9,PKSCORE
    UNPK      OSCORE,PKSCORE
    MVZ       OSCORE+2(1),OSCORE
     :
     :
    PKSCORE   DS    D

6.  TESTOUT   DS    0CL80
    CCT       DS    CL1'-'
              DS    CL18' '
    MESG      DC    CL25'YOUR SCORE FOR TEST-1 IS '
    SCORE     DS    CL3
              DS    CL33
```

7.
```
PERRECD  DTFCD  DEVADDR=SYSIPT,IOAREA1=INBUFF,DEVICE=2501,   X
               WORKA=YES,EOFADDR=EXIT

         PERRECD    DS    0CL80
         EMPLNUM    DS    CL5
         EMPLNAME   DS    CL31
         DEPTNUM    DS    CL2
                    DS    CL1' '
         JOBTITLE   DS    CL20
                    DS    CL5' '
         SERVICE    DS    CL2
                    DS    CL14
```

8. VAL: F1 F0 F2 F3

9. FLD: F0 F0 F2 C0

10. ACE: 5C F6 F5 D9

11. NUM: 00 00 11 5D

18. X'402021202020'

19. **1,234.56

20. bbb002.13

21. X'402020202020'

22. X'40202120206B202020'

23. a. BAL   8,MODULE2
    b. BAL   9,MODULE1   NOTE: d. returns to b.
    c. BR   9   and
    d. BR   8   c. returns to B EXIT

24. MAINLINE   MODULE2
```
    BAL  5,MODULE2          BAL  7,MODULE3
    BAL  6,MODULE1           :
    B    EXIT               BR   5
```
    MODULE1   MODULE3
```
     :                       :
     :                       :
    BR   6                  BR   7
```

Appendix G: Answers to Asterisked Exercises

CHAPTER 5

```
1.                L      5,N120
       PGMLOOP    BAL    10,READIN
                  BAL    10,PROCESS
                  BAL    10,OUTPUT
                  BCT    5,PGMLOOP
                   :
                   :
       N120       DC     F'120'
```

3. $0000\ 01C2_{16}$

4. $0000\ 0063_{16}$

5. $0000\ 05DC_{16}$

6. $FFFF\ FAA_{16}$

7. $FFFF\ FDE9_{16}$

CHAPTER 6

1.	B	CHKPOINT		BNL	STEP1
2.	BNL	COMPUTE		BNH	LINE42
3.	BNH	ROUTE8		A	5,PAYMT
4.	BNE	MODULE14		BL	TWO
5.	BL	THREE		S	3,N10
6.	BNL	SUBTRACT		BNH	ADD
7.	BM	PATH20		BP	LINE10
8.	BM	ROUTINE1		BP	STMT2
9.	B	LINE70		BM	PASS5

	——MAJOR——	——MINOR——	
10.	(BP 0010)	BNZ 0111	BNM 1011
12.	(BP 0010)	BNZ 0111	BNM 1011
13.	(BM 0100)	BNZ 0111	BNP 1101
16.	(BP 0010)	BNZ 0111	BNM 1011
18.	(BZ 1000)	BNM 1011	BNP 1101

CHAPTER 7

2.
```
          CLC   PREVKEY,CURRKEY      compare control fields
          BNE   BREAK                if not equal, break
          B     SKIP                 else skip break
BREAK     A     9,THREE              add 3 to line counter
          BAL   PNTSUBTL             print subtotal
          SR    7,7                  set subtotal to zero
          MVC   PREVKEY,INPKEY       set control fields equal
SKIP      continue...
```

4. There is no previous division for the first read. The input division is moved to previous division to avoid a break on the first record.

CHAPTER 8

1. 05 72 91 6C   4 bytes

3. 00 06 3C   3 bytes

5. 03 6C   2 bytes

7. 00 00 08 0D   4 bytes

9. 00 00 01 23 45 6C   6 bytes

11. 00 00 00 4D   4 bytes

	Storage	Condition Code
13.	NBR: 0C	1000
15.	VALU: 06 0C	0010
16.	(CNT and STOR do not change)	1000
18.	N10: 00 00 00 05 0C	no change
20.	NUM: 00 00 00 4C 00 0C	no change
23.	N10: 00 00 00 05 0D	no change
25.	VALU: 00 5C	0010
28.	NEG: 01 5D	0100
30.	NUM: 00 00 00 00 9C 3C	no change

CHAPTER 9

2. Since update processing involves changing or adjusting fields in the master record, the transaction must be set up to handle any one field or all fields. This necessity is clear when one considers adding a new record to the master file: Before a record can be added, the program must have access to all the fields. Hence, all fields must be coded in the transaction.

7. When a disk file is updated, we cannot see the results. But, we can write a program to read and print the file to verify that the update performed as desired and that the contents of the file are correct.

10. Yes. Since we cannot delete a record that doesn't exist, the program logic catches the error in the BADTRN segment of the UPDATE PROCESSING module and prints the UNMATCHED TRANS error message.

INDEX

A (Add) instruction, 63, 173
ABEND (abnormal end), 289
Accumulator, 38
Addition statements
    binary, 63–64, 173
    packed-decimal, 173, 246–247
Address (storage), 36
Addressability, 72
AP (Add Packed) instruction, 173, 246–247
AR (Add Register) instruction, 63–64, 173
Arithmetic comparisons, 171, 173
Arithmetic/Logic Unit (ALU), 4
Assembler
    coding format, 44
    language, 43
    processor, 14

B (Branch) instruction, 176
BAL (Branch and Link) instruction, 111
BALR (Branch and Link Register) statement, 72
Base 2 (binary), 22
Base 10 (decimal), 20
Base 16 (hexadecimal), 29
BCT (Branch on Count) instruction, 130–131
BE (Branch on Equal) instruction, 172, 173, 175, 252
BH (Branch on High) instruction, 172, 173, 175, 252
Binary

addition rules, 24
conversion: binary to decimal, 22
conversion: binary to hexadecimal, 29
number system, 22
operations, 54
subtraction rules, 25
Bit (binary digit), 26
BL (Branch on Low) instruction, 172, 173, 186, 252
BLKSIZE (block size), 92, 93
BM (Branch on Minus) instruction, 173, 189
BNE (Branch on Not Equal) instruction, 172, 173, 175, 252
BNH (Branch on Not High) instruction, 172, 173, 177, 252
BNL (Branch on Not Low) instruction, 172, 173, 186, 252
BNM (Branch on Not Minus) instruction, 173, 189
BNP (Branch on Not Positive) instruction, 173, 188
BNZ (Branch on Not Zero) instruction, 173, 188
Boundary alignment, 57
BP (Branch on Positive) instruction, 173, 188
BR (Branch Register) instruction, 112
Branching
    conditional, 170, 172
    selection (decision processing), 172
    statements, 172

    unconditional, 111, 112, 170, 176
Buffer (see I/O buffer)
Byte, 26
BZ (Branch on Zero) instruction, 173, 187

C (Compare) instruction, 171, 173, 176
Carriage control characters, 10, 92
Central processing unit (CPU), 3, 4, 5
Character
    defined, 6, 26, 34, 91
    comparisons (see Logical comparisons)
    constants, 57
    variables, 61
Characters per inch (CPI—printer), 10, 11
CLC (Compare Logical Character) instruction, 171, 172, 173–174
CLI (Compare Logical Immediate) instruction, 171, 173, 185
CLOSE macro, 94, 140
Coding format (Assembler)
    continuation field, 44, 45
    defined, 44
    label field, 44, 45
    opcode (operation code) field, 44, 45
    operand field, 44, 45
    sequence number field, 44, 45
Collating sequence, 34

Comments (statement and line), 45
Comparison statements, 171
Computer
  defined, 2
  memory, 5, 26
  system 3
Condition code, 171, 172, 252
Constants
  character, 57
  defined, 55
  fullword, 55
  halfword, 56
  hexadecimal, 58
  packed-decimal, 244–245
Continuation (program statement), 44, 45
Control break, 220–221
Control field, 220, 267
Control group, 220
Control unit, 4
CP (Compare Packed) instruction, 171, 173, 252
CR (Compare Register) instruction, 171, 173, 186
CSECT (Control Section) statement, 70, 72
CTLCHR (Control Character), 92
CVB (Convert to Binary) instruction, 141
CVD (Convert to Decimal) instruction, 95–96

D (Divide) instruction, 76–77
Data, 2, 36
Data definition (see DC statement)
Data names (program variables)
  rules for creating, 44–45
Data organization (structure), 5, 90
Database, 5, 7, 90
DC (Define Constant) statement, 55
  character, 56
  fullword, 55
  halfword, 56
  hexadecimal, 58
  packed-decimal, 244–245

DCB (data control block), 91–93
DDNAME (data definition name), 93
Debugging (errors), 8, 11, 15, 42
Decimal
  number system, 20
  conversion: decimal to binary, 23
  conversion: decimal to hexadecimal, 31
Desk checking, 8
DEVADDR (device address), 92
DEVICE, 92, 273
Digit bits, 35
Division statements
  binary, 76–77, 78–79
  packed-decimal, 250–252
Dividend, 76–79, 250–252
Divisor, 76–79, 250–252
DOS (disk operating system), 72, 91, 137, 138
Doubleword (D-type), 26, 60
DP (Divide Packed) instruction, 250–252
DR (Divide Register) instruction, 78–79
DS (Define Storage) statement
  character, 60–61
  doubleword, 60–61
  fullword, 60–61
  halfword, 60–61
  hexadecimal, 60–61
  packed-decimal, 245
DSORG (disk organization), 93
DTF (define the file), 91–92, 139, 273
Dump (see PDUMP)

EBCDIC, 34
ED (Edit) instruction, 107–110
Edit mask, 107
Edit pattern, 107–110
END statement, 70, 72
End-user, 3

EODAD (end of data address), 93
EOFADDR (end of file address), 92
EOJ statement, 69, 72
EQU statement, 100–101
Error log (see Sequential file)
Error(s)
  diagnostics, 15
  logical, 13
  syntax, 13, 15
  updating, 300–312
Expanded form, 21

Fields, 6, 91, 105–106
File
  defined, 6, 90
  master, 267
  transaction, 267
Fill character (editing), 108
Fixed-point binary operations (see Binary operations)
Flag (programming), 170
Fullword (F-type), 26, 55

Generations (program languages), 36
GET macro, 99, 138, 139

Halfword (H-type), 26, 56
Hardware, 2, 4
Hexadecimal
  addition, 32
  conversion: hexadecimal to decimal, 30
  conversion: hexadecimal to binary, 30
  number system, 29
  subtraction, 33
Hierarchical organization (see Data organization)
High-level languages, 36
Housekeeping functions (operations), 15, 72

Information, 2
Input, 2, 60
Input device, 3, 4
I/O (Input/Output) buffer, 92, 139

Index

IOAREA (input/output area), 92
IOCS (input/output control system), 91, 140
Iteration, 129–130

JCL (job control language), 137
Job, 137
Job control statements, 137

L (Load) instruction, 61
Label (name field)
  field, 44
  rules for creating, 44–45
Leading decision, 130
Line counter, 209
Lines per inch (LPI—printer), 10
Linkage editor, 15
Load module, 15, 16
Loader, 15, 16
Location counter, 72
Logic design, 8
Logical comparisons, 171, 172
Loop (program)
  body of loop, 130
  counter, 130
  counter-controlled, 130
  defined, 129
Looping read, 232
Low-level languages, 36
LR (Load Register) instruction, 62–63
LRECL (logical record length), 93
LTR (Load and Test Register) instruction, 173, 189–190

M (Multiply) instruction, 73–74
Machine code, 41–42
Machine language, 38
MACRF (macro form), 93
Macro, 67
Mainline control, 112, 115
Memory (main storage), 5, 14
Memory allocation table, 39
Modular structured programming, 101, 110, 117, 158
Module, 100, 110, 158

MP (Multiply Packed) instruction, 249–250
MR (Multiply Register) instruction, 74–75
Multiplicand, 73–75, 250
Multiplier, 73–75, 250
Multiplication statements
  binary, 73–74, 74–75
  packed-decimal, 249–250
MVC (Move Character) instruction, 106–107
MVI (Move Immediate) instruction, 98
MVZ (Move Zone) instruction, 95, 97–98

Name field (*see* Label)
Negative binary integers (*see* Two's complement notation)
Numeric comparisons (*see* Arithmetic comparisons)
Numeric constants (*see* DC statement)

Object module, 14, 15
Opcode (operation code), 37, 44, 45
Opcode conversion table, 39
OPEN macro, 94, 139
Operand, 37, 38, 44, 45
Operand address, 40, 41
Operating system, 3
Operation, 36, 37
OS (operating system), 91, 137, 138
Output, 2, 60
Output device, 3, 4, 5

PACK instruction, 140, 242
Packed-decimal format, 95, 242
Packed-decimal operations, 242, 243–244
Page break, 209
Page counter, 209
PDUMP (partial dump) macro, 67–69
Physical end (*see* END statement)
Positional notation, 21

Priming read, 223, 232
PRINT statement, 72
Printer spacing chart, 10
Problem analysis, 7
Problem definition, 7
Procedural language, 36, 37
Program(s)
  application, 2-3
  coding, 8
  custom-made, 3
  defined, 2
  documentation, 8
  logic, 7, 8
  packaged, 3
  source, 14
  testing, 8
  utility (system), 3
Program development process, 7
Programmer, 2
Programming guidelines, 158
Programming loop (see Loop)
Pseudocode, 8
PUT macro, 99

Quotient, 76–79, 250–252

RECFORM (record format), 273
Record
  defined, 6, 91, 105, 137, 139
  key, 267
  master, 267–268
  transaction, 267–268
Register
  even/odd pair, 73–75, 76–79
  general purpose, 44
  tracking use, 157
Relative addressing, 252
Remainder (division), 76–79, 250–252
Report (printer output)
  column headings, 12
  detail lines (body of report), 9, 12
  page titles, 12
  planning guidelines, 12
  summary lines, 13
  total lines, 13

S (Subtract) instruction, 65, 173
Secondary storage medium
  disk, 5
  tape, 5
Scratch-pad memory, 38
Sequence number field, 44, 45
Sequential file
  creation, 267, 269
  disk file (DTF), 273
  error log, 301
  maintenance, 267
  processing, 269
  updating, 268
Selection (see Branching)
Selection character (editing), 108
Sign
  binary division, 76
  binary integer, 26
  packed-decimal, 242
  zone-decimal, 35
Sign bits, 97
Significant start character (editing), 108
Software
  application, 3
  system, 3

SP (Subtract Packed) instruction, 173, 249
SR (Subtract Register) instruction, 65, 173
ST (Store) instruction, 66
START, 38, 39, 40
Storage
  allocate, 38
  area, 60–61
  device, 4
  fixed-length, 60
  internal, 2, 4
  secondary, 5
  unit, 4
  variable-length, 60
Structured program development (see Program development process)
Structured programming (see Modular structured programming)
Subtotal (processing), 220
Subtraction statements
  binary, 65, 173
  packed-decimal, 173, 249
Symbolic code, 43
Symbolic language, 36
System unit, 3

Top-down
  design, 115, 117, 158
  programming, 115
Trailing decision, 130
Transaction code, 289
Two's complement notation, 27, 28, 56
TYPEFLE (type file), 273

UNPK (Unpack) instruction, 95, 96
USING statement, 72

Variable data
  binary, 60
  packed-decimal, 245
Variable-length data
  character (string), 57, 61
  hexadecimal, 58, 61
  packed-decimal, 244
VERIFY, 273

WORKA (work area), 92

ZAP (Zero and Add Packed) instruction, 173, 247–248
Zone bits, 35, 97, 243
Zone character (see Zone bits)
Zone-decimal format, 35, 95